Why Nations Go to War

Fifth Edition

Why Nations Go to War

Fifth Edition

John G. Stoessinger
Trinity University

New York   St. Martin's Press

For my son
Richard
and
his generation

Senior editor: Don Reisman
Project editor: Elise Bauman
Production supervisor: Chris Pearson
Cover design: Darby Downey
Cover photo: UPI/Bettmann Newsphotos

For information, write:
St. Martin's Press, Inc.
175 Fifth Avenue
New York, NY 10010

ISBN: 0-312-01882-7

Published and distributed outside North America by:

MACMILLAN EDUCATION LTD.
Houndmills, Basingstoke, Hampshire RG21 2XS
and London
Companies and representatives throughout the world.

ISBN: 0-333-52486-1

Even in our sleep
Pain that we cannot forget
Falls drop by drop upon the heart
Until in our own despair
Against our will
Comes wisdom
Through the awful grace of God.

AESCHYLUS

Preface

The global landscape has brightened considerably since the fourth edition of *Why Nations Go to War* appeared. Relations between the Soviet Union and the United States are markedly improved, a direct result of the exchange of visits between Ronald Reagan and Mikhail Gorbachev in 1987, during which they managed to sign a modest but significant disarmament treaty. The new détente began to extend to other parts of the world as well, including Europe, Asia, Africa, and Central America. Even the United Nations has experienced a new resurgence. I have examined these welcome developments in the conclusion of this new edition.

Only the Middle East has continued on its melancholy course of violence. A fierce Palestinian uprising has made the Arab-Israeli conflict even more intractable. Lebanon, torn apart by a bevy of factions, has become virtually ungovernable. And the Iran-Iraq war, although brought to an end at last after eight years of bloody slaughter, has now assumed the dubious distinction of being one of this century's most terrible conflicts, with more than one million casualties on both sides. Over one hundred thousand of these were children who believed they were going to Paradise if they fell on the field of battle. This disaster constitutes a new case study in this revision: "The Price of Martyrdom."

As we examine the tapestry of crises in the Middle East and in the Persian Gulf, we must bear in mind not only the "objective" causes, but also the personalities that tend to unleash wars. Who are these people that are dragging us to the abyss? What can we do to stop them? If we cannot stop them, can we limit the damage they are able to inflict?

I first wrote this book in order to transmit an understanding of twentieth-century warfare to my students. Over the past fifteen years, I have received a multitude of letters from students and teachers all over the world. Many of these contained suggestions for improvement that have found their way into the present edition. Thus, this book is more than an updated version of its earlier editions; it now represents a common quest for more fundamental answers to the question of why nations go to war.

Wars seem to occur in generational cycles. The war between Catholics and Protestants more than three centuries ago was fought for thirty years. The recent conflict involving the French, Americans, and Vietnamese in Indochina, the struggle between Hindus and Moslems on the Indian subcontinent, and the modern forty years' war fought between Arabs and Israelis in the Middle East—all these seem to run their course within a single generation.

As I write these lines, it is my fervent hope that future historians will not regard the Persian Gulf the way today's historians regard the Balkans: as a prologue to world war. Accordingly, I hope that my seventh case study will serve as a warning. And I hope too that the present generation, chastened by holocaust and war, may be more determined than its forebears to say no.

I would like to thank the following individuals who offered suggestions to St. Martin's for the fifth edition of my book: Charles F. Gruber, Marshall University; Michael Kelley, University of Central Arkansas; and Jose Sanchez, Adelphi University. Don Reisman, Heidi Schmidt, and Elise Bauman of St. Martin's Press provided invaluable editorial assistance.

John G. Stoessinger

Introduction

This book attempts to take a new look at the age-old scourge of war. Ever since I was a student, I have found most explanations of war somehow wanting. I read that wars were caused by nationalism, militarism, alliance systems, economic factors, or by some other bloodless abstraction that I could not understand. Often I was told that war was an ineradicable part of human nature. Having lived through most of the major wars of this century, I wondered if this could be true. I yearned for a deeper understanding, in the hope that insight might bring healing. The conventional wisdom left me totally dissatisfied, both intellectually and emotionally. It somehow always missed the human essence of the problem. After all, wars were begun by people. Yet this personality dimension was seldom given its due weight in traditional books on war. Instead, forces over which people had no control often were enthroned as "fundamental" causes. Out of my need to know the human truth behind the mechanistic forces grew the outline for this book.

I decided to embark on six case studies of the major international wars fought in this century: the two world wars, Korea, Vietnam, India and Pakistan, and the Arab states and Israel. What interested me most in each case was the "moment of truth" when leaders crossed the threshold into war. I decided to "blow up" that fateful moment, to capture it in flight, as it were, in all its awesome tragic meaning. In the process, I sought answers to the questions that have always haunted me: At what moment did the decision to go to war become irreversible? Who bore the responsibility and why? Could the disaster have been averted? Did the six cases, different though they were, reveal some common truths about war in our time?

As a final case study in this revision, I have chosen to examine the Iran-Iraq War. In many ways, this conflict resembles World War I, complete with an arsenal of horrors including trench warfare, poison gas, and the extinction of an entire generation of young men on both sides. When shall we ever learn?

My first unforgettable exposure to World War I was Erich Maria Remarque's classic, *All Quiet on the Western Front,* a book dedicated to the memory of a generation that "had been destroyed by war even though it may have escaped its guns." Yet many old people to whom I spoke about the war remembered its outbreak as a time of glory and rejoicing. Distance had romanticized their memories, muted the anguish, and subdued the horror. I have attempted to recapture the atmosphere of those few weeks in July 1914 that changed the world forever, and I have tried to portray the leading personalities who contributed to the disaster.

I remember well the charismatic nature of Hitler's grip on the German nation. Most of my boyhood years were spent in fleeing from the Nazi terror. I have always been haunted by the personality of Hitler and driven by a need to understand his demon. That is why I chose to examine the attack on the Soviet Union—an assault that witnessed Hitler at the zenith of his power, but also bore the seeds of his ultimate destruction. Why did he launch this suicidal assault? Why did Stalin, who trusted no one, place his trust in Hitler? And what explains the fact that so many German soldiers followed Hitler to their doom in Russia like obedient schoolchildren?

When the Korean War broke out, I remember that I applauded President Harry Truman for repelling the armed aggression from the north. But when General Douglas MacArthur's forces crossed the thirty-eighth parallel into North Korea, I began to wonder. And when the general drove on toward the Chinese border, I shuddered with anxiety that China might intervene. My fear was justified. I have attempted in this case study to recapture each decision separately and to place responsibility where it belongs.

In no war did personalities play a greater role than in Vietnam. I believe that, in the course of a single generation, five American presidents based their policies in Indochina not on Asian realities but on their own fears and, ultimately, on their hopes. Each president made a concrete policy decision that escalated the war and left it in worse shape than before. It is for this reason that this case, like a Greek tragedy, has five "acts," each a virtually new step in a gradually escalating conflict that became the "Thirty Years' War" of our century.

Three of the most dreadful wars of our time were fought on the Indian subcontinent. The human suffering that accompanied them was of a scale so vast as to defy the imagination. I have attempted to study the personalities of the Hindu and the Moslem leaders for whom religious war was just as real in our secular era as it was at the time of the Crusades a thousand years ago.

A Forty Years' War has been fought in this century between Arab and Jew. Six times in a single generation these two peoples have turned on each other with a terrible ferocity. Both Arab and Jewish leaders have seen their cause as just and firmly based on the will of God, morality, and reason. And in the name of two appeals to justice, they have done things to one another that neither side will easily forget. I have attempted to capture the human truth of this great tragedy in which right does not clash with wrong, but with another right.

Upon completing my seven cases and surveying the entire spectacle of war in our time, a number of new themes emerged that I had never seen before. I have presented these in the concluding chapter of this book. A pattern *did* emerge that, I hope, will point to new directions and start a dialogue about humanity's most terrible self-imposed affliction.

Perhaps chaos is a name we give an order that as yet we do not understand. I hope that this book may bring some order to the chaos by presenting some original perspectives. And such insight, I dare hope, may be a first step to liberation.

Contents

The Iron Dice:
World War I

If the iron dice must roll, may God help us.
Theobold von Bethmann-Hollweg
German chancellor, August 1, 1914

Most people do not believe that everything is possible. The emperors and generals who sent their men to war in August 1914 thought in terms of weeks, not months, let alone years. "You will be home before the leaves have fallen from the trees," the German Kaiser told his troops in early August; at the same time, members of the czar's Imperial Guard wondered whether they should take along their dress uniforms for their victorious entry into Berlin or have them brought to the front by the next courier. Few foresaw the world catastrophe that would snuff out the lives of an entire generation and consign the next to disillusion and despair. When it was all over, no one was who he used to be and, as D. H. Lawrence said, "all the great words were cancelled out." In one of history's consummate touches of irony, one of the few who did see the shadow of war lengthening into years was the chief of the German general staff, Helmuth von Moltke, who predicted "a long and wearisome struggle," but who also believed that sooner or later war was inevitable; on June 1 he saw fit to pronounce that Germany was "ready, and the sooner the better for us."

This theme of inevitability is a haunting and pervasive one. Most of the statesmen who made the crucial decisions behaved like actors in a Greek tragedy. The terrible dénouement was foreseen, but somehow it could not be prevented. Time and again, people shifted responsibility from themselves to an impersonal God or Providence that was deemed to be in ultimate control. In the words of German chancellor Theobold von Bethmann-

Hollweg, on August 1, "if the iron dice must roll, may God help us," or in those of Emperor Francis Joseph of Austria-Hungary: "We cannot go back now." Historians, too, have been affected by this fatalistic attitude. As one leading scholar has summed up his analysis of the outbreak of the war: "All the evidence goes to show that the beginning of the crisis . . . was one of those moments in history when events passed beyond men's control."[1]

The thesis of this chapter is that such a view is wrong: mortals made these decisions. They made them in fear and in trembling, but they made them nonetheless. In most cases, they were not evil people bent on destruction but frightened and entrapped by self-delusion. They based their policies on fears, not facts, and were singularly devoid of empathy. Misperception, rather than conscious evil design, seems to have been the leading villain in the drama.

In this analysis I shall not dwell on the underlying causes of the world war. Not only have these been discussed exhaustively by leading historians,[2] but I seriously question whether they can be related directly and demonstrably to the fateful decisions that actually *precipitated* the war. For example, historians are virtually unanimous in their belief that the system of competitive alliances dividing Europe into two camps in 1914 was a principal factor that caused the war to spread. This strikes me as a mechanistic view that does not leave enough room for psychological and personality considerations. On July 5 Germany gave her ally Austria-Hungary full support to punish Serbia for the assassination of the Austrian crown prince. By late July, however, when Austrian policy threatened a general mobilization in Russia on Serbia's behalf, Germany attempted to restrain her ally. In this attempt she failed, and the result was world conflagration. But had the German Kaiser or his chancellor *succeeded* in restraining the Austrians, historians would have had to credit the alliance system with the *prevention* of a war. In other words, a study of the leading personalities of the time and the manner in which they perceived one another may be a more fruitful analysis than to postulate such abstractions as alliance systems, militarism, or nationalism.

The crucial events to be examined on the threshold of war are the German pledge of support to Austria in her policy toward Serbia; Austria's ultimatum to Serbia and the rejection of the

Serbian response; Germany's efforts to mediate and to restrain Austria; and the actual outbreak of general war on August 1, precipitated by Germany's declaration of war on Russia and the invasion of Luxembourg and Belgium.

The Kaiser's Fateful Pledge

The news of the assassination of the Austrian crown prince Franz Ferdinand on June 28, 1914, reached the German Kaiser on his yacht near Kiel. According to an eyewitness, Wilhelm II turned deathly pale as he heard the fatal news from Sarajevo.[3] He had been drawn to the Austrian archduke and his wife and had just returned from visiting the couple at their castle. Franz Ferdinand's intentions to marry a lady-in-waiting had aroused the sullen opposition of the aged emperor, Francis Joseph, who had consented only on the condition that the marriage would be a "morganatic" one, that is, the couple's children would be deprived of the right of succession to the throne. This act of renunciation had embittered Franz Ferdinand, a condition further aggravated by the condescension of the Austrian court toward his wife Sophie.

Kaiser Wilhelm was a moody man with a mercurial temper. The romantic predicament of his Austrian friend had appealed to him, and he had formed a deep and apparently genuine personal attachment. He was deeply shaken when he heard that the archduke's last words to his wife were "Sophie, Sophie, do not die, live for our children,"[4] before death claimed them both, and his fury and indignation toward the Serbians were thoroughly aroused. In his marginal comments, he described them as "bandits" and "murderers." In addition to his personal grief, he believed that the assassination represented a profound threat to the monarchical principle. Hence, it is not surprising that Admiral von Tirpitz reports in his *Memoirs* the Kaiser's conviction that the Russian czar would not support "the assassins of royalty."[5] The crowned heads of Europe would have to take a common stand against the threat of regicide. With characteristic impetuosity, the Kaiser wanted Austria to punish Serbia as quickly as possible. He was convinced that the entire civilized world, including Russia, would be sympathetic. He put it in no uncertain terms: "Matters must be cleared up with the Serbians and that soon. That is self-evident and the plain truth."[6] On July 5 he took the fateful step of assuring Austria that she could count on Germany's "faithful support" even if the punitive action she was planning to take against Serbia would bring her into conflict with Russia. In other words, the Kaiser issued Austria-Hungary a blank check. Before he went off on a vacation cruise the next morning, he exclaimed confidently: "I cannot imagine that the old gentleman in Schönbrunn will go to war, and most certainly not if it is a war over the Archduke Franz Ferdinand."[7]

The incredible fact is that the German Kaiser had not the slightest idea of what the Austrians would do. Impelled by a generous impulse of loyalty to his dead friend, he offered what he thought would be moral support to the aggrieved party. That this guarantee would entail military support never seriously occurred either to him or to the German military and governmental apparatus that fully supported his move. Even more important, the Kaiser believed that a common loyalty to monarchy would be a stronger bond than the links of ethnic kinship; in other words, that the czar would support the Kaiser against his fellow Slavs in Serbia. On both these counts Wilhelm II proved to be terribly mistaken.

The Kaiser used a special term for his pledge to Austria: *Nibelungentreue*. There is no adequate English translation for this term. The *Nibelungen* are mystical German sagas peopled with heroes whose highest virtues are honor, courage, and loyalty. The pledge of a *Nibelung* is a blood bond that is sacred and irrevocable; once given, it can never be retracted. Wilhelm's cousin, Ferdinand I of Bulgaria, understood its significance when he observed:

> I certainly do not like my cousin Kaiser Wilhelm, but I feel sorry for him all the same. Now he will be dragged into the whirlpool, be entangled, and he will have to fight, whether he wants to or not. That is all he gets out of his Nibelungentreue.[8]

The Kaiser's decision to support Austria-Hungary under any circumstances demonstrated an extraordinary confusion of personal ethics and political judgment. His friendship with the arch-duke prompted him to place the fate of his nation in the hands of another power. His view of the Russian czar as a kindred-spirited fellow monarch led him to assume that such a relinquishment of control carried no risk whatever. And his romanticism robbed him of all flexibility in the emerging crisis.

It is not true, as many historians have stated, that the Kaiser wanted war. Nor is it true, as his definitive biographer has said, that he "succumbed to a power he had not reckoned with: the power of Fate; had it not been for that, the war would never have started."[9] Such thinking is guilty of blind determinism. The Kaiser was indeed to blame. His flaw was both moral and political, for his form of loyalty demanded sacrifice beyond himself. It offered up the German nation, and it emboldened the senile monarchy of Austria-Hungary to take a desperate gamble. The cliché of the saber-rattling Kaiser is misleading. What is closer to the truth is that he permitted others to rattle and ultimately use the saber for him.

The Austrian Ultimatum to Serbia

During the tense days of July 1914, the fate of Austria-Hungary was in the hands of three men: Emperor Francis Joseph, his foreign minister, Count Leopold von Berchtold, and the chief of staff, Conrad von Hötzendorff.

At the time of the Sarajevo assassination Francis Joseph was an exhausted old man. The wars he had waged in the past had ended in defeat or loss of territory. In his declining years he was embittered by personal disasters: the murder of his wife, the tragic death of his son, and now the murder of his nephew. "Everyone is dying around me," he said mournfully. There is little doubt that above all he wished his life to end in peace. Shortly after the assassination of Franz Ferdinand, he spoke of plans for a summer respite needed to regain his strength. Evidently he had no expectation of even a local war with Serbia. When Conrad von Hötzendorff urged mobilization measures, after receiving Kaiser Wilhelm's promise of support on July 5, the emperor refused to approve them, pointing out the danger of an attack from Russia and the doubtfulness of German support. During the next three weeks, however, Francis Joseph's strength began to fail, and his signature affixed to the crucial documents laid before him by his foreign minister revealed a trembling and uncertain hand. More important, the marginal annotations no longer showed the probing mind of earlier years. One distinguished historian even maintains that the foreign minister dispatched the crucial ultimatum to Serbia "without the knowledge or approval of Francis Joseph."[10] While this is difficult to prove, it is likely that the aged sovereign no longer fully grasped the consequences of the policies that Count Berchtold and his chief of staff were now pursuing.

Conrad von Hötzendorff, Austria-Hungary's chief of staff and head of the militarist party in Vienna, believed passionately in the need to preserve his nation's status as a great power. Even before Sarajevo he feared the disintegration of the Habsburg empire from either internal decay or violent overthrow by its enemies. If Austria-Hungary accepted this final insult, then the dual monarchy would indeed become a "worm-eaten museum piece." Thus Serbia had to be dealt a punishing blow quickly, before the situation deteriorated even further. Von Hötzendorff's own words are illuminating:

> For this reason, and not as vengeance for the assassination, Austria-Hungary must draw the sword against Serbia. . . . It (is) not a question of knightly duel with "poor little" Serbia, as she like(s) to call herself, nor of punishment for the assassination. It (is) much more the highly practical importance of the prestige of a Great Power. . . . The Monarchy ha(s) been seized by the throat, and ha(s) to choose between allowing itself to be strangled and making a last effort to prevent its destruction.[11]

In the view of Austria-Hungary's chief of staff, then, the monarchy's status as a great power was in desperate peril. Both pride and prestige motivated his policy.

Count Leopold von Berchtold, the foreign minister, has been described by Sidney B. Fay as "as helpless and incompetent a person as was ever called to fill a responsible position in time of danger."[12] The record of his behavior during the critical weeks of July 1914 reveals a striking difference between his attitude toward Serbia before July 5, the date of the Kaiser's blank check to Austria, and his approach to the problem after that date. When informed of the tragedy of Sarajevo, Berchtold vacillated. He hesitated to take military action against Serbia for fear that the Kaiser would not support him, but he shared von Hötzendorff's conviction that something had to be done to preserve Austria's great power status. The Kaiser's pledge served to resolve Berchtold's indecision, and the promise of German support enabled him to use the Sarajevo assassination as the final justification for clearing up Austria's Serbian problem once and for all. He drafted an ultimatum that he was certain Serbia would reject. Protected by Germany, he could then deal a mortal blow without fear of Russian intervention.

Count Berchtold's outstanding character trait seems to have been his duplicity. Though outraged by Sarajevo, he took no action until he received the German guarantee, and then went a great deal further than the Kaiser could possibly have wanted. Austria-Hungary's failing prestige could now be buttressed by a German guarantee. With the German *Nibelungentreue* translated into an ironclad commitment, Germany could thus be made to pay the price of Austria-Hungary's last and fateful effort to remain a world power.

Berchtold seems to have been the main, possibly even the sole, author of the Serbian ultimatum. He communicated its general tenor to Berlin, and the Kaiser, incredibly enough, did not demand to see the precise text. Thus, when Berchtold transmitted the note to Serbia, Wilhelm was faced with a fait accompli. The terms of the ultimatum were stern and unyielding: they included demands for the dissolution of Serbian nationalist groups, the dismissal of key military officers, the arrest of leading political figures, and the right for Austria-Hungary to implement these measures to her complete satisfaction. Serbia was given forty-eight hours to respond or else face the consequences.

The Serbian prince regent Peter and his ministers were deeply shaken by the harshness of the ultimatum. They suspected that it was a pretext to eliminate Serbia as a sovereign state. After all, even though the assassins were Slav nationalists with Serbian ties, they were subjects of the empire, and the assassination itself had taken place on Austro-Hungarian soil. In desperation, the prince regent cabled the following plea to the Russian czar:

> We are unable to defend ourselves and beg your Majesty to come to our aid as soon as possible. The much-appreciated goodwill which your Majesty has so often shown toward us inspires us with the firm belief that once again our appeal to your noble Slav heart will not pass unheeded.[13]

The Serbian ministers then began to work around the clock on their reply. They argued bitterly over the intent of the ultimatum. A minority felt that the demands were honestly calculated to exact punishment for the assassination and to guarantee Austria's future security, but the majority was convinced that the document had been framed deliberately to elicit a rejection. The final reply was actually conciliatory and accepted most of the Austrian demands. Only those that would virtually have abrogated Serbia's sovereignty were treated somewhat evasively. The consensus was reached within minutes of the deadline. To add to the tension, the only remaining typewriter broke down, and the final text was copied out in a trembling hand by a secretary. Just before the deadline of 6 P.M. July 25, Nikola Pashich, the Serbian interior minister, arrived at the Austrian embassy in Belgrade with the reply. Baron W. Giesl, the Austrian ambassador, was under strict instructions from Berchtold to break off diplomatic relations unless Serbia yielded on every point. He hurriedly glanced at the document, noted the Serbian qualifications on some of the demands, and immediately dispatched a note to Pashich informing him that Austria-Hungary had severed diplomatic relations with Serbia. The note overtook Pashich during his return to the ministry, and he found it there on his arrival. So great was Giesl's eagerness that he and the entire staff of the Austrian legation managed to catch the 6:30 P.M. train from Belgrade.

The news reached Emperor Francis Joseph two hours later at his summer villa in Ischl. According to an eyewitness, the old man looked at the message, sank into a chair, and muttered in a choked voice: *"Also doch!"* (so it has come about after all).[14] Berchtold now convinced the broken man of the need to order partial mobilization. On July 28, Austria-Hungary officially declared war on Serbia. One day later Belgrade was under bombardment.

During these fateful days the Kaiser was cruising on his yacht in the North Sea. He showed so little interest in the matter that he did not even ask to see the text of the Serbian reply until the morning of July 28, a few hours before Austria declared war. After reading it, he jotted the following words in the margin:

A brilliant performance for a time-limit of only 48 hours. This is more than one could have expected! A great moral success for Vienna; but with it every reason for war drops away, and Giesl ought to have remained quietly in Belgrade! After such a thing I should never have ordered mobilization.[15]

To his secretary of state, Gottlieb von Jagow, Wilhelm issued the following instruction:

I propose that we say to Austria: Serbia has been forced to retreat in a very humiliating manner and we offer our congratulations; naturally, as a result, every cause for war has vanished.[16]

A few hours later, however, when Austrian bombs fell on Belgrade, Kaiser Wilhelm was compelled to face the dreadful consequences of the heedless pledge to Austria he had made less than a month before.

The Closing Trap

The war that broke out on July 28 was a localized conflict between Serbia and Austria-Hungary. The Austrians gambled that it would remain so. Count Berchtold was convinced that there was nothing to fear from Russia; after all, the czar, who lived in fear of assassination himself, was sure to sympathize with a determined Austrian move against Serbia for the cause of monarchy. And even if this assumption was incorrect, then a swift and decisive military victory over Serbia would confront the czar with a fait accompli. But most important, Berchtold was sure that the Kaiser's guarantee to Austria would prevent Russian intervention. Thus the war would remain localized and could safely be brought to a quick and successful conclusion.

It now becomes essential to this analysis to consider the actual situation in Russia at the time of Sarajevo. Russia's foreign policy turned on the shoulders of three men: Czar Nicholas II, Foreign Minister Sergei Sazonov, and the minister of war, Vladimir Sukhomlinov.

The czar, though kind and considerate in personal relations, was the epitome of apathy and indifference in matters of public policy. Barbara Tuchman offers a devastating vignette describing the czar's reaction to the news of Austrian and German plans for mobilization. "Nicholas listened," she writes, "and then, as if waking from a reverie, said gravely, 'God's will be done.' "[17] His main concept of government was to preserve intact the absolute monarchy bequeathed to him by his father. The czarina had fallen under the spell of the magnetic personality of Rasputin, and the imperial court was totally out of touch with the people whom the monarchy was supposed to govern.

Sazonov, the czar's foreign minister, was a highly emotional man who had entered the diplomatic service when frail health forced him to abandon his original intention to become a monk. The German ambassador at St. Petersburg described him as "filled with glowing patriotism bordering on chauvinism. When he talk[ed] of past events in which he thought Russia suffered injustice, his face assumed an almost fanatical expression."[18] According to another eyewitness, his lips trembled with emotion when he once remarked that he could not survive another defeat such as Russia had suffered in her war with Japan.[19]

The man responsible for Russia's preparations for war was the minister of war Sukhomlinov, a pleasure-loving man in his sixties. Sazonov, who disliked him intensely, said that "it was very difficult to make him work but to get him to tell the truth was well-nigh impossible."[20] He held office at the whim of the czar and through the artful cultivation of Rasputin. Naturally lazy, he left his work largely to subordinates and, in the words of the French ambassador, Maurice Paléologue, kept "all his strength for conjugal pleasures with a wife 32 years younger than himself," whom he had married after a sensational divorce scandal. The evidence for the divorce was supplied by an Austrian named Altschiller, who then became a close friend of the minister. In January 1914 Altschiller was exposed as Austria's chief espionage agent in Russia. Totally unreceptive to new ideas, Sukhomlinov prided himself on not having read a military manual in twenty-five years. The phrase "modern war" irritated him. "As war was," he said, "so it has remained." As a result, he clung stubbornly to obsolete theories and ancient glories and believed unquestioningly in the supremacy of the bayonet over the bullet.

This, then, was the trio of men to whom the prince regent of Serbia appealed for help against Austria-Hungary. The popular response in Russia to the Austro-Serbian rupture was extremely heated. On July 26 crowds chanting "Down with Austria" and

"Long live Serbia" marched through the streets of St. Petersburg. Hostile demonstrations were held in front of the Austrian embassy, and the police had to protect the diplomatic staff from being attacked by the incensed crowd. The czar, when informed of the ultimatum, displayed mild irritation and requested Foreign Minister Sazonov to keep him informed. Sazonov's own reaction, however, was explosive: *"C'est la guerre Européenne."* He was convinced that the ultimatum was a pretext for Austrian aggression against Serbia. When Count S. Szápáry, the Austro-Hungarian ambassador at St. Petersburg, attempted to defend his country's action by emphasizing the need for a common stand against revolutionary agitation and regicide, Sazonov shouted heatedly: "The fact is, you want war and you have burned your bridges. You are setting Europe on fire."[21] Sazonov was particularly infuriated by Berchtold's methods: the shortness of the time limit, the humiliating demands, and the infringements on Serbia's sovereignty. By the time the German ambassador, Count Friedrich von Pourtalès, called on Sazonov in support of his Austrian colleague, the Russian foreign minister had worked himself into a towering rage. His fury was such that Pourtalès expressed the fear that he was blinded by his hatred of Austria. "Hate," replied Sazonov, "is foreign to my nature. I do not hate Austria; I despise her." And then he exclaimed: "Austria is seeking a pretext to gobble up Serbia; but in that case Russia will make war on Austria."[22]

General Sukhomlinov too had no doubt that Austria would invade Serbia after the time limit expired. He felt that a war between Austria and Serbia would mean a war between Austria and Russia and therefore between Germany and Russia. As one of his aides put it: "One does not send such an ultimatum except when the cannons are loaded."[23] These Russian perceptions of Austrian intentions produced the next logical step for Russia: mobilization.

In conjunction with its declaration of war against Serbia, Austria-Hungary had mobilized eight out of a total of sixteen army corps. By this action Berchtold hoped not only to administer a decisive military defeat to Serbia but also to frighten off Russia from intervening. Sazonov, however, viewed this partial mobilization as directed against Russia and so decided to order a partial mobilization of his own. He hoped that quick Russian action would deter Austria from attacking Serbia in the first place. Thus, both the Austrian and Russian decisions to mobilize a part of their armies were essentially bluffs designed to deter the other side.

When the Kaiser was informed of the Austrian declaration of war and the partial Russian mobilization, his indifference gave way to growing panic. The implications of his blank check policy now became painfully clear. He decided to make a determined effort to localize the Austro-Serbian war and to act as mediator between Austria and Russia. In this attempt he was encouraged by Sir Edward Grey, the British foreign secretary, who was becoming increasingly nervous as tensions grew with every passing hour.

The Kaiser took the most direct possible route: he sent a telegram to his cousin Czar Nicholas II. The following excerpt reveals his conciliatory intent:

> It is with the gravest concern that I hear of the impression which the action of Austria against Serbia is creating in your country. . . . With regard to the hearty and tender friendship which binds us both from long ago with firm ties, I am exerting my utmost influence to induce the Austrians to deal straightly to arrive at a satisfactory understanding with you. I confidently hope you will help me in my efforts to smooth over difficulties that may still arise.
>
> Your very sincere and devoted friend and cousin.
>
> Willy[24]

In the past direct personal messages of this kind had been helpful in steering the Russian and German ships of state through troubled waters. At the same time, Bethmann, acting on the Kaiser's instructions, dispatched to Berchtold another telegram asking him to halt the Austrian armies in Belgrade and not spread the war.

The Russian leadership too was eager to prevent the Austro-Serbian conflict from escalating into a Russo-German war. Sazonov told General von Chelius, the German military plenipotentiary in St. Petersburg, that "the return of the Kaiser has made us all feel easier, for we trust in His Majesty and want no war, nor does Czar Nicholas. It would be a good thing if the two Monarchs should come to an understanding by telegraph."[25] Accordingly,

Nicholas sent to his German cousin the following telegram, which crossed that sent by Wilhelm:

> Am glad you are back. In this most serious moment, I appeal to you to help me. An ignoble war has been declared on a weak country. The indignation in Russia shared fully by me is enormous. I foresee that very soon I shall be overwhelmed by the pressure brought upon me and be forced to take extreme measures which will lead to war. To try and avoid such a calamity as a European war, I beg you in the name of our old friendship to do what you can to stop your allies from going too far.
>
> Nicky[26]

Wilhelm's response to this telegram was another wire asking his cousin not to take military measures that "would be looked upon by Austria as threatening."[27] Nicholas wired back the following message:

> Thank you heartily for your quick answer. The military measures which have now come into force were decided five days ago for reasons of defense on account of Austria's preparations. I hope from all my heart that these measures won't in any way interfere with your part as mediator which I greatly value. We need your strong pressure on Austria to come to an understanding with us.[28]

This last communication, which was received by the Kaiser on July 30, completely destroyed his sense of balance. In growing panic, he wrote the following comments in the margins of the czar's wire:

> According to this the Czar has simply been tricking us with his appeal for assistance and has deceived us. . . . Then I must mobilize too. . . . The hope that I would not let his mobilization measures disturb me in my role of mediator is childish, and solely intended to lure us into the mire. . . . I regard my mediation action as brought to an end.[29]

In short, the Kaiser believed that the czar had used the German mediation effort to get a five-day head start in his own military preparations behind Wilhelm's back. The "Willy-Nicky" telegrams had simply bought time for the Russians. By the afternoon of July 30 the Kaiser's panic took on a quality of paranoia. At

1 P.M. a telegram had arrived from Lord Grey, who warned that "if war breaks out, it [would] be the greatest catastrophe that the world has ever seen."[30] Wilhelm's response was to scribble in the margin: "This means they will attack us; Aha! The common cheat."[31] In the Kaiser's view, England was combining threat with bluff "to separate us from Austria and to prevent us from mobilizing, and to shift responsibility of the war."[32]

Wilhelm's response to both Austrian and Russian general mobilization was to place the blame on England. At the very moment when Lord Grey desperately attempted to avert a general war, the Kaiser saw the British at the head of a plot to attack and destroy Germany. In an extraordinary and revealing marginal comment on one of Lord Grey's diplomatic notes, Wilhelm wrote:

> The net has been suddenly thrown over our head, and England sneeringly reaps the most brilliant success of her persistently prosecuted, purely anti-German world policy, against which we have proved ourselves helpless, while she twists the noose of our political and economic destruction out of our fidelity to Austria, as we squirm isolated in the net.[33]

This British plot, which included Russia and France, to exterminate Germany was absolutely real to the Kaiser. The time to strike back had come. "This whole business must now be ruthlessly uncovered," the Kaiser exclaimed to Bethmann, "and the mask of Christian peaceableness publicly and brusquely torn from its face in public, and the pharisaical hypocrisy exposed on the pillory."[34] The entire world must unite against "this hated, lying, conscienceless nation of shopkeepers; for if we are to be bled to death, England shall at least lose India."[35]

This was the basis on which Kaiser Wilhelm made his decision to strike first. On July 31 the Kaiser proclaimed a "state of threatening danger of war" and issued a twelve-hour ultimatum to Russia demanding demobilization. When the Russian leadership refused to comply, Wilhelm promptly ordered full mobilization. The iron dice had begun to roll.

The Iron Dice

As emperors and statesmen on all sides gradually lost control over the deepening crisis, generals and military staffs began to dominate the scene. During the final period before the outbreak of general war, one appalling fact becomes terrifyingly clear: the unrelenting rigidity of military schedules and timetables on all sides. All these had been worked out in minute detail years before, in case war should come. Now that it was imminent, each general was terrified lest his adversary move first and thus capture the initiative. Everywhere, then, military staffs exerted mounting pressure on their chiefs of state to move schedules ahead so as to strike the first blow. What each plan lacked to an astonishing degree was even a small measure of flexibility. In the words of the chief of the mobilization section of the Russian general staff, for example, "the whole plan of mobilization is worked out ahead to its final conclusion and in all its detail . . . once the moment is chosen, everything is settled; there is no going back; it determines mechanically the beginning of war."[36] This was not only an accurate description of the situation in Russia, but also in Austria, France, and, most particularly, in Germany.

In Russia, the czar vacillated between full mobilization, which would make retreat very difficult, and partial mobilization, which left some room for maneuver. When informed of the Austrian bombardment of Belgrade on the afternoon of July 29, he decided to order full mobilization. That evening, however, Wilhelm's telegram arrived in which he pleaded with the czar not to take the military measures that would precipitate a calamity. Pondering the telegram, the czar now felt that he had made a mistake in signing the ukase for general mobilization. He decided to cancel the order and substitute another one for partial mobilization. At this point the Russian generals became extremely alarmed. Minister of War Sukhomlinov, chief of staff General Ianushkevich, and chief of mobilization General Dobrorolski all were convinced that a suspension of general mobilization would give the enemy the opportunity to mobilize more quickly than Russia. The czar nonetheless remained firm, and toward midnight of July 29 the order for partial mobilization was released.

The three generals, however, refused to yield. On the following morning they won Sazonov over to their point of view. The foreign minister in turn promised to win over the czar. The chief of staff asked Sazonov to telephone him at once from Peterhof to inform him as to whether or not he had succeeded. If Sazonov's news was positive, the chief of staff would convert the partial mobilization to a general one and immediately thereafter "retire from sight, smash my telephone and generally take all measures so that I cannot be found to give any contrary orders for a new postponement of general mobilization."[37]

It took Sazonov approximately one hour to convince the czar. The arguments he used were essentially those of the generals. The foreign minister telephoned the chief of staff as promised and added: "Now you can smash the telephone. Give your orders, General, and then—disappear for the rest of the day."[38]

We have already seen Berchtold's role in persuading Emperor Francis Joseph of Austria-Hungary to agree to partial mobilization against Serbia. Berchtold, in turn, was under the influence of Austria's chief of staff, Conrad von Hötzendorff, who hoped to deter Russia through a quick military victory and thus keep the war localized. He was ready, however, to risk intervention by Russia, and so he insisted on the mobilization of eight army corps, or approximately half the Austrian armed forces. He also worked out a plan to convert partial to full mobilization with a minimum of delay, which in fact he did when the news of Russian general mobilization reached Vienna. Encouraged by a telegram from the German chief of staff, Helmuth von Moltke, urging general mobilization, von Hötzendorff decided to push the button on July 31 instead of on August 1, the date agreed upon in an audience with Emperor Francis Joseph. As head of Austria's militarist party, von Hötzendorff had great faith in the ability of his army to deliver a crushing blow to Serbia and, if necessary, to capture the initiative in a military campaign against Russia.

In Germany the Kaiser waited anxiously for a Russian reply to his ultimatum. When the deadline of twelve noon on August 1 passed without word, Wilhelm's remaining balance collapsed and paranoia again took over. Hearing the news of the Russian mobilization, Wilhelm burst into a tirade without any connection to reality:

The world will be engulfed in the most terrible of wars, the ultimate aim of which is the ruin of Germany. England, France, and Russia have conspired for our annihilation . . . that is the naked truth of the situation which was slowly but surely created by Edward VII. . . . The encirclement of Germany is at last an accomplished fact. We have run our heads into the noose. . . . The dead Edward is stronger than the living I![39]

A short time before he decreed general mobilization at 5 p.m. on August 1 the Kaiser confided to an Austrian officer: "I hate the Slavs. I know it is a sin to do so. We ought not to hate anyone. But I can't help hating them."[40]

Wilhelm's hatred of the Slavs kept his mind attuned to a war with Russia. But his general staff, in particular its chief, Helmuth von Moltke, thought differently. For several years, the German generals had been committed to the Schlieffen Plan—the product of Count Alfred von Schlieffen—one of the most illustrious disciples of the nineteenth-century Prussian strategic thinker Karl von Clausewitz. The Schlieffen Plan envisaged a German attack on France through Belgium as the most promising first strike in the event of the outbreak of a general European war. The fact that such a move would violate the neutrality of Belgium hardly bothered the German generals. Caught between his personal desire to begin a military campaign with a devastating blow against Russia and the plan of his general staff to invade Belgium and France, the Kaiser, like Bismarck before him, began to dread the specter of a two-front war. In the meantime, however, mobilization had been ordered, and the gigantic German war machine, prepared for years for this day, had begun to roll. Barbara Tuchman paints a vivid picture of this machine:

Once the mobilization button was pushed, the whole vast machinery for calling up, equipping, and transporting two million men began turning automatically. Reservists went to their designated depots, were issued uniforms, equipment, and arms, formed into companies and companies into battalions, were joined by cavalry, cyclists, artillery, medical units, cook wagons, blacksmith wagons, even postal wagons, moved according to prepared railway timetables to concentration points near the frontier where they would be formed into divisions, divisions into corps, and corps into armies ready to advance and fight. One army corps alone—out of the total of 40 in the German forces—

required 170 railway cars for officers, 965 for infantry, 2960 for cavalry, 1915 for artillery and supply wagons, 6010 in all, grouped in 140 trains and an equal number again for their supplies. From the moment the order was given, everything was to move at fixed times according to a schedule precise down to the number of train axles that would pass over a given bridge within a given time. Confident in his magnificent system, Deputy Chief of Staff General Waldersee had not even returned to Berlin at the beginning of the crisis but had written to Jagow: "I shall remain here ready to jump; we are all prepared at the General Staff; in the meantime there is nothing for us to do!" It was a proud tradition inherited from the elder, or "great" Moltke who on mobilization day in 1870 was found lying on a sofa reading *Lady Audley's Secret.*[41]

With the momentum of mobilization directed toward the French frontier, the Kaiser's fear of a two-front war rose to a frenzy. Desperately he looked for a way out, and indeed it seemed that at the last minute the opportunity was offered to him. A colleague of Theobold von Bethmann-Hollweg's suggested the proposal of autonomy for the French province of Alsace in exchange for a pledge of French neutrality. With France neutral, England would remain neutral as well, and the Kaiser could turn his forces against Russia. Prince Karl Max Lichnowsky, the German ambassador in London, did indeed report that England would observe neutrality if Germany refrained from attacking France.

The Kaiser seized this chance for a one-front war and immediately sent for Moltke, who had just put the mobilization order into effect. The trains had already begun to roll toward France as a car, sent out specially to fetch Moltke, brought the perplexed chief of staff to the imperial palace. Wilhelm quickly explained the situation and then announced to Moltke: "Now we can go to war against Russia only. We simply march the whole of our army to the East."[42]

Moltke, the successor of Schlieffen, had planned for this day for a decade. In 1914, at the age of sixty-six, he was still living in the shadow of his illustrious uncle, the victor over France in 1870. This burden had taken its toll: the younger Moltke tended toward melancholy, was a poor horseman, and was a follower of Christian Science. Introspective by nature, he carried Goethe's *Faust* in a pocket of his military tunic, and was an ardent reader of contemporary literature. Military decisions were agonizing for him, and he reached them only after searing self-doubt. The emotional cost of making them was so great that he found it next to impossible to alter, let alone reverse, them. In short, he totally lacked flexibility.

When the Kaiser told Moltke of his plan, the chief of staff was aghast. "Your Majesty," he exclaimed, "it cannot be done." When pressed for a reason, Moltke explained:

> The deployment of millions cannot be improvised. If Your Majesty insists on leading the whole army to the East it will not be an army ready for battle but a disorganized mob of armed men with no arrangements for supply. Those arrangements took a whole year of intricate labor to complete and once settled, it cannot be altered.[43]

The vision of 11,000 trains wrenched into reverse was simply too much for Moltke to bear. He refused the Kaiser point-blank. "Your uncle would have given me a different answer," Wilhelm said bitterly. This statement, Moltke wrote afterward, "wounded me deeply," but did not change his opinion that the job "could not be done."[44] In fact, it could have been done, as Barbara Tuchman reveals in *The Guns of August:* "the German General Staff, though committed since 1905 to a plan of attack upon France first, had in their files, revised each year until 1913, an alternative plan against Russia with all the trains running eastward." General von Staab, the chief of the German Railway Division, was so shocked by Moltke's "it cannot be done" that he wrote a book about it after the war. In this work von Staab showed painstakingly how, given notice on August 1, he could have turned most of the armed forces around and deployed them against Russia by mid-August.

Be that as it may, Moltke convinced the Kaiser on that fateful August 1 that the German machine that had begun to roll toward the west could no longer be stopped, let alone reversed. The Kaiser made one final effort: he dashed off a telegram to King George of England informing him that due to "technical reasons" mobilization could no longer be countermanded; he also stated that if both France and England would remain neutral, he would "employ [his] troops elsewhere." Simultaneously, Wilhelm ordered his aide-de-camp to telephone German headquarters at Trier, a point near the Luxembourg border where German troops were scheduled to cross the frontier at any moment. Moltke, according to his memoirs, thought that his "heart would break."[45] The railways of Luxembourg were essential to his timetable, since they ran into Belgium and from there into France. He "burst into bitter tears of abject despair," and refused to sign the order countermanding the invasion of Luxembourg. While he was sulking, another call came from the Kaiser, summoning him to the palace. On his arrival there, Wilhelm informed Moltke that a negative response about the prospects of English neutrality had been received from Prince Karl Max Lichnowsky. "Now you can do what you like," the Kaiser said to Moltke. The chief of staff later reported that he "never recovered from the shock of this incident. Something in me broke and I was never the same thereafter."[46]

As it turned out, the Kaiser's final effort had been too late. His phone order to Trier had not arrived in time. German soldiers had already crossed the border into Luxembourg and had entered the little town of Trois Vierges, named for the three virgins who symbolized faith, hope, and charity.

At the same time, Count Pourtalès, the German ambassador at St. Petersburg, presented the Kaiser's declaration of war to Sazonov. According to Maurice Paléologue, the French ambassador, Sazonov responded by exclaiming: "The curses of the nations will be upon you!" to which the German replied: "We are defending our honor."[47] The night before, Admiral von Tirpitz had wanted to know why the Kaiser found it necessary to declare war on Russia at all since no immediate invasion of Russia was planned and the entire thrust of the German strategy was directed westward. To this question the naval minister never received a satisfactory answer. Nor can we know with certainty what would have happened if Moltke had acquiesced to the Kaiser's order to turn the army around and march toward the east. At the very least, however, valuable time would have been gained. Quite possibly, the outbreak of general war might have been postponed or even averted. But the unrelenting logic of a military schedule foreclosed that possibility.

In France a similar confrontation between a statesman and a general occurred. Premier René Viviani, haunted by the fear that war might erupt by accident, through "a black look, a brutal word, a shot," took an extraordinary step on July 30 and ordered a 10-kilometer withdrawal along the entire French-German border, from Switzerland to Luxembourg. In Viviani's words, France took a chance "never before taken in history." The French commander in chief, General Joseph Joffre, agreed but reached the opposite conclusion. Trained to seize the offensive, he regarded the withdrawal as suicidal and pleaded with the premier to mobilize. By the morning of August 1, he had declared that since each twenty-four-hour delay before general mobilization would mean a 15- to 20-kilometer loss of territory, he would refuse to take the respon-sibility as commander. Several hours later, he had his way and the premier authorized full mobilization.

England was the only major European power that had no mili-tary conscription. The cabinet hoped to keep the nation out of war, but it also realized that England's national interest was tied to the preservation of France. As Sir Edward Grey put it in a typical understatement: "If Germany dominated the continent, it would be disagreeable to us as well as to others, for we should be isolated."[48] As the tension mounted, the cabinet became increas-ingly divided. The man who most clearly saw the imminent out-break of war on the continent was First Lord of the Admiralty Winston Churchill. On July 28 Churchill ordered the fleet to sail to its war base at Scapa Flow, and thus prepared it for possible action and probably saved it from a surprise torpedo attack. When, on August 1, Germany declared war on Russia, Churchill asked the cabinet to mobilize the fleet instantly. Encountering no opposition, he went to the Admiralty and promptly issued the order to activate the fleet.

We see, then, that the chiefs of state of every European nation involved in a military alliance were pressed by their general staffs to mobilize. The generals, under the relentless pressure of their self-imposed timetables, stridently demanded action lest even one crucial hour be lost to the enemy. The pressure on the brink was such that ultimately the outbreak of war was experienced not as a world tragedy but as a liberating explosion.

Conclusion

It is my conviction that during the descent into the abyss, the perceptions of statesmen and generals were absolutely crucial. For the sake of clarity and precision, I should like to consider the following dimensions of this phenomenon: (1) a leader's perception of himself; (2) his perceptions of his adversary's character; (3) his perceptions of the adversary's intentions; (4) his perceptions of the adversary's power and capabilities; and (5) his capacity for empathy with his adversary.

All the participants suffered from greater or lesser distortions in their images of themselves. They tended to see themselves as honorable, virtuous, and pure, and the adversary as diabolical. The leaders of Austria-Hungary probably provide the best illustration of this. Berchtold and von Hötzendorff perceived their country as the bastion of European civilization. They saw an Austria-Hungary fighting not only for its national honor but for its very existence against an enemy who had it "by the throat." The possibility of losing prestige and sinking to the status of a second-class power was anathema to the two Austrian leaders. Hence, they perceived it essential to take a firm and fearless stand that, in their minds, would make a potential enemy back down. The fact that not only Serbia, but Russia too, perceived the Austrian action as aggression never seriously perturbed either Berchtold or his chief of staff. If aggression is defined as the use of force against the territory of another nation in violation of the wishes of that nation's people, then indeed the Austrian move against Serbia fits that definition. Yet the Austrians never saw their action in that light, and charges of aggression were simply ignored. In their zeal to defend Austria's honor and to ensure her status as a major power, Berchtold and von Hötzendorff stepped over the edge of a precipice. Their sights were so set on their goal that they failed to pay attention to the world around them; they virtually ignored the reactions of their ally, Germany, and those of their potential adversaries, Russia, England, and France. In their eagerness to vindicate the image of Austria as a virile nation, they led their country to destruction.

Diabolical enemy images were rampant during the crisis, but probably the clearest and most destructive of these was entertained by Kaiser Wilhelm. Before the crisis had reached the boiling point, the Kaiser's efforts to mediate between Austria and Russia were carried out fairly rationally and constructively. But when the czar decided to mobilize, Wilhelm's deep-seated prejudices against the Slavic peoples broke through and sent him into a frenzy. As tensions mounted, this frenzy assumed paranoid proportions and was finally redirected, of all things, toward England, which at that very moment was making every effort to preserve the peace. Wilhelm saw devils in both Russia and England; this perception, more than any other, led to his decision to strike first.

All the nations on the brink of the disaster expected the worst from their potential adversaries. The Russian leadership provides a case in point. Because the czar and his generals perceived themselves threatened by Austria, Sazonov, who "did not hate Austria, but despised her," responded with threats of hostile action. As Berchtold and von Hötzendorff, and later the Kaiser, perceived the Russians' hostility, they too escalated their hostile behavior. These acts convinced the Russians that their initial perceptions had been correct. Thereafter, the diplomatic exchanges became increasingly negative and threatening, and not even the "Willy-Nicky" telegrams were able to save the situation. When a nation perceives another nation as its enemy, and does so hard enough and long enough, the perception will eventually come true.

Perceptions of power during the crisis were particularly revealing. During the early phases, leaders notoriously tended to exaggerate their own power and perceive their enemies as weaker than they really were. Wilhelm's pledge to Austria, for example, displayed a fundamental contempt for Russia's military power and an exaggerated confidence in his influence on the Russian leadership. Similarly, the Austrians had contempt for Russia's military machine, which they perceived as more cumbersome and weaker than it actually was. As stress mounted, however, these perceptions gradually changed, and were soon replaced by acute fears of inferiority. Interestingly enough, these fears did not deter any of the participants from actually going to war. At the boiling point, all leaders tended to perceive their own alternatives as more restricted than those of their adversaries. They saw their own options as limited by necessity or "fate," whereas those of the adversary were characterized by many choices. This may help explain the curiously mechanistic quality that pervaded the attitudes of statesmen everywhere on the eve of the outbreak: the "we cannot go back now" of Francis Joseph; the "iron dice" of Bethmann-Hollweg; and the absolute determinism and enslavement to their timetables of the military leaders, who perceived the slightest advantage of the enemy as catastrophic.

Everywhere, there was a total absence of empathy; no one

could see the situation from another point of view. Berchtold did not see that, to a Serbian patriot, Austria's action would look like naked aggression. He did not see that, to the Russian leadership, war might seem the only alternative to intolerable humiliation, nor did he see the fateful mood swings of his ally, the German Kaiser, from careless overconfidence to frenzied paranoia. Wilhelm's growing panic and total loss of balance made any empathy impossible. And the Russians' contempt for Austria and fear of Germany did likewise.

Finally, one is struck with the overwhelming mediocrity of the personalities involved. The character of each of the leaders, diplomats, or generals was badly flawed by arrogance, stupidity, carelessness, or weakness. There was a pervasive tendency to place the preservation of one's ego before the preservation of the peace. There was little insight and no vision whatsoever. And there was an almost total absence of excellence and generosity of spirit. It was not fate or Providence that made these people fail so miserably. It was their own evasion of responsibility. As a result of their weakness, a generation of Europe's young men was destroyed. The sins of the parents were truly visited on the sons, who forfeited their lives. Of all the cruelties that people have inflicted on one another, the most terrible has always been brought by the weak against the weak.

NOTES

1. F. H. Hinsley, *Power and the Pursuit of Peace* (London: Cambridge University Press, 1963), p. 296.

2. See, for example, Sidney Bradshaw Fay, *The Origins of the World War,* 2 vols. (New York: 1928–1930); Luigi Albertini, *The Origins of the War of 1914,* 3 vols. (London: 1952–1957); or Fritz Fischer, *Griff nach der Weltmacht* (Hamburg: 1961).

3. René Recouly, *Les Heures Tragiques d'Avant Guerre* (Paris: 1923), p. 19.

4. Fay, *op. cit.,* Vol. 2, p. 126.

5. Grand Admiral von Tirpitz, *My Memoirs* (London: Hurst and Blackett, 1919), pp. 241–242.

6. Fay, *op. cit.,* Vol. 2, p. 209.

7. Joachim von Kürenberg, *The Kaiser* (New York: Simon & Schuster, 1955), p. 293.

8. *Ibid.,* p. 295.
9. *Ibid.,* p. 430.
10. Fay, *op. cit.,* Vol. 2, p. 253.
11. *Ibid.,* pp. 185–186.
12. Fay, *op. cit.,* Vol. 1, p. 469.
13. *Les Pourparlers Diplomatiques* (Serbian Blue Book) 16/29 juin–3/16 août (Paris: 1914), p. 37.
14. Freiherr von Margutti, *Vom Alten Kaiser* (Vienna: 1921), p. 404.
15. Karl Kautsky (ed.), *Die Deutschen Dokumente zum Kriegsausbruch* (Berlin: 1919), p. 271.
16. *Ibid.,* p. 293.
17. Barbara Tuchman, *The Guns of August* (New York: Macmillan, 1962), pp. 59–60.
18. Pourtalès to Bethmann, August 23, 1910, cited in Fay, *op. cit.,* Vol. 1, p. 265.
19. Mühlberg, German ambassador in Rome, to Bülow, June 11, 1909, cited in Fay, *ibid.*
20. *Diplomatische Aktenstücke zur Vorgeschichte des Krieges* (Austrian Red Book of 1919) (Vienna: 1919), p. 16.
21. *Ibid.,* p. 19.
22. *Ibid.*
23. Kautsky, *op. cit.,* p. 291.
24. *Ibid.,* p. 335.
25. *Ibid.,* p. 337.
26. *Ibid.,* p. 366.
27. *Ibid.,* p. 359.
28. *Ibid.,* p. 390.
29. *Ibid.*
30. *Ibid.,* p. 321.
31. *Ibid.*
32. *Ibid.*
33. *Ibid.,* p. 354.
34. *Ibid.,* p. 350.
35. *Ibid.*
36. S. Dobrorolski, *Die Mobilmachung der russischen Armee, 1914* (Berlin: 1921), p. 9.
37. Cited in Fay, *op. cit.,* Vol. 2, p. 470.
38. *Ibid.,* p. 472.
39. Cited in Tuchman, *op. cit.,* p. 75.
40. *Ibid.,* p. 74.
41. *Ibid.,* pp. 74–75.
42. *Ibid.,* p. 78.
43. *Ibid.,* p. 79.
44. *Ibid.*

45. *Ibid.,* p. 81.
46. *Ibid.*
47. *Ibid.,* p. 83.
48. *Ibid.,* p. 91.

SELECTED BIBLIOGRAPHY

CHURCHILL, WINSTON. *The World Crisis, 1911–1914.* New York: Scribner, 1928.

EARLE, EDWARD M. (ed.). *Makers of Modern Strategy.* Princeton: Princeton University Press, 1943.

FAY, SIDNEY B. *The Origins of the World War.* 2 vols. New York: Free Press, 1966.

GOERLITZ, WALTER. *History of the German General Staff.* New York: Praeger, 1955.

HERMANN, CHARLES F. (ed.). *International Crisis: Insights from Behavioral Research.* New York: Free Press, 1972.

HOLSTI, OLE R. *Crisis, Escalation, War.* Montreal and London: McGill-Queen's University Press, 1972.

KÜRENBERG, JOACHIM VON. *The Kaiser.* New York: Simon & Schuster, 1955.

TUCHMAN, BARBARA T. *The Guns of August.* New York; Macmillan, 1962.

2

Barbarossa: Hitler's Attack on Russia

You will never learn what I am thinking. And those who boast most loudly that they know my thought, to such people I lie even more.
Adolf Hitler, to Lieutenant-General
Franz Halder, August 1938

The most distrustful persons are often the biggest dupes.　Cardinal de Retz, Seventeenth Century

Sigmund Freud once remarked that if a little child had the physical strength to do so, it would smash everything in its path that aroused its displeasure. The key to an understanding of Hitler's invasion of Russia is more likely found in the realm of psychology than in political science or strategic thought. Hitler was not interested in just defeating Russia; it was not even important to him to conquer and incorporate her into the grand design of his Third Reich that was to last for a thousand years. What he really yearned to do, with all the passion of his demonic nature, was to destroy Russia altogether—to crush her government, pulverize her economy, enslave her people, and eliminate her as a political entity. His determination to destroy Russia was unalterable regardless of Stalin's policy toward Germany; thus, the German assault would have been unleashed sooner or later.

It was this childlike single-mindedness that made Hitler's attack on Russia so utterly destructive and so difficult to comprehend. Stalin was indeed afraid that Hitler might attack some day, but he believed that the Führer would first present him with an ultimatum to which a rational response might be made. The Soviet leader did not believe that Hitler would attack no matter what, nor was he alone in this belief. The great majority of world leaders and intelligence services had misperceived Hitler's intentions just as badly.[1] Thus Hitler achieved almost complete strategic and tactical surprise in his attack on Soviet Russia. Stalin, that least trusting, most cunning and devious of men, had actually placed his trust in the rationality of Hitler, the least rational of men. The mystery of this war lies therein. What led Hitler to this utterly self-destructive decision to invade? What was the basis of Stalin's trust in a man who had broken every promise and violated every pledge? What psychological interplay between these two evil geniuses pitted them against each other in mortal combat? The answers to these questions unlock some of the mysteries that continue to surround the outbreak of one of the bloodiest and most terrible wars in modern history.

Hitler and Russia

Hitler's intention to conquer Russia was first made public in his memoirs, *Mein Kampf,* which were published in 1924, the year of Lenin's death. Here he made known his ambition to acquire *Lebensraum* in the east:

> We terminate the endless German drive to the South and West of Europe, and direct our gaze towards the lands in the East. . . . If we talk about new soil and territory in Europe today, we can think primarily only of Russia and its vassal border states. The colossal empire in the East is ripe for dissolution, and the end of the Jewish domination in Russia will also be the end of Russia as a state.

To understand Hitler's growing hatred for Russia, one must appreciate the fact that he paved his road to power with Communist blood. As the German population grew polarized between right and left, due to the deepening economic crisis and a wave of unemployment, Hitler began to perceive the Communists as his only serious obstacle and, next to the Jews, his worst enemies. His storm troopers confronted them in innumerable street battles, beer hall skirmishes, and fistfights in crowded meeting halls. Since Russia was the citadel of the Communist movement, Hitler's fury against the Soviet Union became an obsession. What began as a desire merely to conquer Russia changed over the years to a deep emotional need to destroy her.

As a young artist in Vienna, Hitler had accumulated a fair amount of knowledge of English, French, and Italian history and culture, but there is no evidence that he had the slightest acquaintance with Russian civilization or that he ever read a book by a Russian writer. To him, Russia was a vast land beyond the pale of civilization, inhabited by ignorant peasants and their savage Bolshevik masters. Shortly after beginning the invasion of Russia, he said: "The Bolsheviks have suppressed everything that resembles civilization, and I have no feeling at all about wiping out Kiev, Moscow, and St. Petersburg."[2] This attitude crystallized during the years of his struggle for power. By the time he became chancellor, it had congealed into an idée fixe.

Hitler's first years in power brought him into gradually escalating conflict with the Soviet Union, and with every confrontation his fury against Bolshevism soared to new heights. One of his first acts on becoming chancellor in 1933 was to abrogate a long-standing mutual rearmament agreement that had strengthened both the German and the Soviet armies. Three years later, Hitler persuaded Japan to sign the Anti-Comintern Pact, which contained a number of secret military provisions directed against Russia. Late in 1936 Hitler confronted Stalin on the field of battle for the first time, albeit indirectly, by sending thousands of airmen, artillerymen, and tank crews, thinly disguised as volunteers, to fight in the Spanish Civil War. But it was the annexation of Czechoslovakia in 1939 that revealed, for the first time, Hitler's mindless hatred for the Slavic peoples in all its merciless brutality.

In Operation Green, the blueprint for the invasion of Czechoslovakia, Hitler had written: "It is my unalterable decision to smash Czechoslovakia in the near future." To his generals, he explained this move as the first step toward a larger "reckoning with the East." Much has been written about Hitler's interview with Dr. Emil Hácha, the hapless president of Czechoslovakia, that took place shortly before the German armored columns entered Prague; during the conversation Hácha fainted and had to be revived with a hypodermic needle. But what many historians generally fail to consider is the fierceness of Hitler's rage against the Czechoslovak statesman. Dr. Paul Schmidt, the interpreter who was present at the time, was struck by Hitler's ferocious hatred and commented on it afterward.[3] This hatred seems not to have been manufactured just for the purpose of intimidating Hácha; it evidently sprang from deep and genuine emotional wellsprings. Its very intensity apparently had a profound psychological impact on Hácha and contributed to his political capitulation.

Arthur Schopenhauer, in his book, *The World as Will and Idea,* advanced the argument that blind, unreasoning will is the most powerful human force. Reason is simply a "light that the will had kindled for itself" in order better to attain the object of its drive. Perhaps this may explain the paradox of Hitler's decision in 1939 to ally himself temporarily with Stalinist Russia, the country that, above all others, he passionately wanted to destroy. After Czechoslovakia, the next Slavic country on his timetable of destruction was Poland. But to crush Poland quickly and without risk Hitler needed the acquiescence of Stalin. An alliance with Stalin would also enable Hitler to complete his conquest of Western Europe without the risk of a two-front war. With the resources of all Europe at his command, the task of annihilating Russia would then be simple. In short, Hitler allied himself with Stalin in order to crush him more effectively later in a war of total annihilation.

In August 1939 Hitler instructed his foreign minister, Joachim von Ribbentrop, to explore with Stalin the possibility of a nonaggression pact, complete with a "supplementary protocol" that would divide up and apportion Poland between the two dictators. When, after a week, no response had arrived from the Kremlin, Hitler himself took the initiative and wrote Stalin a letter in which he in effect asked the Soviet leader to hurry, as a German invasion of Poland was imminent:

> The tension between Germany and Poland has become intolerable. . . . A crisis may arise any day. Germany is at any rate determined from now on to look after the interests of the Reich with all the means at her disposal.[4]

On August 21, in a letter addressed to "The Chancellor of the German Reich, A. Hitler," Stalin replied that he would receive Ribbentrop in Moscow on August 23. On the following day, in a state of euphoria, Hitler addressed his generals and announced his plans for the imminent destruction of Poland:

> I shall give a propagandist cause for starting the war. Never mind whether it is plausible or not. The victor will not be asked, later on,

whether we told the truth or not. In starting and waging war, it is not Right that matters but Victory. Have no pity. Adopt a brutal attitude. . . . Complete destruction of Poland is the military aim. To be fast is the main thing. Pursue until complete annihilation. The start will be probably ordered for Saturday morning.[5]

Saturday was August 26, and the attack on Poland was to take place only two days after the signing of the Nazi-Soviet pact. Hitler was in no mood to lose time in his plans to destroy another Slavic country.

The Hitler-Stalin pact was duly signed in Moscow on August 23. The attached Secret Additional Protocol divided up Poland and assigned to the Soviet sphere of influence Finland, Estonia, Latvia, and part of Rumania. Nine days later Hitler invaded Poland, and England and France declared war on Germany. Stalin now hoped that his three enemies would exhaust each other in a long and bloody war and that he could simply sit by and watch their agonizing deaths.

To Stalin's growing dismay, however, Hitler's armies made short shrift of most of Western Europe. The goal of annihilating Russia lay in Hitler's mind like bedrock; and not for a moment did he consider abandoning it. In fact, a mere three months after signing the nonaggression pact with Stalin, Hitler informed a group of high military officers that he would move against the Soviet Union immediately after the conquest of Western Europe. General Franz Halder, who kept a copious diary, recorded on October 18, 1939, that Hitler had instructed his generals to regard conquered Poland as "an assembly area for future German operations."

As Hitler observed that Stalin's attitude toward territorial conquest began to resemble his own, his rage against Bolshevik Russia gradually assumed frantic proportions. Stalin's attack on Finland in late 1939 sparked an emergency meeting with his generals in Berlin at which Hitler demanded that an attack on Russia be launched by the autumn of 1940. The desperate protestations by the entire general staff that such a short schedule would pose insuperable logistical problems made Hitler postpone the projected assault until the spring of 1941. To make matters worse, while Hitler was busy conquering Denmark and Norway in the spring of 1940, Stalin imposed Red Army bases on the three

Baltic states of Estonia, Latvia, and Lithuania. In June Stalin took the provinces of Bessarabia and Bukovina away from Rumania and one month later, on July 21, he simply annexed the three Baltic states. That same day, in a raging speech to his generals, Hitler ordered immediate feasibility studies for the conquest of Russia.

Hitler's obsession with the Soviet Union now began to color his view of Britain. So desperate was he to destroy Russia that he told his generals in July 1940 that Britain's stubborn determination to continue the war could only be explained by her hope that Russia would enter the war. Hence, Hitler argued, Russia had to be destroyed first, since the road to London passed through Moscow: "If Russia is smashed, Britain's last hope will be shattered. . . . In view of these considerations Russia must be liquidated, spring 1941. The sooner Russia is smashed, the better."[6] In early August, Hitler ordered *Aufbau Ost* (Buildup East), his plan "to wipe out Russia's very power to exist."[7] The destruction of the Soviet Union came first. Operation Sea Lion, the planned invasion of Britain, had to wait.

Thus Hitler's hatred of Russia blinded him completely to the strategic realities that prevailed in the summer of 1940. Stalin had absolutely no intention of helping Britain in her plight. It is quite conceivable that Hitler could have dealt Britain a fatal blow had he not been mesmerized by his need to annihilate the Soviet Union at all costs. Winston Churchill recognized this only too well when he wrote to Franklin D. Roosevelt at the time that the continuation of the war "would be a hard, long, and bleak proposition." Thus Hitler's boundless hatred for the Slavic peoples was responsible for one of the greatest blunders of his career.

In the autumn of 1940 Hitler issued a directive to transfer large segments of the Wehrmacht to the east. Strict orders were given to keep these transfers secret so as not to arouse Stalin's suspicions. Accordingly, the German military attaché in Moscow was instructed to inform the Soviet government that the massive troop transfers were merely efforts to replace older men who were being released to industry. In the words of General Alfred Jodl, "these regroupings must not create the impression in Russia that we are preparing an offensive in the East."[8]

Hitler was so infuriated by Stalin's annexation of the two Rumanian provinces that, in late August 1940, he ordered five panzer and three motorized divisions plus airborne troops to seize the Rumanian oil fields. Moscow was not consulted, and in late September Soviet foreign minister Vyacheslav Molotov warned Hitler that the Soviet Union still had interests in Rumania. He also complained that the Germans had sent reinforcements to Norway via Finland, countries he considered to be in the Soviet sphere of influence. In October Ribbentrop asked Stalin to send Molotov to Berlin so that "the Führer could explain personally his views regarding the future molding of relations between the Reich and the Soviet Union." He hinted that Hitler intended to propose a scheme that would in effect divide up the world among the four leading dictatorships. As he put it euphemistically: "It appears to be the mission of the Four Powers—the Soviet Union, Italy, Japan, and Germany—to adopt a long-range policy by delimitation of their interests on a world-wide scale."[9] Stalin accepted the invitation on behalf of Molotov, and on November 12 the Soviet foreign minister, eager for a more advantageous division of the spoils, and apparently quite unaware of *Aufbau Ost*, arrived at Berlin's main railroad station, which was decorated for the occasion with the hammer and sickle flying side by side with the swastika. It was this meeting between Hitler and Molotov that provided the final spark to Operation Barbarossa, the invasion of Russia.

Dr. Paul Schmidt, Hitler's interpreter, left a vivid account of the Berlin meeting. It seems that during the morning of November 12 Ribbentrop was given the task of explaining Hitler's conception of the "new order" to Molotov. The Führer, he said, had concluded that all four allies should expand in a southerly direction. Japan and Italy had already done so, and Germany would seek new *Lebensraum* in Central Africa. The Soviet Union, too, might "turn to the South for the natural outlet to the open sea which was so important to her." "Which sea?" Molotov asked laconically. Ribbentrop had no answer. In the afternoon it was Hitler's turn. In Schmidt's words, "the questions hailed down upon Hitler; no foreign visitor had ever spoken to him in this way in my presence."[10] The precise Bolshevik with the pince-nez wanted to know what Hitler was up to in Finland and demanded that German troops be pulled out. In addition, he wanted clarification regarding Soviet interests in Bulgaria, Rumania, and Turkey. Hitler was too taken aback to answer and proposed to adjourn the meeting until evening. At the dinner meeting, the Führer did not make an appearance, leaving Ribbentrop to entertain the Russian. This he did by expounding at length on the imminent collapse of Britain and the great opportunity, in which the Soviet Union would share, to divide up the remnants of the British Empire. At almost that very moment, according to Dr. Schmidt, the air-raid sirens began to sound and Ribbentrop and his guest were forced to run for shelter somewhat unceremoniously. British bombers had raided Berlin. When Ribbentrop, sitting in the air-raid shelter, repeated again that the British were finished, Molotov asked: "If that is so, why are we in this shelter, and whose are these bombs which fall?"[11]

The next day, after Molotov's departure, Hitler was beside himself with rage. "Stalin is clever and cunning," he told his generals. "He demands more and more. He is a cold-blooded blackmailer. A German victory has become unbearable for Russia. Therefore: she must be brought to her knees as soon as possible."[12] On December 18, Hitler dictated the secret directive that became the basis for Operation Barbarossa:

> The German Armed Forces must be prepared, even before the conclusion of the war against England, to crush Soviet Russia in a rapid campaign. . . . I shall issue orders for the deployment against Soviet Russia eight weeks before the operation is timed to begin. Preparations . . . will be concluded by May 15, 1941. It is of decisive importance that our intention to attack should not be known.[13]

Thus May 15 was set as the date for the destruction of Russia. Throughout the winter Hitler was preoccupied with the military planning for Barbarossa. He decided to penetrate the Soviet Union with two gigantic armies, one to conquer Leningrad in the north and the other to attack Kiev in the south. Moscow, in Hitler's view, would inevitably fall once the rest of Western Russia had been conquered. Only nine copies of this directive were made, one for each of the three armed services and the others kept under guard at Hitler's headquarters. The Führer demanded that the number of officers privy to the secret be kept as small as possible. "Otherwise the danger exists that our preparations will become known and the gravest political and military disadvantages result."[14] There is no evidence whatsoever that any of the generals who were taken into Hitler's confidence objected to Barbarossa. Halder, the chief of the general staff, noted in his diary in December 1940 that he was full of enthusiasm for the Russian campaign. Several weeks later, in February 1941, Halder submitted such an optimistic assessment of German chances to annihilate the Red Army in short order that Hitler exclaimed jubilantly: "When Barbarossa commences, the world will hold its breath and make no comment."[15] He then called for the operation map in order to put the finishing touches on his plans for the massacre that was to begin on May 15.

During this crucial period two events took place that prompted Hitler to postpone the invasion of Russia by five weeks. It is of the utmost importance to consider these events, since the postponement of the invasion probably spelled the difference between victory and defeat.

In October 1940 Mussolini, eager for martial glory of his own, decided to invade Greece in a surprise attack. When Hitler visited his fellow dictator in Florence on October 28, Mussolini met him at the railroad station and announced triumphantly: "Führer, we are on the march! Victorious Italian troops crossed the Greco-Albanian frontier at dawn today!"[16] According to Schmidt, who was present, Hitler managed to control his rage. Shortly thereafter, however, the Italian campaign turned into a rout, and by January 1941 Mussolini had to ask Hitler humbly for military assistance. Hitler complied, and by April 1941 Nazi tanks rattled into Athens and the swastika flew from the Acropolis. The price of this diversionary maneuver, however, amounted to twelve German divisions mired down in Greece.

The second and even more pivotal event was a coup d'état that took place in Yugoslavia on March 26, 1941. During that night the government of the regent, Prince Paul, who had come close to being a puppet of Hitler, was overthrown. Peter, the young heir to the throne, was declared king, and the Serbs made it quite clear on the following day that Yugoslavia's subservience to Germany had ended.

According to William Shirer, the Belgrade coup threw Hitler into one of the wildest rages of his life.[17] He took it as a personal affront from a Slavic nation that existed only at his whim. Calling his generals into immediate session, Hitler announced that "no diplomatic inquiries [would] be made, and no ultimatum presented."[18] Yugoslavia would be crushed with "unmerciful harshness." He ordered Goering to "destroy Belgrade in attacks by waves" and also ordered the immediate invasion of Yugoslavia. Then he announced to his generals the most fateful decision: "the beginning of the Barbarossa operation will have to be postponed by up to four weeks."[19]

Once again, none of the generals present objected. But six months later, when German troops were hit by deep snows and Arctic temperatures in front of Moscow, three or four weeks short of what General Halder thought they needed for final victory, the chief of staff was to recall with deep bitterness that the postponement of Barbarossa was probably the most catastrophic military decision of the entire war. In order to vent his personal revenge on a small Slavic nation, the Nazi leader had thrown away the opportunity to annihilate the Soviet Union. Hitler too realized this shortly before his death. Like the Roman emperor Augustus, shouting to a pitiless sky, "Varus, give me back my legions," Hitler, in the underground bunker of the Reich chancellery with the Russians only several blocks away, was said to have screamed in anguish at a portrait of Frederick the Great: "Give me back my four weeks!"

On March 30, 1941, the number of Wehrmacht officers fully apprised of Barbarossa suddenly jumped to approximately 250. The occasion was a long speech delivered by Hitler in the new Reich chancellery in Berlin. The subject was the coming massacre of the Soviet Union, now rescheduled to begin on June 22, 1941. The basic purpose of the speech was to prepare the generals for a war of total annihilation. Hitler described the coming campaign as a war to the death between two opposing ideologies. The struggle would be conducted with merciless harshness, and no quarter would be given. Breaches of international law would be excused since Russia had not participated in the Hague Conference and thus had no rights under it. Soviet commissars who surrendered were to be executed. In conclusion, Hitler stated, "I do not expect my generals to understand me, but I shall expect them to obey my orders."[20] None of the generals in Hitler's audience asked any questions, nor was there any discussion. Five years later at Nuremberg, when the question of the notorious Commissar Order was brought up, several generals confessed that they had been horrified but had lacked the courage to object.

During the final weeks before the invasion, Hitler alternated between detailed military planning and indulgence in fantasies of what he would do to the hated Russians. "In a few weeks we shall be in Moscow," he declared, "there is absolutely no doubt about it. I will raze this damned city to the ground and I will make an artificial lake to provide energy for an electric power station. The name of Moscow will vanish forever."[21] Russian tradition, history, and culture would cease to exist. No Russian books, except perhaps agricultural handbooks, would be published, and Russian children would be given just enough instruction in their schools to understand the orders of their German masters. All Russian Jews would perish, and the population of Russia would be drastically reduced through starvation and mass executions. On the morning after the summer solstice, the German army would smash into Russia. Long before the winter solstice, Russia would disappear from the map.

Hermann Goering was placed in charge of the economic exploitation of the Soviet Union. On May 23, 1941, Goering issued a directive in which he announced that most of Russia's food production would go to Germany, and the Russian population would be left to starve:

> Any attempt to save the population from death by starvation . . . would reduce Germany's staying power in the war. As a result, many millions of persons will be starved to death if we take out of the country the things necessary for us. This must be clearly and absolutely understood.[22]

Once again, there is no evidence that any of Goering's subordinates who prepared the spoliation of Russia during that pleasant German spring of 1941 voiced any protest.

When the order to invade the Soviet Union was finally given at 3 A.M. on June 22, Hitler was the absolute master of the most formidable fighting machine the world had ever seen: 154 German divisions, not to mention Finnish and Rumanian detachments, were massed on the Russian border; 3,000 tanks and 2,000 airplanes were ready for battle; generals fresh from a succession of victories were in command of the Wehrmacht. It seemed that nothing could prevent Hitler's entry into Moscow before the end of the summer.

In addition, the attack was a complete surprise, due not so much to Hitler's discretion as to Stalin's stubborn refusal to believe that a surprise attack was imminent. During the night of the invasion, Moscow slept peacefully. As dawn broke, the commander of a small Soviet frontier post was awakened by artillery fire. When he called the general in command to report the shelling, the reply was: "You must be insane." By this time, the Germans had overrun the post and advanced deep into Russia.

Examining these events, one is struck by Hitler's private and personal involvement in the war against Russia. The need to destroy the hated Slavic nation was an oppressive presence that blinded him completely to the strategic realities in Russia, both before and after the invasion. Perhaps the most revealing document on this subject is a letter that Hitler wrote to Mussolini on June 21, a few hours before the German troops poured into Russia. As Hitler wrote:

> Since I struggled through to this decision, I again feel spiritually free. The partnership with the Soviet Union . . . was nevertheless often very irksome to me, for in some way or other it seemed to me to be a break with my whole origin, my concepts and my former obligations. I am happy now to be relieved of these mental agonies.[23]

Thus German soldiers, sure of a summer victory, entered Russia wearing their light uniforms. No provisions had been made to procure winter clothing nor had preparations been made to cope with the Russian winter. Men and machines were tooled to perfection, but only for another *Blitzkrieg.* The lessons of Charles XII of Sweden and of Napoleon Bonaparte, who had met their doom in the snows of Russia, were ignored. Yet Hitler chose for his greatest military venture two symbols whose murky significance is strange indeed. Barbarossa, after whom he named the campaign, had been a crusader of the Holy Roman Empire who had failed in his mission to the East and drowned. His corpse and the site of his burial were lost. Even more peculiar was the choice of June 22 as the day of reckoning. As Hitler never mentioned the fate of the Grand Armée in its retreat from Moscow in 1812, it has never been established whether he knew that this was the anniversary of Napoleon's invasion of Russia almost a century and a half before.

Stalin and Germany

Today, when one thinks of the Russo-German war, the images that come most quickly to mind are the Soviet victory at Stalingrad and the ultimate triumph of Soviet arms in Berlin in 1945. What is remembered less readily is that "the scale of the disaster wrought by the German invaders in the first hours, days, weeks, and months of the war can be considered unprecedented in the history of modern warfare."[24] One month after the beginning of the invasion, the German Army Group Center was within 200 miles of Moscow; Army Group North was moving toward Leningrad; and Army Group South was approaching Kiev, the capital of the Ukraine. Most of the Soviet air force had been destroyed, much of it on the ground during the first five days. More than half a million prisoners had been taken by the advancing German armies. By midsummer of 1941 German troops controlled Soviet territory amounting to more than twice the size of France. While there can be no doubt about the determined resistance and dogged fighting spirit of the Red Army, it is likely that in the last analysis the Soviet Union was saved by her immense space, manpower, resources, and, perhaps most important, by the Russian winter.

The haunting question that arises when one contemplates the disaster of June 1941 is: How was it possible for Hitler to achieve such complete strategic and tactical surprise when Stalin had received an abundance of intelligence information warning of the imminent attack? Without a doubt, Stalin "received more and better information on the approaching danger, even on specific details of date and hour of invasion, than did any other leadership of an attacked country in the history of modern warfare."[25] Winston Churchill, who personally warned Stalin several times, was so appalled by the Russian's heedlessness that he reached the conclusion that "Stalin and his commissars showed themselves to be the most completely outwitted bunglers."[26]

Soviet prewar predictions of the likely course of a Nazi-Soviet war were separated from reality by an unbridgeable gulf. In the summer of 1939 there appeared in the Soviet Union a novel by N. Shpanov, entitled *The First Strike—The Story of a Future War,* in which a Fascist air attack on Russia was repulsed by Soviet fighters within half an hour. Ten hours later the Soviet air force reported the destruction of the entire German war-making potential. Considering that this fictional war story seems to have been widely believed in the Soviet Union, one can appreciate that the reality of the summer of 1941 took on the dimensions of a colossal nightmare and produced a "mental vacuum and a terror of the unexplainable."[27] Yet an explanation must be sought in the personality of the absolute ruler of the Soviet Union—Josef Stalin.

Probably the single most important reason for the disaster was the Great Purge of the 1930s. Though all sectors of Soviet society were crippled by the unprecedented terror unleashed by Stalin after the death of Sergei Kirov in 1934, the officer corps of the Red Army was virtually decimated. General Shmushkevich, chief of the Soviet air force and senior military officer before the Nazi invasion, was executed a mere two weeks before the German assault.

It is likely that, even if Stalin had heeded the numerous intelligence warnings of the Nazi attack, he could not have averted the disaster completely. The Great Purge was a horrible bloodletting; many more senior officers were killed during those years than during four years of war against Nazi Germany.[28] Arrests of senior officers in 1936 commenced the assault. In 1937 a group of the highest-ranking officers of the Red Army, including General Tukhachevsky, were arrested, tried as "foreign agents," and shot. A crescendo of executions took place under the direction of the head of the Secret Police, N. I. Yezhov, until that "lord high executioner" was himself executed in 1939 and replaced by Lavrenti Beria. During these years the Soviet military establishment sustained terrible and irreplaceable losses. Moreover, the professional competence of the Red Army, not to speak of its morale, deteriorated to dangerously low levels. By 1940 about one-fifth of the positions of unit and subunit commanders were vacant; military schools could neither fill vacancies nor provide reserves.[29] At the time of the invasion, only 7 percent of all Soviet officers had received higher military education, and 37 percent had not even completed military training; 75 percent had occupied their posts for less than a year.[30] Careers were made and broken with dizzying speed, and inexperienced men often reached the apex of command, not out of professional competence but because of political favor and the personal whim of the supreme commander, Josef Stalin. The purge produced an atmosphere of overwhelming fear;

the knowledge of the possible consequences of a single misstep gave rise to a situation in which decisions on trivial as well as grave matters ultimately gravitated to the center of all power— Stalin. By 1941 military policy had in effect been reduced to preparing proposals for Stalin, asking permission from Stalin, appealing for help to Stalin, and, above all, to executing the orders of Stalin.[31] Even after the invasion, the Soviet generals feared Stalin more than they feared the Germans. Top field commanders, responsible for the lives of close to 700,000 troops almost certain to be annihilated in the trap at Kiev in 1941, refused to risk Stalin's anger by requesting permission to withdraw. Very much like Field Marshal Friedrich von Paulus at Stalingrad, who feared Hitler's anger more than Soviet guns, the Russian generals preferred to take their chances with the Nazis rather than run the risk of Stalin's wrath. The Soviet leader's control over the Red Army in 1941 was as complete as Hitler's dominance over the Wehrmacht.

What compelled Stalin to these purges, which almost broke the backbone of Russia's fighting forces in her hour of supreme trial? The evidence suggests that Stalin placed the security of his power within the Soviet state above all else, including the security of the nation from foreign attack. Essentially, the purges were designed to eliminate not only all actual but also all potential opposition to Stalin's absolute rule. Conveniently enough, many victims of the purge, some of whom were made to testify at the notorious Moscow Trials, were depicted as "paid agents of the capitalist powers." The attention of the Russian people was thus deflected from their real domestic problems to imaginary dangers that lurked outside Soviet borders. Stalin stopped the engine of destruction only when it threatened, in its mad momentum, to get out of hand completely, but not before it had almost destroyed the very fabric of society.

In his famous "secret speech" to the Twentieth Party Congress in 1956, Nikita Khrushchev accused Stalin of empty boasts about Russia's fighting ability in 1941 and chastised him for failing to heed the many clear warnings of Nazi intentions in word and deed that were made available to him before the invasion. He challenged Stalin's qualifications as a military commander, and citing his nervousness and hysteria, Khrushchev noted that for two weeks after the invasion Stalin had been in a state of nervous collapse and "ceased to do anything whatever" except sulk. But he reserved his strongest words for Stalin's disastrous annihilation of military cadres during the years of the Great Purge. This, said Khrushchev, almost cost the Soviet Union its existence as a sovereign nation.

Stalin's role as war leader was elevated after Khrushchev's ouster in 1964, but condemnation of the purge has remained official Soviet policy. As a more balanced picture of the man who ruled Russia for a quarter of a century slowly emerges, it seems that his role in the "Great Patriotic War" will remain controversial. The Great Purge, however, will probably continue to be regarded both inside and outside the Soviet Union as Stalin's greatest crime and greatest blunder.

A second major cause for the disaster of June 1941 was Stalin's decision to ally himself with Hitler in 1939. Stalin justified the pact on the occasion of his first broadcast to the Soviet people after the invasion. In this message, delivered on July 3, Stalin said:

> We secured peace for our country for one and a half years, as well as an opportunity of preparing our forces for defense if fascist Germany risked attacking our country in defiance of the pact. This was a definite gain for our country and a loss for fascist Germany.[32]

In short, Stalin argued that his deal with Hitler had given Russia the same breathing spell that Czar Alexander had secured from Napoleon at Tilsit in 1807 and that Lenin had wrested from Germany at Brest-Litovsk in 1917. This argument merits detailed and objective consideration.

During the early 1930s Stalin began to cast about for allies to counter the rising threat of Hitler. He sought mutual security pacts and promoted popular front alliances between Communist parties and other anti-Fascist groups within other nations. By 1938, however, Stalin felt increasingly insecure in his temporary alliance with Britain and France. He may even have suspected that Britain aimed at encouraging Hitler to strike to the east to provoke a death struggle between the Soviet Union and Germany. In any event, the Anglo-French fiasco at Munich confirmed the Soviet leader's suspicion that an alliance with Hitler might be highly advantageous. Stalin calculated that such a pact would safeguard the Nazi dictator's eastern flank and thus give him the green light to launch an offensive against the West. Since, in Stalin's view, Nazi Germany and Western Europe were approximately equal in strength, a mutually exhausting war would give the Soviet Union an opportunity to grow stronger in peace and ultimately absorb both adversaries. In addition, a pact with Hitler would buy time, an essential commodity since the Great Purge had seriously weakened the Soviet military machine. Moreover, the Soviet Union would at last be able to make some territorial gains: half of Poland and the three Baltic states of Latvia, Lithuania, and Estonia. Thus, in 1939, Stalin decided to sacrifice Marxism-Leninism on the altar of Machiavelli.

As it turned out, Stalin's premises included one fundamental miscalculation: it took Hitler not years but weeks to conquer most of Western Europe. So by 1940 Stalin was dismayed to find himself confronted with a Nazi colossus with the resources of most of Western Europe at its disposal. Throughout 1941, 1942, and 1943 Stalin was to complain bitterly that there was no second front in Europe against Hitler and that Russia was forced to bear the sole burden of containing the German army. In 1939 there was still a western front in Europe that could have drawn off the German forces. Nor would Poland have been overrun in two weeks if Stalin had supported her instead of carving her up with Hitler. And most important, there might not have been any war if Hitler had known that he would have had to face the Soviet Union in alliance with England and France. Even his timid generals had warned him at the time that Germany's chances of winning were slim against such a formidable coalition.

Stalin's pact with Hitler was also the result of his contempt for the policies of Britain and France. He argued that he had only done what the two capitalist powers had done the year before at Munich: bought peace and the time to rearm at the expense of a small state. Chamberlain had bought time by sacrificing Czechoslovakia, and so Stalin could do the same and sacrifice Poland. By the time Ribbentrop visited Moscow on August 23, 1939, to sign the pact, Stalin had become so anti-British that he exchanged confidences with his German guest. "The British military mission in Moscow," he told Ribbentrop, "had never told the Soviet government what it really wanted." Ribbentrop responded by saying that Britain had always tried to disrupt good relations between Germany and the Soviet Union. "England is weak," he declared, "and wants to let others fight for her presumptuous claim to world dominion." Stalin eagerly concurred and added: "If England dominated the world, that was due to the stupidity of the other countries that always let themselves be bluffed."[33] After signing the pact, Stalin spontaneously proposed a toast to Hitler: "I know how much the German nation loves its Führer. I should therefore like to drink to the Führer's health."[34] As Ribbentrop was leaving, Stalin took him aside and said: "the Soviet Government takes the new pact very seriously. I can guarantee on my word of honor that the Soviet Union will not betray its partner."[35] In short, Stalin wanted to convey to Hitler that he trusted him more than he had ever trusted the British and French. Less than four weeks later he absorbed his share of Poland.

The Soviet population seems to have been utterly confused by Stalin's *volte-face.* In the following excerpt, a pilot in the Soviet air force, writing after the war, looked back on those "twenty-two strange and incomprehensible months" when the pact was in force:

> The fascists were no longer called fascists—one could not find any trace of this word in the press or in official reports and speeches. Things which we had become accustomed to seeing as hostile, evil, and dangerous . . . had somehow become virtually neutral. This was not stated directly in words but rather crept into our consciousness from the photograph showing Hitler standing beside Molotov, from reports of Soviet oil and Soviet grain flowing from us to fascist Germany, and even from the introduction of the Prussian parade step at that time. Yes, it was difficult to understand what was what![36]

There is little doubt that at the time the pact was signed Stalin had more faith in Hitler than in "Anglo-American capitalism." In this exaggerated trust in his fellow dictator and his equally exaggerated suspicion of Britain and the United States lies yet another key to the riddle of the disaster of June 1941.

During the year preceding the invasion, eighty-four separate warnings about Barbarossa were conveyed to the Soviet Union,[37] and presumably a great number were brought to Stalin's attention. The strongest warning, however, emanated from British and American sources. Because of its source, Stalin in most cases discounted the information, rather than consider it on its merits.

He received with suspicion, or even rejected outright, all information about Hitler's actions that came from the English or the Americans. Since he believed that Britain wanted him to go to war with Germany, he was convinced that all English intelligence about the possibility of imminent war was a fabrication designed to provoke a Russo-German war. When he finally realized the veracity of this "capitalist" intelligence, the time for effective countermeasures had almost passed. A fair sample of these warnings will suffice to demonstrate the depths of Stalin's self-delusion.

The British government attempted to warn Stalin on six separate occasions. On June 25, 1940, Churchill wrote a personal letter to Stalin in which he pointed out that Hitler's insatiable lust for conquest posed a common problem. Ambassador Stafford Cripps delivered Churchill's note and added his own concurring remarks. Stalin, who, according to Cripps, was "formal and frigid," never bothered to reply to Churchill's note. In late February 1941 Cripps, on his own initiative, again warned Molotov, stating that he was convinced that Hitler would attack the Soviet Union before the end of June. Stalin not only dismissed the warning but passed it on privately to the German ambassador. On June 13 a Tass release branded Cripps an *agent provocateur*. On March 30, 1941, Churchill was dismayed by the growing eastward deployment of German forces and again instructed Cripps to warn Stalin with an urgent personal message. Once more, there was no reply from the Kremlin. On June 10 British intelligence had become convinced that Hitler was about to attack and that an explicit warning to Stalin was in order. Accordingly, on that day under secretary Sir Alexander Cadogan summoned Soviet ambassador Ivan Maisky to the Foreign Office, where he proceeded to document a detailed inventory of Germany's recent eastward deployment, giving specific dates and places of movement of division after division.[38] He then announced that "the Prime Minister asked that these data be communicated immediately to the Soviet Government."[39] Maisky recalls in his memoirs that he conveyed this warning to Moscow immediately, adding his own impression to the effect that the report "should give Stalin serious food for thought and lead him urgently to check it and, in any case, give strict instructions to our Western frontier to be on guard."[40] Maisky further recalls his "extreme amazement" when the only apparent response to his own warning was a Tass communiqué issued on June 14 publicly denouncing "the British and foreign press rumors about the imminence of war between the USSR and Germany."[41] On June 13 Anthony Eden, together with Victor Cavendish-Bentinck, the chairman of Britain's Joint Intelligence Committee, saw Maisky once again to warn him. Cavendish-Bentinck added that "he would put his money on 22 June."[42] Finally, at 1 P.M. on Saturday, June 21, Cripps telephoned Maisky to inform him that he now had reliable information that the attack would take place on the following day. Maisky sent a telegram to Moscow and nervously awaited the outcome. By daybreak he had his answer.

No wonder that Churchill, on his first wartime trip to Russia, August 15, 1942, asked Stalin why he had chosen to ignore these repeated warnings. Stalin shrugged and replied: "I did not need any warnings. I knew war would come, but I thought I might gain another six months or so."[43] We know from the memoirs of General Georgi Zhukov, however, who worked closely with Stalin at the time, that the Soviet leader was "strongly prejudiced against information coming from imperialist circles, particularly from Churchill."[44] Ideological blinders prompted Stalin to trust Hitler rather than Churchill.

The Americans too were generous with their intelligence information. On March 1, 1941, Cordell Hull and Sumner Welles tried to warn Soviet ambassador Konstantin Umansky in Washington. According to Hull, Umansky "visibly blanched, averred that he fully realized the gravity of the message and promised to forward it to Moscow immediately."[45] But instead of heeding the warning, Molotov instructed Umansky to inform the German ambassador in Washington that the Americans had evidence of a German plan to attack Russia. Stalin was so fearful of "Anglo-American provocations" that he decided to tattle to the Nazis in order to maintain the precariously balanced Russo-German relationship. What he did not know was that Hitler had already decided to end the entire balancing act.

Britain and the United States, of course, were not the only sources from which Moscow received its information. Stalin had his own man in Tokyo, Dr. Richard Sorge, who conveyed repeated warnings about the imminence of Barbarossa. Leopold Trepper, *le grand chef* of Soviet espionage in Europe, also communicated vital information. Finally, the countless flights by German reconnaissance planes over Soviet territory and unmistakable firsthand reports about German troop movements toward the Soviet border disturbed Stalin's monumental complacency. His response, however, was not to take military defense measures but to engage in special demonstrations of friendliness toward Hitler, to bribe history as it were, in order to postpone what he now began dimly to feel would be a catastrophe. On April 13, 1941, for example, Stalin threw his arm around the German military attaché, Colonel Krebs, at the Moscow railroad station, and said to him: "We will remain friends with you—through thick and thin!"[46] Two days later, Stalin unconditionally accepted Hitler's proposals for the settlement of the border between the two countries. In addition, Stalin continued to supply grain, petroleum, manganese ore, and rubber to blockaded Germany. This compliant attitude struck Hitler as "very remarkable," and indeed it was. In a supreme gesture of conciliation, Stalin closed the embassies of countries conquered by Hitler and proceeded to recognize the pro-Nazi government of Iraq.

On June 14, 1941, the very day that Hitler convened his final military conference for the planning of Barbarossa, Stalin authorized Tass to broadcast a communiqué stating that "rumors of Germany's intention to break the pact and open an attack on the USSR are devoid of all foundation; the recent transfer of German troops is . . . it must be assumed, connected with other reasons which have no bearing on Soviet-German relations."[47] Thus, one week before the invasion, Stalin still refused to face squarely the accumulating evidence.

This evidence suggests the following conclusions about Stalin's failure to prepare for the disaster. First, he perceived British and American warnings as "capitalist provocations" and simply dismissed them. In no case did he bother to examine the evidence on its own merits. When, however, under the weight of irrefutable facts coming in from Soviet sources, Stalin began to realize in early 1941 that Hitler might indeed attack, this realization was too terrifying for him to bear. He then began to engage in appeasing Hitler. As Admiral N. G. Kuznetsov of the Soviet navy recounts:

Stalin acted so as to avoid giving Hitler the slightest pretext for an attack in order not to provoke a war. As a result, when German planes photographed our bases, we were told: Hold your fire! When German air intelligence agents were caught over Soviet fortifications and made to land at our airports, the order was: release them at once![48]

Finally, Stalin believed that if Hitler did decide to attack, he would first present the Soviet Union with an ultimatum. What he did not perceive at all was Hitler's childlike, single-minded determination to destroy Russia regardless of the Soviet leader's actions. Thus Stalin erred in three fundamental ways: he was too blinded by his own ideological biases to credit the veracity of truthful Anglo-American information; he attributed to Hitler a basically rational view of Russo-German relations and was unable to understand the nature of Hitler's irrational and mindless hatred for Russia. And, finally, when the dreadful truth became clear, Stalin found its implications so horrendous that he was simply unable to face the consequences.

Thus, when Hitler struck, Stalin became paralyzed and suffered a nervous breakdown. According to Khrushchev's "secret speech," as well as the memoirs of leading Soviet military men, it took repeated proddings by members of the Politburo to shake Stalin out of his lethargy. But he did finally emerge, and on July 3, with élan restored, he broadcast his first war speech to the Russian people. In the end, despite the horrors of the purges, the blunders of the pact with Hitler, and his blindness toward Hitler's true intentions, Stalin triumphed over Nazi Germany. His hold on reality, though precarious at times, nevertheless remained firm on the field of battle. Hitler, on the other hand, behaved like a compulsive gambler unable to cut his losses, living more and more in fantasy until, when overtaken by reality, he was face-to-face with doom.

Conclusion

How was it possible for Hitler to inflict himself on the German people, to mesmerize them, and to take them with him to disaster in the wastes of Russia?

I am convinced that Hitler's charismatic grip on Germany can best be explained by the authoritarian structure of the German family. Erik Erikson paints a convincing portrait of the typical German father, whose frequent remoteness and tyranny over his children make their maturation process excessively difficult:

> When the father comes home from work, even the walls seem to pull themselves together. . . . The children hold their breath, for the father does not approve of "nonsense"—that is, neither of the mother's feminine moods nor of the children's playfulness. . . .
>
> Later, when the boy comes to observe the father in company, when he notices his father's subservience to superiors, and when he observes his excessive sentimentality when he drinks and sings with his equals, the boy acquires the first ingredient of *Weltschmerz:* a deep doubt of the dignity of man—or at any rate of the "old man." . . .
>
> The average German father's dominance and harshness was not blended with the tenderness and dignity which comes from participation in an integrating cause. Rather, the average father, either habitually or in decisive moments, came to represent the habits and ethics of the German top sergeant and petty official who—"dress'd in a little brief authority"—would never be more but was in constant danger of becoming less; and who had sold the birthright of a free man for an official title or a life pension.[49]

This kind of father, of course, makes the son's adolescence an unusually difficult period of "storm and stress" that becomes a strange mixture of open rebellion and submissive obedience, of romanticism and despondency. For each act of rebellion the boy suffers profound guilt, but for each act of submission he is punished by self-disgust. Hence, the search for identity frequently ends in stunned exhaustion, with the boy's "reverting to type" and, despite everything, identifying with his father. The excessively severe superego implanted by the father in his son during childhood has entrenched itself like a garrison in a conquered city. The boy now becomes a "bourgeois" after all, but suffers eternal shame for having succumbed.

During the 1930s the catalytic agent that offered the possibility of escape from this vicious circle was Adolf Hitler. In the Führer's world the adolescent could feel emancipated. "Youth shapes its own destiny"—the motto of the Hitler Youth—was profoundly appealing to a youth whose psychological quest for identity was often thwarted. Erikson points out that Hitler did not fill the role of the father image. Had he done so, he would have elicited great ambivalence in the German youth. Rather, he became the symbol of a glorified older brother, a rebel whose will could never be crushed, an unbroken adolescent who could lead others into self-sufficiency—in short, a leader. Since he had become their conscience, he made it possible for the young to rebel against authority without incurring guilt. Hermann Goering echoed the sentiments of the Hitler Youth when he stated categorically that his conscience was Adolf Hitler. It was this complete official absolution from guilt that made the German pattern of authoritarianism unique. Parents were to be silenced if their views conflicted with the official doctrines of the Third Reich: "All those who from the perspective of their experience and from that alone combat our method of letting youth lead youth, must be silenced."[50] The young Nazi was taught that he was destined by Providence to bring a new order to the world. Young Nazi women, too, felt a surge of pride to learn that childbirth, legitimate or illegitimate, was a meaningful act because "German women must give children to the Führer." I recall how, on numerous occasions, large groups of young women would march the streets chanting in chorus: "We want to beget children for the Führer!" National socialism made it possible for the young to rid themselves of their deep-seated personal insecurities by merging their identities with the image of a superior and glorious German nation. This image of a common future was well expressed in the famous Nazi marching song, sung by the German soldiers as they advanced into Russia: "Let everything go to pieces, we shall march on. For today Germany is ours; tomorrow the whole world!"

Gregor Strasser summed up Hitler's appeal concisely:

> Hitler responds to the vibrations of the human heart with the delicacy of a seismograph . . . enabling him, with a certainty with which no conscious gift could endow him, to act as a loudspeaker proclaiming the most secret desires, the least permissible instincts, the sufferings, and personal revolts of a whole nation.[51]

It apparently was Hitler's gift to suspend the critical faculty of others and to assume that role for himself alone. He appealed to the deepest unconscious human longings. His premium on harshness and brutality and his rejection of all things civilized and gentle caused those who were victimized by him to strive constantly to be what they were not and to exterminate that which they were. In the end, in fighting for Hitler in Russia, his soldiers and his generals were fighting unconsciously for what appeared to them to be their own psychological integrity. To face themselves and what they had done honestly and without rationalization would have meant the collapse of an entire *Weltanschauung* and complete psychological disintegration. The only way for the German people to break this fatal bond with Hitler was to drink the cup of bitterness to the end and go down with him to destruction.

What was Stalin's role in the Soviet recovery from the initial disaster? No doubt, the Soviet leader received a great deal of help from Hitler. The Nazi leader's policy of treating Russians as subhumans to be shipped as *Ostarbeiter* to the German Reich soon encountered fierce resistance. Early Russian defections to the German side quickly ceased, and the Nazi invaders found themselves confronted by a nation fighting for its survival.

Even more important, Stalin immediately perceived that the Russian soldier would not give his life for Communism, the party, or its leader, but that he would fight to the death for his Russian homeland. In his first broadcast after the invasion on July 3, Stalin appealed to "Comrades, citizens, brothers and sisters, fighters of our Army and Navy" to repel the invaders in a "great patriotic war." This was something new. Stalin had never spoken like this before. He conjured up images of Napoleon and Wilhelm II, who also had been smashed by a people fighting for their motherland. This war, Stalin said, was not an ordinary war between two armies; it was a war of the entire Soviet people fighting against the Nazi hordes. In short, Stalin appealed to the national loyalties, rather than to Communist loyalties, of the Russian population. It was going to be 1812 all over again.

The effect of this speech was electric. Until that time there had always been something artificial in the public adulation of Stalin. After all, he had been associated with forced collectivization and the terror of the Great Purges. But now, after this patriotic appeal, which greatly resembled Churchill's famous "blood, sweat and tears" speech after Dunkirk, the Russian people felt that they had a strong and able war leader. Konstantin Simonov, in his novel *The Living and the Dead,* wrote a poignant description of the impact of Stalin's address on soldiers in a field hospital:

> There was a discrepancy between that even voice and the tragic situation of which he spoke; and in this discrepancy there was strength. People were not surprised. It was what they were expecting from Stalin. They loved him in different ways, wholeheartedly, or with reservations; admiring him and yet fearing him; and some did not like him at all. But nobody doubted his courage and his iron will. And now was a time when these two qualities were needed more than anything else in the man who stood at the head of a country at war.[52]

This passage is particularly remarkable since it was written in 1958, at the height of Khrushchev's "de-Stalinization" drive. But evidently the author was unwilling to distort the truth on this cardinal point. Most Western observers who heard the speech also testified to its critical, even decisive, importance.

After the story of the outbreak of this terrible war is told, one final truth emerges with striking clarity: Hitler ultimately lost the war because he despised everything and everybody including the German people whom he professed to love. In the end, Stalin emerged triumphant despite his blunders and his purges because he was able to convince the Russian people that he loved them and was committed to the preservation of their homeland. Hitler never learned from his mistakes when the fortunes of war began to go against him in Russia. He compounded them again and again until disaster became a certainty. Stalin, on the other hand, did learn from his initial errors and thus was able to turn a rout into a final victory. The war in Russia became the supreme character test for both men and stripped them naked to the core. In Stalin, madness never gained the upper hand; in Hitler, madness conquered.

NOTES

1. Barton Whaley, *Codeword Barbarossa* (Cambridge, Mass.: MIT Press, 1973), p. 7.

2. Robert Payne, *The Life and Death of Adolf Hitler* (New York: Praeger, 1973), p. 430.

3. *Ibid.,* p. 336.

4. Documents on German Foreign Policy, Files of the German Foreign Office, VII, pp. 156–157.

5. Cited in Payne, *op. cit.,* p. 361.

6. Cited in William L. Shirer, *The Rise and Fall of the Third Reich* (Greenwich, Conn.: Fawcett, 1960), p. 1047.

7. *Ibid.*

8. *Ibid.,* p. 1048.

9. *Ibid.,* p. 1053.

10. Paul Schmidt, *Hitler's Interpreter* (New York: Heinemann, 1951), p. 212.

11. Shirer, *op. cit.,* p. 1061.

12. *Ibid.,* p. 1062.

13. *Ibid.,* p. 1063.

14. *Ibid.,* pp. 1064–1065.

15. *Ibid.,* p. 1078.

16. Schmidt, *op. cit.,* p. 220.

17. Shirer, *op. cit.,* p. 1080.

18. *Ibid.*

19. Oberkommando der Wehrmacht (OKW), Minutes of the Meeting, *Trials of War Criminals Before the Nuremberg Military Tribunals,* Vol. 4 of 15 vols. (Washington, D.C.: Government Printing Office, 1951–1952), pp. 275–278.

20. Payne, *op. cit.,* p. 419.

21. *Ibid.,* p. 431.

22. Shirer, *op. cit.,* p. 1093.

23. Cited in *ibid.,* pp. 1114–1115.

24. Severin Bialer (ed.), *Stalin and His Generals* (New York: Pegasus Press, 1969), p. 181.

25. *Ibid.,* p. 180.

26. Winston S. Churchill, *The Second World War* (London: Cassell, 1950–1955), Vol. 3 of 6 vols., p. 316.

27. Bialer, *op. cit.,* p. 179.

28. *Ibid.,* p. 63.

29. *Ibid.*

30. *Ibid.*

31. *Ibid.,* p. 89.

32. Cited in Shirer, *op. cit.,* p. 721.

33. *Ibid.,* p. 718.

34. *Ibid.,* p. 719.

35. *Ibid.*

36. Cited in Bialer, *op. cit.,* pp. 128–129.
37. Whaley, *op. cit.,* pp. 24–129.
38. *Ibid.,* p. 107.
39. *Ibid.,* p. 108.
40. Ivan Maisky, *Memoirs of a Soviet Diplomat: The War, 1939–1943* (New York: Scribner's, 1968), p. 149.
41. *Ibid.*
42. Whaley, *op. cit.,* p. 115.
43. Churchill, *op. cit.,* Vol. 4, p. 493.
44. Georgi K. Zhukov, *Memoirs* (New York: Delacorte, 1971), p. 224.
45. Cordell Hull, *Memoirs* (New York: Macmillan, 1948), p. 968.
46. Cited in Shirer, *op. cit.,* p. 1100.
47. Whaley, *op. cit.,* p. 207.
48. Bialer, *op. cit.,* pp. 199–200.
49. Erik Erikson, *Childhood and Society* (New York: Norton, 1950), p. 289.
50. *Ibid.,* p. 300.
51. Cited in Walter C. Langer, *The Mind of Adolf Hitler* (New York: Basic Books, 1972), p. 205.
52. Alexander Werth, *Russia at War* (New York: Avon Books, 1964), pp. 173–174.

SELECTED BIBLIOGRAPHY

BIALER, SEVERIN (ed.). *Stalin and His Generals.* New York: Pegasus Press, 1969.
ERIKSON, ERIK. *Childhood and Society.* New York: Norton, 1950.
IRVING, DAVID. *Hitler's War.* New York: Viking, 1977.
LANGER, WALTER C. *The Mind of Adolf Hitler.* New York: Basic Books, 1972.
PAYNE, ROBERT. *The Life and Death of Adolf Hitler.* New York: Praeger, 1973.
WAITE, ROBERT G. L. *The Psychopathic God: Adolf Hitler.* New York: Basic Books, 1977.
WERTH, ALEXANDER. *Russia at War.* New York: Avon Books, 1964.
ZHUKOV, GEORGI K. *Memoirs.* New York: Delacorte, 1971.

3

The Temptations of Victory: Korea

This was the toughest decision I had to make as President. Harry S Truman, June 26, 1950

The reasons for the outbreak of the Korean War remain a mystery; we can only speculate about the motivations for the North Korean attack of June 1950. Four possible explanations, given here in descending order of probability, suggest themselves.

The most likely explanation of the attack is that it was a probing action by Stalin against the West. With the establishment of the North Atlantic Treaty Organization (NATO) in 1949 Soviet advances into Western Europe had begun to meet determined resistance. It seemed that the absorption of Czechoslovakia in 1948 might be Stalin's final European triumph. Thus the time had arrived to turn to Asia. Conveniently enough, Secretary of State Dean Acheson, in a speech before the National Press Club in Washington on January 12, 1950, had outlined the "military defense perimeter" of the United States. There was one notable omission: Korea. It is reasonable to assume that Stalin, thus encouraged, ordered the North Koreans to attack the South.

A second possibility is that Stalin sought to create problems not for the United States but for China. Since Mao Tse-tung had come to power in China without the help of Stalin, who at the time was engaged in major purges of Communist parties everywhere, it is likely that the Soviet leader was troubled by Mao's ascendancy. It might be argued that Stalin's pact with Mao in February 1950 was merely a facade and Stalin's order to absorb South Korea an attempt to place China in a Soviet nutcracker. In short, Stalin might not have told the Chinese about the imminent attack. It might have come as much of a surprise to them as it did to the Americans. And if the war did involve the United States, then Stalin would succeed in ruining any possibility of reconciliation between mainland China and America. A Machiavellian plan indeed, but certainly not one that was beyond the Soviet leader's ken.

A Chinese initiative in North Korea presents a third, though unlikely, possibility. Mao Tse-tung had been in power for less than a year and was fully occupied with problems of domestic consolidation. Besides, North Korea was clearly in the Soviet orbit, and China had little, if any, influence there.

Finally, it is possible, though not very likely, that the North Korean attack was an internal affair, initiated by an independent decision of Premier Kim Il Sung, as the Soviet Union has contended. According to this argument, Kim Il Sung, clearly a second-rater next to such powerful Communist leaders as Tito, might have advanced to the front rank with a successful attack on South Korea.

Though the causes of the offensive remain uncertain, it does seem probable that Stalin was behind the North Korean attack. His motives seem less clear. In any event he was sure of a speedy military victory. The North Korean leadership announced that it would win the war before V-J Day in September. Once again a war launched in early summer was to end in victory before the leaves had fallen from the trees.

The focus of this chapter will be the response to the North Korean assault by the United States and the United Nations. The evidence here is abundant, and empirical analysis is possible. The following crucial phases of the American and United Nations responses will be examined: (1) President Truman's decision in June 1950 to commit American forces and the role of the United Nations in initiating the "police action"; (2) General MacArthur's crossing of the thirty-eighth parallel; (3) his drive toward the Chinese border at the Yalu River that precipitated China's military intervention; and (4) the significance of the Korean War in the larger perspective of recent history.

President Truman's Decision

At 4 A.M. on Sunday, June 25, 1950, more than 100,000 North Korean troops charged across the thirty-eighth parallel into South Korea. This event presented the United States with two classical challenges of a genuine crisis: danger and opportunity.

At the time of the North Korean attack, Harry S Truman was sixty-six years old and had served as president for more than five years. Truman had always admired "strong liberal Presidents" and had singled out for his particular affection Thomas Jefferson, Andrew Jackson, Abraham Lincoln, Theodore Roosevelt, and Franklin D. Roosevelt. He saw himself as the champion of the common person and was deeply committed to the liberal tradition in American politics.

Perhaps most significant for the Korean decision was Truman's belief in a strong chief executive. In his view, whenever a president weakly deferred to Congress, the public interest was the real loser. A decade of experience as senator had made Truman wary of the power of special interests in the passage of legislation. Certain decisions, particularly those pertaining to foreign policy, could be made only by the president in a strictly bipartisan manner. His readiness to accept full responsibility for crucial decisions was expressed by the motto inscribed on the triangular block that was always prominently displayed on his desk: "The buck stops here."

Harry Truman was blessed with the capacity to make extremely tough decisions without tormenting afterthoughts. As he wrote in a letter to his mother shortly after he assumed office: "I have to take things as they come and make every decision on the basis of the facts as I have them and then go on from there; then forget that one and take the next."[1] At the time he made the decision to drop the atomic bomb on Japan, he wrote to his sister: "Nearly every crisis seems to be the worst one, but after it's over, it isn't so bad."[2] Critics of President Truman have never asserted that his "resolution [was] sicklied o'er with the pale cast of thought." His advisers admired his readiness to accept full responsibility, though historians for decades to come will undoubtedly regard most of the Truman foreign policy decisions as controversial. In addition, Truman was deeply committed to the United

Nations: "As long as I am President," he declared on May 10, 1950, "we shall support the United Nations with every means at our command."[3]

Secretary of State Dean Acheson, fifty-seven years old at the time of the Korean crisis, had been in office for almost a year and a half. Acheson's relationship with Truman was excellent; he thought of himself as "the senior member of the Cabinet" and was completely loyal to the president. Truman, in turn, had great confidence in Acheson's judgment, and in disagreements between the secretary of state and other members of the cabinet almost always ruled in Acheson's favor.

The secretary of state also admired his president's ability to make difficult decisions. "The decisions are his," wrote Acheson, "the President is the pivotal point, the critical element in reaching decisions on foreign policy. No good comes from attempts to invade the authority and responsibility of the President."[4] A secretary of state, in Acheson's view, should be the "principal, unifying, and final source of recommendation" on foreign policy matters to the president. Acheson's admiration for Truman was rooted in his belief that the more difficulty a problem presented, the less likely one decision was right. As he put it:

> The choice becomes one between courses all of which are hard and dangerous. The "right" one, if there is a right one, is quite apt to be the most immediately difficult one. . . . In these cases the mind tends to remain suspended between alternatives and to seek escape by postponing the issue.[5]

Acheson saw it as his duty to give the president the "real issues, honestly presented, with the extraneous matter stripped away,"[6] but the decision was the president's: "Ultimately, he must decide."[7] Finally, like his chief, Acheson was committed to the United Nations. On June 22, 1950, only two days before the North Korean attack, he had declared before a Harvard commencement audience that the United States would give its "unfaltering support to the United Nations."[8]

At 11:20 P.M. on Saturday, June 24, Dean Acheson telephoned President Truman at his home in Independence, Missouri, where he was spending a quiet weekend with his wife and daughter. "Mr. President, I have very serious news," the secretary of state reported, "the North Koreans have invaded South Korea."[9] He explained that a few minutes earlier a cable had been received from John J. Muccio, the United States ambassador to South Korea, advising that North Korean forces apparently had launched "an all-out offensive against the Republic of Korea."[10]

Acheson recommended an immediate emergency meeting of the United Nations Security Council. The president concurred and expressed his strong conviction to bring the issue of the invasion before the United Nations. A few minutes later, Assistant Secretary of State John D. Hickerson telephoned the home of Ernest A. Gross, the United States deputy representative to the United Nations and, failing to reach him, telephoned the secretary-general of the United Nations, Trygve Lie.

Trygve Lie, the first secretary-general, had been active in Norwegian labor politics for many years before his election to the UN post. He was known as a man of strong convictions who did not hesitate to take positions on explosive issues. Only a few months before the Korean crisis, he had provoked the extreme displeasure of the American government by publicly supporting the application of the People's Republic of China for membership in the United Nations. By summer, his relations with the host country had deteriorated even further because of Senator Joseph McCarthy's probe for disloyal Americans in the United Nations Secretariat.[11] Upon hearing of the invasion, Lie reproached the Soviet Union, "My God," he exclaimed, "that's a violation of the United Nations Charter!"[12] He immediately decided to cable a request for full information to the United Nations Commission on Korea, whose observers were actually on the scene. In the meantime, Acheson and a small group of State Department officials in Washington considered possible courses of action.

What is most striking about these early American responses is the unanimous agreement that the United States would have to respond to the North Korean challenge through the United Nations. Ambassador Philip C. Jessup summarized these first reactions: "We've got to do something, and whatever we do, we've got to do it through the United Nations."[13] At 2 A.M. on Sunday, Secretary Acheson again telephoned the president and informed him that a group of officials in the State Department had drafted a resolution charging North Korea with a "breach of the peace" and an "act of aggression" and asking the UN Security Council to put an end to the fighting. President Truman approved the draft, and at 3 A.M. Ambassador Gross telephoned Secretary-General Lie requesting a meeting of the Security Council by early afternoon.

During the early hours of Sunday morning, top officials at the United States Mission to the United Nations, under the guidance of Ambassador Gross, planned the American strategy for the Security Council meeting. Gross, greatly worried about a possible Soviet veto that would paralyze the council, made contingency plans for initiating an emergency session of the General Assembly within twenty-four hours. The delicate problem of whether the operative paragraph of the resolution should take the form of an "order" or a "recommendation" to the Security Council was sidestepped when Gross suggested that the phrase "call upon" be employed. This language was diplomatically strong, but kept the precise legal status of the resolution somewhat in doubt. Another problem was resolved by midmorning when a message from the United Nations Commission on Korea became available. The commission reported a "serious situation which [was] assuming the character of full-scale war." Since sole reliance on American sources might have created difficulties in the Security Council, this United Nations source provided a most welcome basis for factual information. By noon the Americans were ready for the meeting.

Shortly after 11 A.M. Dean Acheson arrived coatless at the State Department. This was unusual behavior for Acheson, who had been named "Best-Dressed Man of the Year" in 1949. Reporters thus deduced that the situation was most serious. Indeed, Acheson had just learned from military intelligence sources at General Douglas MacArthur's headquarters in Tokyo that the North Korean attack seemed like an "all-out offensive" and that "the South Koreans seemed to be disintegrating."[14] At 2:45 P.M. he telephoned the president, who now decided to return to Washington without delay. At the Kansas City airport, the president was described by reporters as "grim-faced," and one of his aides privately told a reporter: "The boss is going to hit those fellows hard."[15]

According to his *Memoirs,* Truman spent most of the journey to Washington alone in his compartment, reflecting on the "lessons of history." The North Korean attack, in his view, was only another link in the chain of aggressive acts by the German, Italian, and Japanese military adventurers that had led to World War II. There was no doubt in the president's mind that a Soviet probing action was behind the North Korean invasion. Unless Communist belligerency was deterred promptly and effectively, a third world war between Communist and non-Communist states was inevitable. In addition, the principles of the United Nations, ratified with such high hopes in 1945, would have to be affirmed through a collective response to aggression.[16] Thus Truman would act through the United Nations if possible, but without it if necessary. While still airborne, the president sent a message to his secretary of state instructing him to arrange a dinner conference at Blair House to which leading State and Defense Department officials were to be invited. At that very moment, the UN Security Council was beginning its emergency session. Present in the council chamber were the representatives of China, Cuba, Ecuador, Egypt, France, India, Norway, the United Kingdom, the United States, and Yugoslavia. The Soviet Union, conspicuous by its absence, was boycotting the Security Council to express its opposition to the presence of Nationalist China.

Secretary-General Lie informed the council that, judging from information submitted by the United Nations Commission on Korea, he believed that North Korea had violated the charter. He then went on to say that he considered it "the clear duty of the Security Council to take steps necessary to re-establish peace and security in that area."[17] Immediately after the secretary-general had made his statement, Ambassador Gross proceeded to read the American draft resolution to the assembled delegates. He "called upon" North Korea to cease hostilities and to withdraw to the thirty-eighth parallel; he also "called upon" all member states "to render every assistance to the United Nations in the execution of this resolution."[18] Though no mention was made of the Soviet Union, American officials were convinced that it was behind the North Korean move. As Edward W. Barrett, assistant secretary of state for political affairs, put it, "the relationship between the Soviet Union and the North Koreans [was] the same as that between Walt Disney and Donald Duck."[19] At 5:30 P.M. the council was ready to vote on the American draft resolution. The final vote would have been unanimous save for a single abstention: Yugoslavia. Several delegates, believing that the United Nations was fighting for its very life, actually risked their political futures by deciding to vote in the absence of instructions from their governments.[20] Independent voting of this nature was most unusual.

In spite of strong UN support, neither President Truman nor his secretary of state had any illusions about the situation. Both men knew that the United States would have to take unilateral military initiatives if the North Korean attack was to be stemmed successfully.

President Truman landed in Washington "in a grim mood." "That's enough," he snapped at reporters who crowded around him to take pictures; "we've got a job to do!"[21] Before departing for Blair House, he stated that he was not going to let the North Korean attack succeed and that he was going to "hit them hard."[22] Thirteen of the nation's top diplomatic and military leaders, including the Joint Chiefs of Staff, awaited the president at Blair House, and by dinner time Truman and Acheson were in complete agreement on the main proposals to be presented at the meeting.

After dinner the president opened the discussion by calling on the secretary of state to advance suggestions for consideration by the conference. He encouraged all those present to voice their opinions freely. Acheson then proceeded to make four specific recommendations: (1) that General MacArthur be authorized to furnish South Korea with generous supplies of military equipment; (2) that the air force be authorized to cover and protect the evacuation of American civilians; (3) that consideration be given to strengthening the role of the UN Security Council; and (4) that the Seventh Fleet be interposed between Formosa and the Chinese mainland.[23]

There was complete agreement on Acheson's first recommendation. As General Omar Bradley put it: "This is the test of all the talk of the last five years of collective security."[24] In view of the sparseness of information from the battle area, however, no one recommended that American ground forces be committed at that moment. "No one could tell what the state of the Korean army was on that Sunday night," the president later noted in his *Memoirs*.[25] Accordingly, as an interim measure, General MacArthur was authorized to give the South Koreans whatever arms and equipment he could spare. There was no disagreement whatsoever over the second recommendation, which was Ambassador

Muccio's main concern. As Defense Secretary Louis A. Johnson put it, the measure was more of an "assumption" than a "decision." So far as the role of the United Nations was concerned, the president emphasized that in this crisis the United States was "working for" the world organization. He added that he would wait for the Security Council resolution to be flouted before taking any additional measures, though he instructed the Chiefs of Staff to "prepare the necessary orders" to make American forces available should the United Nations request them.[26] Finally, there was full agreement that the Seventh Fleet be used to restrain the Chinese Communists as well as the Chinese Nationalists from military operations that might widen the theater of war. The conference closed with a strong sense of resolve that the United States was prepared, under the United Nations banner, to take whatever measures were required to repel the invasion.

By Monday morning the situation had hardened. Ambassador Gross reported from the United Nations that there seemed to be growing support among the delegates for sterner measures to enforce North Korean compliance with the Security Council Resolution of June 25. Meeting with reporters in Washington, President Truman pointed to Korea on a large globe in his office and said to an aide: "This is the Greece of the Far East. If we are tough enough now, there won't be any next step."[27] Members of the White House staff commented on the president's mood of grim resolution. By 2 P.M. the military situation in Korea had grown so desperate that President Syngman Rhee placed a personal telephone call to Washington to plead with President Truman to rescue his government from complete disaster. The president and secretary of state met in seclusion during the afternoon to plan the next steps. By evening they had agreed that the situation had become serious enough to warrant another full-scale conference at Blair House at 9 P.M.

"There was no doubt! The Republic of Korea needed help at once if it was not to be overrun," President Truman recalled in his *Memoirs* about the second conference.[28] Unless such help was immediately forthcoming, no further decisions regarding Korea would be necessary. Accordingly, the president proposed that the navy and air force be instructed to give the fullest possible support to the South Korean forces south of the thirty-eighth parallel. In addition, the president recommended stepped-up military aid to the Philippines and the French forces engaged in fighting Communist Vietminh troops in Indochina. No mention was made of ground troops in Korea, but it was clear that American sea and air cover were logical preludes to such a commitment. It was thought unlikely that strong naval and air support would give the South Koreans sufficient superiority to render a ground commitment unnecessary. Ambassador Gross believed that the Security Council resolution could be "stretched" to cover the president's recommendations. The problem of possible Soviet or Chinese countermoves was discussed and the conclusion reached that neither the Soviet Union nor China was likely to intervene directly in Korea. Once again, the conferees drew historical parallels this time from the Greek crisis of 1947 and the Berlin crisis of 1948, when resolute American resistance had been successful. Support for the president's position was unanimous. As Defense Secretary Johnson was to recall later:

> If we wanted to oppose it, then was our time to oppose it. Not a single one of us did. There were some pointing out the difficulties ... and then the President made his decision which . . . I thought was the right decision.[29]

Ambassador Jessup recalled that he "felt proud of President Truman," and General Bradley explained that "we did it so we wouldn't have one appeasement lead to another and make war inevitable."[30] The president confided to Acheson that "everything I have done in the last five years has been to try to avoid making a decision such as I had to make tonight."[31] In his *Memoirs* he later recalled that "this was the toughest decision I had to make as President."[32]

By Tuesday, June 27, General MacArthur had been notified of the president's decision. He reacted with pleasant surprise, since he had not expected such forceful action. At noon the president and Acheson briefed a group of congressional leaders on the most recent developments. The responses in both the Senate and House were overwhelmingly favorable. While a few congressmen and senators questioned the president's authority to make these decisions without prior congressional approval, not a single legislator openly doubted the wisdom of the decision.

During the afternoon attention shifted from Washington to the

United Nations. At 3 P.M. the Security Council met in one of the most dramatic sessions of its short history. There was considerable apprehension in the United States Mission that Ambassador Yakov A. Malik of the Soviet Union would be present in order to cast a veto. A great deal of thought had been given to this possibility, and various contingency procedures that would mobilize the General Assembly were under active consideration. Just before the Security Council meeting Ambassadors Gross and Malik were lunching with Secretary-General Lie and other UN delegates. As the delegates rose from the table, Lie approached Malik and told him that the interests of the Soviet Union demanded his participation in the meeting. "No, I will not go there," the Soviet delegate replied. Outside the restaurant Ambassador Gross heaved a huge sigh of relief.[33]

The Soviet absence from the council on that fateful afternoon has been the subject of a great deal of speculation. Most likely, it was a blunder. The cumbersome Soviet processes for making decisions probably had left Malik without instructions on what to do in the Security Council. Hence his only option was to be absent from the council altogether.

Chief delegate Warren R. Austin read the text of the American resolution, which had been approved personally by President Truman. Its operative paragraph recommended "that Members of the United Nations furnish such assistance to the Republic of Korea as may be necessary to repel the armed attack and to restore international peace and security in the area."[34] The council had before it another report from the United Nations Commission on Korea that stated that the North Korean regime was carrying out a "well-planned, concerted, and full-scale invasion of South Korea."[35] The council postponed a vote twice because the delegates of India and Egypt were waiting for instructions. Finally, just before midnight, the Security Council passed the American-sponsored resolution, with the United Kingdom, France, China, Cuba, Ecuador, and Norway in support, Egypt and India abstaining, Yugoslavia in opposition, and the Soviet Union absent. The Security Council had recommended military measures be taken to stem the North Korean assault. At almost precisely the time of the voting, Seoul, the capital of South Korea, was taken by the North Korean army.

On the following morning President Truman chaired a meeting

of the National Security Council in Washington. Before the council was a report from General MacArthur stating that "the United States would have to commit ground troops if the thirty-eighth parallel were to be restored."[36] The president signed a bill to extend the Selective Service Act, but stopped short of ordering American ground forces into combat in Korea. That afternoon, with the loud acclaim of the press, General MacArthur flew to Korea to conduct a personal reconnaissance of the military situation. *The New York Times* commented editorially that:

> Fate could not have chosen a man better qualified to command the unreserved confidence of the people of this country. Here is a superb strategist and an inspired leader; a man of infinite patience and quiet stability under adverse pressure; a man equally capable of bold and decisive action.[37]

The president decided to wait for the general's report from the scene of battle before taking the crucial step of committing ground forces.

MacArthur, with a small group of advisers, surveyed "the dreadful backwash of a defeated and dispersed army" during a convoy ride toward Seoul. The roads were clogged with thousands of southbound refugees, who were probably unaware that MacArthur was passing through. The South Korean army seemed to be in a state of complete and disorganized rout.[38] During his flight back to Tokyo the general drafted a report to the president in which he made his position absolutely clear:

> The only assurance for holding the present line and the ability to regain the lost ground is through the introduction of United States ground combat forces into the Korean battle area.... Unless provision is made for the full utilization of the Army-Navy-Air team in this shattered area, our mission will at best be needlessly costly in life, money and prestige. At worst, it might even be doomed to failure.[39]

Specifically, the general declared that if the president gave the authorization, he could "hold Korea with two American divisions."[40]

At the same time that MacArthur was drafting his report the president held a press conference in Washington. One reporter wanted to know whether the United States was at war or not. "We are not at war," the president replied. When another reporter queried the president whether "it would be possible to call the American response a police action under the United Nations," Truman responded that this was exactly what it was. The action was being taken to help the United Nations repel a raid by a "bunch of bandits."[41] Later that evening, President Truman and Acheson considered President Chiang Kai-shek's offer to send 33,000 Chinese Nationalist troops to Korea. The president was not inclined to accept the offer but delayed making a final decision.

General MacArthur's urgent recommendation to commit American ground forces in Korea reached Washington at dawn on June 30. "Time is of the essence and a clear-cut decision without delay is essential," the general insisted. At 5 A.M. Secretary of the Army Frank Pace, Jr., communicated MacArthur's recommendation to the president. Without hesitation, Truman approved the commitment of one regimental combat team. During the morning he met with the secretary of state and top military officials. At that conference it was decided to decline politely the Chinese Nationalist troop offer and to give General MacArthur "full authority to use the troops under his command."[42]

On the afternoon of June 30 Ambassador Austin informed the UN Security Council of the latest American decision. He emphasized again that the American action was being taken under the United Nations banner. Other members, however, would have to contribute if the Korean police action was to be a genuine collective security measure. The United States had taken the lead in protecting the UN Charter; now it was up to the others to assume their share of the responsibility.

In response to the Security Council Resolution of June 27, Secretary-General Lie had sent a cable to all member states asking for information on the nature and amount of assistance each member state was prepared to give. Of the fifty-nine replies, he felt fifty-three were generally favorable.[43] In concrete and specific terms, however, actual military contributions were slow to arrive. Within two weeks of the request, naval and air units from the United Kingdom, Australia, and New Zealand were actively involved, and units from the Netherlands and Canada were on their way. By the middle of September Lie had reported that fourteen members other than the United States had contributed ground forces. From the beginning, the United States had borne the main brunt of the fighting, with the Republic of Korea in second place. By services, the American contribution was 50.32 percent of the ground forces, 85.89 percent of the naval forces, and 93.38 percent of the air forces. The respective contributions of South Korea were 40.10 percent, 7.45 percent, and 5.65 percent.[44] From these figures it is clear that the contributions of other UN members were small indeed. Though military contributions from member nations remained disproportionate throughout the Korean War, it must be noted that thirty governments did render supplementary assistance in the form of field hospitals, blood plasma, rice, and soap. Iceland, for example, made a contribution of cod-liver oil for the troops.

In view of the predominant role played by the United States, the Security Council decided on July 7 to establish a "Unified Command" under the leadership of the United States and authorized this command to use the United Nations flag. On the following day President Truman designated General MacArthur as supreme commander of the United Nations forces. However, the general also retained his title of Commander in Chief of United States Forces in the Far East; MacArthur viewed his connection with the United Nations as nominal and continued to receive his instructions directly from the president. On August 1, when Yakov Malik, the Soviet delegate, returned to the Security Council and assumed the presidency of that body, the council went into eclipse. On September 6 the Soviet Union cast its first veto on the Korean problem and thus removed any further possibility of using the Security Council to direct the UN action in Korea.

When the UN General Assembly met in mid-September, it was confronted with a dramatic change in the military situation in Korea. On September 15 General MacArthur had executed a daring amphibious landing at Inchon that had taken the North Koreans by complete surprise. Two weeks later the North Koreans were in full retreat, and the United Nations forces, in hot pursuit, had reached the thirty-eighth parallel. The question now facing the United States and the UN General Assembly was whether the UN forces should cross into North Korea. Suddenly a desperate crisis had been resolved, and an attractive new opportunity had arisen: the invader was on the run and could now be taught a lesson. This prospect, however, raised serious tactical as well as policy questions that had to be resolved quickly. The relationship between the United States and the United Nations needed to be clarified, especially the role of the supreme commander, General MacArthur. The possible responses of the two great Communist powers, China and the Soviet Union, to a UN crossing of the parallel had to be weighed. In short, the sudden successes of MacArthur's forces presented entirely new challenges. But these events were to precipitate a massive military intervention by China only a few weeks later, and—in General MacArthur's words—an "entirely new war."

General MacArthur's Gamble

Two explosive events brought the United Nations forces face to face with China on the battlefields of Korea: first, the crossing of the thirty-eighth parallel in October and, second, the drive toward the Chinese border at the Yalu River in November. Crucial to both events was the personality of General MacArthur, who was widely acclaimed as, and probably believed himself to be, America's greatest living soldier. The startling success of his Inchon landing had made the general's confidence in his own military genius unshakable. President Truman and Secretary of State Acheson had full confidence in America's most honored soldier and believed the armed might of the United States to be invincible. Nevertheless, United Nations Unified Command was badly mauled in its first encounter with Chinese troops, and MacArthur suffered the worst defeat in his entire military career. An analysis of the outbreak of this "entirely new war" may help to explain this paradox.

As the United Nations forces approached the parallel, the problem of whether to cross it presented the Unified Command with an acute dilemma. On the one hand, it was impossible to achieve total defeat of the North Korean invaders if the United Nations forces were not allowed to cross the parallel. It could be argued that the North Korean attack destroyed the sanctity of the thirty-eighth parallel as a boundary and that the "hot pursuit" of the invader was therefore perfectly in order. On the other hand, if the mission of the Unified Command was merely to "repel the armed attack," then the case could be made that the UN forces should not be permitted to cross into territory that was not a recognized part of the Republic of Korea before the North Korean attack. Moreover, there was the important question: Who was to decide whether United Nations forces should cross the parallel, and if so, for what purpose and within what limits? Finally, there was on record an explicit warning that had been made by Indian Ambassador K. M. Panikkar in Peking. If United Nations forces crossed the parallel, China probably would enter the war.[45]

In view of these conflicting considerations, there was considerable initial confusion over the matter. President Truman's first response on September 22 was to let the United Nations make the decision.[46] Less than a week later, however, he apparently changed his mind and instructed Secretary Acheson to declare that the resolutions passed by the Security Council in June and July gave the Unified Command the necessary authority to cross the parallel. This was also the position taken by General MacArthur and the Joint Chiefs of Staff. MacArthur, in particular, was of the opinion that the resolution of June 27 extended ample authority to cross the parallel. He felt that he required broad and flexible powers and that any restrictions placed on him would be rendered ineffective by the needs to ensure the safety of his troops. This view evidently impressed the president and his top advisers. As it turned out, it was never seriously disputed by most of the other member states of the United Nations.

When the UN General Assembly met in late September, most delegations were quite willing to follow the leadership of the United States. In view of the fact that the United States had been the first to come to the assistance of South Korea, and had now apparently reversed the scales of battle in favor of the UN forces, this willingness to accept the American lead was considered quite natural. Ambassador Austin set forth the American position in a major speech before the General Assembly on September 30. He argued the case for crossing the parallel in the strongest possible terms:

The artificial barrier which has divided North and South Korea has no basis for existence either in law or in reason. Neither the United Nations, its Commission on Korea, nor the Republic of Korea recognizes such a line. Now, the North Koreans, by armed attack upon the Republic of Korea, have denied the reality of any such line.[47]

The United States took the lead in drafting an eight-power resolution calling for the taking of appropriate steps "to insure conditions of stability throughout Korea" and "the establishment of a unified, independent and democratic Government in the sovereign State of Korea."[48] Apart from the Soviet bloc, there was little opposition, and the final vote on October 7 was 47 in favor, 5 opposed, and 7 abstentions.[49] The UN General Assembly had now placed its seal of approval on the twin American objectives: to destroy the North Korean forces and to unify the entire country under the flag of the UN command.

On October 8 General MacArthur, speaking as United Nations commander in chief, called on the North Korean army to surrender and "cooperate fully with the United Nations in establishing a unified, independent, democratic government of Korea."[50] He informed the North Korean authorities that, unless a favorable response was immediately forthcoming, he would "at once proceed to take such military action as may be necessary to enforce the decrees of the United Nations." The ultimatum was drafted personally by MacArthur, and the style and phraseology were unmistakably his own.

There is no evidence to suggest that President Truman's position on the question of crossing the thirty-eighth parallel differed from MacArthur's. The president and his top aides felt that by its aggression North Korea had forfeited any right that it might previously have had to prevent the execution of the UN's decree by force. Neither the fact that the UN General Assembly lacked the legal authority to legislate decrees nor that its recommendation of October 7 had been only partially accepted deterred the American leadership from declaring its own military objectives as identical with those of the United Nations. And neither the presence of Soviet advisers with the North Korean army down to the battalion level nor the stern warning issued by China deterred General MacArthur from crossing the parallel and initiating a rapid advance toward the Chinese border at the Yalu River.

South Korean troops crossed the parallel into the North on October 1, and the first American forces, the United States First Cavalry Division, followed suit on October 7. Ambassador Panikkar issued his warning on October 2, and on October 10 China's Foreign Minister Chou En-lai announced that "the Chinese people [would] not stand idly by in this war of invasion." These warnings received only passing attention in Washington and Tokyo.

The tendency among American government officials was to dismiss them as Chinese bombast.

On October 15, however, President Truman and General MacArthur met on Wake Island. As a result of the increasing frequency of Chinese warnings, the president had become sufficiently concerned to ask the general for a professional assessment about the possibility of Chinese intervention. MacArthur considered this possibility remote:

> Had they interfered in the first or second month, it would have been decisive. We are no longer fearful of their intervention. We no longer stand hat in hand. The Chinese have 300,000 men in Manchuria. Of these, probably not more than 100 to 125,000 are distributed along the Yalu River. They have no Air Force. Now that we have bases for our Air Force in Korea, if the Chinese tried to get down to Pyongyang, there would be the greatest slaughter.[51]

Four days later, when MacArthur's forces entered Pyongyang, the State Department also came to the conclusion that Chinese intervention in Korea was "unlikely." In the opinion of one leading authority:

> This assessment was by no means confined to the department over which Acheson presided. It was shared alike by the President, the Joint Chiefs of Staff, members of the National Security Council, General Walter Bedell Smith, Director of Central Intelligence, prominent senators, congressmen, and political pundits of all hues. If questioned, that amorphous character "the man in the street" would have expressed the same opinion.[52]

Nevertheless, at the very time that the American leadership denied the possibility of Chinese intervention, the Chinese Fourth Field Army crossed the Yalu and penetrated the ragged mountain terrain of North Korea.

Truman and MacArthur were convinced that China neither would nor could intervene in Korea and believed that their frequent pronouncements of America's nonaggressive intentions would reassure the Chinese leaders. On November 16 the president declared that the United States had "never at any time entertained any intention to carry hostilities into China."[53] He added that "because of the long-standing American friendship for the people of China, the United States [would] take every honorable step to prevent any extension of the hostilities in the Far East."[54] Thus American policymakers chose to view the tension between America and China as a passing phenomenon and felt that assurances of goodwill toward China would suffice to insulate the Korean conflict from Chinese intervention. Operating on the assumption of long-standing Sino-American friendship, both Truman and MacArthur were deeply astonished at the rising tone of violence in Chinese statements during the month of October. They simply did not see the intervention coming. That the illusion of a firm Sino-American friendship underlying a Communist veneer persisted in the face of growing evidence to the contrary suggests that the United States was not yet prepared to take the new China seriously. Her statements were not as yet considered credible. So far as Ambassador Panikkar's warning was concerned, neither Truman nor MacArthur took it seriously. Truman viewed it as "a bold attempt to blackmail the United Nations" and later observed in his *Memoirs* that "Mr. Panikkar had in the past played the game of the Chinese Communists fairly regularly, so that his statement could not be taken as that of an impartial observer."[55]

On the other side of the Yalu, the Chinese leaders regarded the United States as the heir to Japan's imperialist ambitions in Asia. They became increasingly convinced that only a powerful intervention in Korea would prevent the United States from invading China. As one scholar of Chinese-American relations has noted:

> While Secretary Acheson was talking about the traditional friendship of America, the Chinese Communists were teaching their compatriots that from the early nineteenth century onward the United States had consistently followed an aggressive policy toward China which culminated in her support for Chiang Kai-shek in the civil war and her present actions in Korea and Taiwan. The Chinese people were told to treat the United States with scorn because she was a paper tiger and certainly could be defeated.[56]

Truman, MacArthur, and the State Department perceived a China that no longer existed. The conviction that China would not intervene represented an emotional rather than an intellectual conclusion, an ascription to the enemy of intentions compatible with the desires of Washington and Tokyo.[57] This misperception lay the groundwork for a military disaster of major proportions.

If the Americans misperceived Chinese intentions by refusing to take them seriously, the Chinese erred in the opposite direction. The world, as viewed in Peking, was rife with implacable American hostility. Not only were American troops marching directly up to the Chinese border at the Yalu River, but the United States was protecting the hated Nationalist regime on Taiwan and was aiding the French against the revolutionaries in Indochina. In addition, the United States was rehabilitating and rearming Japan. With this outlook, the Chinese leaders not surprisingly regarded verbal protestations of goodwill on the part of the United States as a mockery.

Most basic to an understanding of MacArthur's drive to the Yalu was his peculiar misperception of China's power. Even though he characterized China as a nation lusting for expansion, MacArthur had a curious contempt for the Chinese soldier. He equated the thoroughly indoctrinated, well-disciplined Communist soldier of 1950 with the demoralized Nationalist soldier of 1948. To be blunt, he did not respect his enemy, and this disrespect was to cost him dearly. Far from regarding the Chinese as military equals, MacArthur insisted that "the pattern of the Oriental psychology [was] to respect and follow aggressive, resolute and dynamic leadership, to quickly turn on a leadership characterized by timidity or vacillation."[58] This paternalistic contempt for the military power of the new China led directly to disaster in October and November 1950. The story is worth examining in some detail.

On October 26, to the accompaniment of fierce bugle calls, shrill whistles, and blasts from shepherds' horns, the Chinese launched a surprise attack on South Korean and American forces some 50 miles south of the Chinese border. The results were devastating. Several United Nations regiments were virtually decimated. Nevertheless, Major General Charles A. Willoughby, MacArthur's main intelligence officer, voiced the opinion on the following day that "the auspicious time for Chinese intervention [had] long since passed" and that "there [was] no positive evidence that Chinese Communist units, as such, [had] entered Korea."[59] On November 1 the Chinese initiated a massive attack against the

United States Third Battalion and virtually tore it apart. Then, after shattering the United States Eighth Cavalry, the Chinese abruptly broke contact and withdrew.

MacArthur's reaction to these events demonstrates how difficult it is for an old, but stubbornly entrenched, misperception to yield to reality. On the day of the Chinese disengagement, his estimate of total Chinese strength in Korea was between 40,000 and 60,000 men.[60] In fact, as of October 31, the Chinese had deployed, with utmost secrecy and within short distances of the American forces they were about to strike, almost 200,000 men.[61] Some of these had crossed the Yalu before the Wake Island meeting between Truman and MacArthur.

The Chinese troops had done what MacArthur had deemed impossible. They had moved by night in forced marches, employed local guides and porters, and used the barren and hostile terrain of the North Korean hills to their advantage. They had then launched their assault on MacArthur's unsuspecting army. When the Chinese temporarily withdrew, MacArthur immediately ascribed this turn of events to the heavy casualties the enemy had sustained. In MacArthur's view, the Chinese needed to rest, and so a golden opportunity was at hand for a second and victorious American drive to the Yalu.

In retrospect, it is clear that:

> The Chinese withdrawal in early November was designed to encourage the enemy's arrogance; to lure the UN forces deeper into North Korea, where their tenuous supply lines could be interdicted and where units separated from one another by the broken terrain could be isolated and annihilated. This was the nature of the deadly trap which P'eng, at his Shenyang headquarters, was setting for the overconfident general in the Dai Ichi Building in Tokyo.[62]

Thus, MacArthur, believing that he was faced with 40,000 instead of 200,000 Chinese soldiers whom he believed were badly in need of rest after their encounter with the American army, advanced northward again for the "final offensive." The Chinese watched for three weeks until finally, on November 27, they attacked in overwhelming force, turning the American advance into a bloody rout. Thus a peasant army put to flight a modern Western military force commanded by a world-famous American general. In one bound China had become a world power, and the image of the Chinese ward, almost half a century in the making, was finally shattered at a cost of tens of thousands of battle casualties on both sides. MacArthur, incredibly enough, did not learn much from the experience. In the words of his aide-de-camp, Major General Courtney Whitney, the general "was greatly saddened as well as angered at this despicably surreptitious attack, a piece of treachery which he regarded as worse even than Pearl Harbor."[63] The stark truth was that MacArthur had fallen blindly into the trap of his own misperceptions.

The paternalistic attitude of American leaders toward Communist China died hard. It remained extremely difficult for the United States to admit that the new China was growing in power and was fiercely hostile, and that this attitude was more than a passing phenomenon. Many rationalizations were invoked to explain this disturbing new presence on the world scene. Communism was viewed as somehow "alien" to the "Chinese character." It would pass, leaving the "traditional friendship" between China and America to reassert itself—although the paternalism implicit in this traditional relationship was never admitted.[64] At other times, Chinese hostility to the United States was explained as the result of the evil influence of the Soviet Union:

> On November 27, immediately following Mr. Vyshinsky's statement of charges of aggression against the U.S., the United States representative in this Committee [one of the United Nations], Ambassador Dulles . . . with a feeling of sadness rather than anger, said one could only conclude that the Soviet Union was trying to destroy the long history of close friendship between China and the United States and to bring the Chinese people to hate and, if possible, to fight the United States.[65]

One of the more bizarre examples of this attempt to maintain old attitudes in the face of bewildering new facts was the brief flurry of articles in the press during December 1950 reporting the possibility of a United Nations military action in China—directed not against the Chinese people but against the Mao faction, which was presumed to be their oppressor. A headline in *The New York Herald Tribune* proclaimed "Declaration of State of War Against Mao's Faction Urged"; the text of the article read that "So far as can be determined now, the action of the UN will not be one of war against China or the Chinese people but against one faction in China, namely the Communists."[66] How this distinction was to be put into effect on the battlefield was never made clear, and apparently the utterly unrealistic nature of the proposal led to its early death. Nevertheless, the distinction between the Chinese people and their Communist leaders persisted for some time. On December 29, 1950, in a statement for the Voice of America, Dean Rusk, then assistant secretary of state for Far Eastern affairs, accused the Chinese Communists of having plotted the North Korean assault. The press reported that "As all American officials have done consistently, Mr. Rusk drew a distinction between the Chinese people, for whom the United States has a long tradition of friendliness, and their Communist rulers."[67] By denying that the new government of China had a power base and a measure of popular support, the United States tried to maintain intact its old illusions about the historical relationship between the two nations. But it had been the relationship between predator and hunted, a fact that had never been admitted.

Indian Ambassador Panikkar detected this blind spot in the American picture of China. He noted that in the early days of the Korean War, the Western military attachés in Peking had been utterly confident that Chinese troops could not possibly stand up to the Americans. He noticed that the defeat in late November came as a profound shock to the Americans, and their attitude thenceforth was very different.[68] In a good summation of the problem, he stated: "China had become a Great Power and was insisting on being recognized as such. The adjustments which such a recognition requires are not easy, and the conflict in the Far East is the outcome of this contradiction."[69]

The Chinese intervention in the Korean War provides a good illustration of the practical, operational consequences of divergent perceptions in world affairs. These perceptions are in effect definitions of the situation at hand. Once the situation has been defined, certain alternatives are eliminated. One does not conciliate an opponent who is perceived as implacably hostile; hence, the Chinese Communists felt in the end that they had no resort but to intervene in Korea. One does not credit the threats of an opponent whose powers one perceives as negligible; hence, the United States viewed even specific Chinese warnings as bluff. One does not compromise with an opponent whose ideology is perceived as antithetical to one's own values; hence, the United States and China remained poised on the brink of potentially disastrous conflict, neither one accepting the other's perception of its world role as legitimate. This was the central significance of the "entirely new war" that was to ravage the peninsula for another eighteen months.

Conclusion

The outbreak of the Korean War may be divided into three separate and distinct phases: the decision to repel the North Korean attack; the decision to cross the thirty-eighth parallel; and MacArthur's drive to the Yalu River that provoked the Chinese intervention. In my judgment, the first decision was correct, the second dubious, and the third disastrous.

When President Truman made his decision to commit American ground forces in Korea, Stalin was still alive and the global Communist movement still intact. China and the Soviet Union had just concluded an alliance. Korea was a test of whether the Communist movement could, by direct invasion, impose itself on the territory of another political entity, or whether that attack could be stemmed through collective action led by the United States.

The president's early decisions were firm, yet graduated: a full week elapsed between his initial response and the infantry commitment. During that week his top advisers were fully heard on several occasions, and their support remained virtually unanimous throughout. The North Koreans had ample opportunity to stop their invasion and thus avoid a full-scale collision with American power. Instead, they pressed the attack and escalated the ferocity of the initial encounter. Finally, even though the president "jumped the gun" on the United Nations by twenty-four hours, he genuinely perceived his action as taken on behalf of the principle of collective security set forth in the United Nations Charter.

Temptation beckoned when the tide of battle turned decisively in favor of the Unified Command. Initially, neither President Truman nor General MacArthur contemplated the seizure of

North Korea, but the success of the Inchon landing provided the opportunity to turn the tables and invade the invader. At this critical juncture, the general, now speaking as a "United Nations commander," insisted on forging ahead, and the president gave his permission. The United Nations was treated rather cavalierly, as little more than an instrument of American policy, and although the UN secretary-general and most member nations accepted their role rather meekly, they had serious inner doubts. A United Nations victory, had it occurred, would clearly have been a victor's peace.

Disaster struck at the Yalu largely because of the hubris of General MacArthur. The UN commander lacked all respect for the new China and preferred instead to act out of hopes and fears rather than realities and facts. By provoking the Chinese intervention, MacArthur probably prolonged the war by another eighteen months and turned it into one of the bloodiest conflicts in recent history. Aside from the 34,000 American dead, South Korea suffered over 800,000 casualties, and North Korea more than 500,000. The Chinese suffered appalling losses of 1.5 to 2 million men. The war ended indecisively in a draw, with the two Koreas remaining fully armed dictatorships, bitterly hostile to one another.

Yet, paradoxically, the violent clash between the United States and China at the Yalu River might in one sense have contributed to long-run improved relations between the two countries, for the effectiveness of China's intervention in Korea established her as a power to be reckoned with. It shattered once and for all the patronization that had previously characterized the American view of China. One cannot, of course, answer with certainty the question of whether China and America would have gone to war over Vietnam in the 1960s if they had not fought in Korea. But it is highly probable that the Korean War served as a powerful corrective and thus as a restraining memory.

In the Korean War the victim of aggression was tempted by aggression and succumbed to the temptation. The United Nations became a party to the war and remained identified with one side in the conflict to the end. Since its identity became fully merged with the American cause, it lost the power to be a truly neutral mediator in Korea. This is perhaps the clearest lesson of the outbreak of this war: as the United Nations was captured by one of the parties to the conflict and made into its instrument, all sides suffered in the long run, and particularly the United Nations itself. No objective entity could now be called on to serve as referee or buffer. Hence, the fighting stopped only through exhaustion, when both sides finally despaired of victory.

One afterthought: Kim Il Sung, the man who launched the North Korean attack in 1950, remains in charge four decades later. Still a second-rater when compared with other Communist leaders, Kim has periodically attempted to enhance his image by printing excerpts from his memoirs in the Western press. The question of whether he might be tempted to try another 1950 has made vigilance at the thirty-eighth parallel a continuing priority.

NOTES

1. Harry S Truman, *Memoirs* (Garden City, N.Y.: Doubleday, 1955), Vol. 1 of 2 vols., p. 293.

2. *Ibid.,* p. 433.

3. Raymond Dennett and Robert R. Turner (eds.), *Documents on American Foreign Relations* (Princeton: Princeton University Press, 1951), p. 4.

4. Dean G. Acheson, "Responsibility for Decision in Foreign Policy," *Yale Review* (Autumn 1954), p. 12.

5. *Ibid.,* p. 7.

6. *Ibid.*

7. *Ibid.*

8. *Department of State Bulletin,* 23, 574 (July 1950), 17.

9. Truman, *op. cit.,* Vol. 2, p. 332.

10. Department of State, *United States Policy in the Korean Crisis,* Far Eastern Series, No. 34 (Washington, D.C.: Government Printing Office, 1950), p. 1.

11. For a full treatment of this subject, see John G. Stoessinger, *The United Nations and the Superpowers,* 3rd ed. (New York: Random House, 1973), Chap. 3.

12. Cited in Glenn D. Paige, *The Korean Decision* (New York: Free Press, 1968), p. 95.

13. *Ibid.,* p. 100.

14. *The New York Herald Tribune,* June 26, 1950.

15. *The New York Times,* July 2, 1950.
16. Truman, *op. cit.,* Vol. 2, pp. 332ff.
17. United Nations Security Council, Fifth Year, *Official Records,* No. 15, 473rd Meeting (June 25, 1950), p. 3.
18. *The New York Times,* June 26, 1950.
19. *Ibid.*
20. Paige, *op. cit.,* p. 120.
21. *The Chicago Tribune,* June 26, 1950.
22. *Ibid.*
23. Paige, *op. cit.,* p. 127.
24. Truman, *op. cit.,* Vol. 2, p. 334.
25. *Ibid.,* p. 335.
26. *Ibid.*
27. Beverly Smith, "The White House Story: Why We Went to War in Korea," *Saturday Evening Post* (November 10, 1951), p. 80.
28. Truman, *op. cit.,* Vol. 2, p. 337.
29. Cited in Paige, *op. cit.,* p. 179.
30. *Ibid.*
31. Smith, *op. cit.,* p. 80.
32. Truman, *op. cit.,* Vol. 2, p. 463.
33. Paige, *op. cit.,* p. 203.
34. United Nations Document S/1508, June 26, 1950.
35. United Nations Document S/1507, June 26, 1950.
36. Roy E. Appleman, *South to the Naktong, North to the Yalu* (Washington, D.C.: Government Printing Office, 1960), p. 34.
37. *The New York Times,* June 29, 1950.
38. Courtney Whitney, *MacArthur: His Rendezvous with History* (New York: Knopf, 1956), p. 327.
39. *Ibid.,* pp. 332–333.
40. Marguerite Higgins, *War in Korea* (Garden City, N.Y.: Doubleday, 1951), p. 33.
41. Paige, *op. cit.,* p. 243.
42. Truman, *op. cit.,* Vol. 2, p. 343.
43. *United Nations Bulletin* (July 15 and August 1, 1950), pp. 50–53, 95, 99.
44. Leland M. Goodrich, *Korea: A Study of U.S. Policy in the United Nations* (New York: Council on Foreign Relations, 1956), p. 117.
45. K. M. Panikkar, *In Two Chinas* (London: Allen and Unwin, 1955), p. 110.
46. *The New York Herald Tribune,* September 22, 1950.
47. UN General Assembly, *Official Records,* Fifth Session, First Committee (September 30, 1950), p. 39.

48. *Ibid.*
49. The negative votes were cast by Byelorussia, Czechoslovakia, Poland, the Ukraine, and the USSR. Abstaining were Egypt, India, Lebanon, Saudi Arabia, Syria, Yemen, and Yugoslavia.
50. *The New York Times,* October 9, 1950.
51. U.S. Senate, *Military Situation in the Far East,* Hearings before the Committee on Armed Services and the Committee on Foreign Relations, 82nd Cong., 1st Sess. (1951), p. 3483.
52. Samuel B. Griffith II, *The Chinese People's Liberation Army* (New York: McGraw-Hill, 1967), p. 124.
53. *The New York Times,* November 17, 1950.
54. *Ibid.*
55. Truman, *op. cit.,* Vol. 2, p. 362.
56. Tang Tsou, *America's Failure in China,* 1941–1950 (Chicago: University of Chicago Press, 1963), p. 578.
57. Griffith, *op. cit.,* p. 124.
58. Douglas MacArthur, Message to Veterans of Foreign Wars, August 28, 1950.
59. *Military Situation in the Far East, op. cit.,* p. 3427.
60. Griffith, *op. cit.,* p. 134.
61. *Ibid.,* p. 129.
62. *Ibid.,* p. 134.
63. Whitney, *op. cit.,* p. 394.
64. Allen S. Whiting, *China Crosses the Yalu* (Stanford: Stanford University Press, 1960), pp. 169–170.
65. United States Mission to the United Nations, Press Release No. 1129, February 2, 1951.
66. *The New York Herald Tribune,* December 6, 1950.
67. *The New York Herald Tribune,* December 30, 1950.
68. Panikkar, *op. cit.,* p. 117.
69. *Ibid.,* pp. 177–178.

SELECTED BIBLIOGRAPHY

DE RIVERA, JOSEPH. *The Psychological Dimensions of Foreign Policy.* Columbus, Ohio: Merrill, 1968.

GOODRICH, LELAND M. *Korea: A Study of U.S. Policy in the United Nations.* New York: Council on Foreign Relations, 1956.

PAIGE, GLENN D. *The Korean Decision.* New York: Free Press, 1968.

STOESSINGER, JOHN G. *Nations in Darkness: China, Russia, America.* 4th ed. rev. New York: Random House, 1985.

TRUMAN, HARRY S. *Memoirs.* 2 vols. Garden City, N.Y.: Doubleday, 1955.
WHITING, ALLEN S. *China Crosses the Yalu.* Stanford: Stanford University Press, 1960.
WHITNEY, COURTNEY. *MacArthur: His Rendezvous with History.* New York: Knopf, 1956.

4

A Greek Tragedy in Five Acts: Vietnam

If you look too deeply into the abyss, the abyss will look into you.   Friedrich Nietzsche

Vietnam has been the Thirty Years' War of the twentieth century. In the course of a single generation five American presidents misperceived reality in Indochina and substituted their own phantoms, first called fear and later called hope. These fears and hopes obscured reality until they produced a nightmare that could not be denied: the longest war in American history and the most divisive conflict domestically since the Civil War.

I do not believe that history will show that five evil men deceived their people and led them into war in Indochina. I do believe, however, that each of these five men, in his own particular way, made a concrete policy decision that escalated the war and contributed to the ultimate disaster. It is for this reason that this chapter will deal with the Vietnam war in five "acts," each to be seen as a "quantum leap" in a gradually escalating conflict.

In retrospect, the tragedy of the American encounter with Vietnam is plain. But the question remains whether it was an example of Greek tragedy, "the tragedy of necessity," where the feeling aroused in the spectator is "What a pity it had to be this way" or of Christian tragedy, "the tragedy of possibility," where the feeling aroused is "What a pity it was this way when it might have been otherwise." The main thesis of this chapter is that in Vietnam the misperceptions of five presidents transformed a tragedy of possibility into a tragedy of necessity.

Act One: Truman—Asia Was Not Europe

President Truman's perception of Indochina underwent profound changes between 1945 and 1952. In 1945, when hostilities erupted between France and Ho Chi Minh, the president was decidedly sympathetic to the latter. He regarded the war as France's problem and what France deserved for her colonial ambitions. An American OSS officer who had worked closely with Ho Chi Minh for several months before V-J Day had described him as an "awfully sweet guy whose outstanding quality was his gentleness."[1] This perception was much like that of President Franklin D. Roosevelt during World War II. Roosevelt had openly opposed the return of French power to Indochina and had advocated some form of international trusteeship for the area. If the fighting in Indochina was a colonial war, it followed that the United States should disapprove of France. This remained American policy under Roosevelt's successor. In 1947 President Truman urged France to end the war and resisted all French appeals for assistance, insisting, for example, that American-produced propellers be removed from the British aircraft given by Britain to the French troops fighting against Ho Chi Minh.[2]

When President Truman's perception, and that of the American leadership in general, did change, the reversal was based not on actual events in Indochina but on developments completely outside the area. In 1948 America's concept of its world role changed profoundly. Crisis followed crisis, from Berlin, to Greece, and to Czechoslovakia, and the division between East and West crystallized and hardened. The concepts of an "iron curtain" and "containment" came to pervade the entire American view of foreign affairs. The chasm between East and West appeared deeper by the day, and President Truman, architect of the North Atlantic Treaty, began to see himself as the leader of an embattled "free world" resisting the expansion of a ruthless totalitarianism.

The threat in Europe was undeniable, and President Truman's response to it was, on the whole, not exaggerated. The Truman Doctrine probably saved Greece and Turkey from Soviet conquest, and the North Atlantic Treaty in all likelihood stopped Stalin from overrunning Western Europe. The new American definition of the European situation, however, spilled over to encompass the entire globe. Having recognized a mortal threat in the heart of Europe, the American leadership soon came to redefine *all* conflicts throughout the world as part of the same struggle. Truman, in effect, decided to transplant the containment policy from Europe to Indochina.

Inexorably, the United States came to believe that the "frontiers" of the free world included Asia as well. In October 1948 the House Foreign Affairs Subcommittee on World Communism issued a report calling China the active theater of the Cold War. The report said that the Communists were using China as a testing ground for tactics they might employ to take over the world and recommended a "guarantee of territorial and political integrity" to the Chinese Nationalists.[3]

This shift in outlook implied an American redefinition of the "true" nature of Ho Chi Minh as well:

> In this country, it is only now beginning to be understood that in any Asiatic nationalist movement connected with Moscow through its leadership, the totalitarian-imperialist trend must inevitably kill native nationalism. . . . His [Ho Chi Minh's] Indochinese independence has become the means to another end: Russian conquest of the Southeast Pacific.[4]

On June 17, 1949, *The New York Herald Tribune* stated flatly that "Ho Chi Minh is a Comintern agent whom the French rate as an authentic political genius." This redefinition did *not* coincide with any objective developments in the Indochinese conflict. It coincided instead with an extraneous event: the Communist victory in China. The sense of betrayal that the American public felt over the loss of China intensified the anxieties arising from the Cold War. Thus peril in Europe, compounded by betrayal in China, produced a strongly emotional reevaluation of the United States' relationship to Southeast Asia.

Hence American failure in China was attributed to the machinations of a worldwide conspiracy. From 1949 onward the American press reflected a shift in attitudes such that the perceptual grid of Cold War categories was ultimately superimposed on the older conflict in Indochina. This grid gradually eclipsed all awareness of the nationalist origins of the Ho Chi Minh insurgency. It even erased American recollections of the colonial conditions that had sparked the revolt until, finally, the original disapproval of France as an imperial power disappeared altogether in a redefinition of the French as "defenders of the West."

One by one the ambiguities disappeared. "Nationalist rebels" were steadily amalgamated with the Communist threat. Bao Dai, once referred to as the "nightclub emperor" and described as a man irretrievably tainted by his close association with the French colonial regime, was now officially considered as "offering more opportunity to the Vietnamese people to develop their own national life than a leader who must obey the orders of international Communism."[5] On February 2, 1950, the *Department of State Bulletin* asserted that the recognition of Ho Chi Minh by the USSR, China, North Korea, and the European nations ended any speculation as to the fate of Vietnam under Ho, who was now described as a lifelong servant of world Communism.

Since the definition of what was going on in Indochina had changed, it was only natural that there should be a closely related shift in ideas of what should be done. Now that the deadly enemy was seen at work in Southeast Asia, President Truman was eager to keep the French in Indochina. In May 1950 the Griffin mission recommended an aid program of $23 million in economic assistance and $15 million in military aid to the French in Indochina.[6] A few days after the outbreak of the Korean War President Truman authorized the first shipments of aircraft to Indochina. In addition, $119 million in military aid was made available to France under the Mutual Defense Assistance Program. This aid increased to $300 million in 1952. Thus, before he left the presidency in 1953, Harry Truman had underwritten the French war effort in Indochina.

By 1951 the American leadership and large segments of the American public perceived France as the free world's frontline ally in the fight against Communism in Southeast Asia. "That the French are making a tremendous effort to hold Indochina for the free world is better understood now than it was a short time ago," stated *The New York Times* in an editorial on September 24, 1951. The reevaluation was even made retroactive: "A bitter and bloody struggle between Communist forces and French Union troops has been racking Indochina for six years," declared the State Department's Office of Public Affairs in 1951.[7] And in

March 1952, a State Department official stated that "in this battle to preserve their country from Communism, France is contributing financially and militarily. . . . French soldiers and resources have borne the brunt of this brutal attack."[8]

By early 1952 the Cold War grid was firmly in place. No longer was Southeast Asia viewed as the arena of an anticolonial revolt; it had now become part of the global East-West power struggle. On January 25, 1952, the *Christian Science Monitor* stated in an editorial that "no one planned that, after a stalemate in Korea, there should be a new trial of strength in the southward projection of Asia," implying that the Indochinese conflict had begun *after* the outbreak of the Korean War. The editorial concluded by imposing the Cold War dichotomy in full force: "Indochina is a place which is bound to be occupied eventually either by East or West. The strategic prizes are so great that the issue must be joined and eventually settled."

While President Truman's attention in Asia was, of course, focused primarily on Korea, by 1950 he believed that the French were fighting for the free world in Indochina just as the United Nations was fighting for it in Korea. He never committed combat troops to Southeast Asia as he did to Korea, but he authorized material aid in 1950 and raised the level of this assistance steadily until he left office in 1953. By that time the United States was paying almost one-third of the total cost of the French war effort in Indochina. President Truman had transferred his Cold War images from Europe to Southeast Asia and based his policies there on facile analogies rather than specific Asian realities. But Asia was not Europe, and what had worked in Europe would turn out to be a disaster in Indochina.

Act Two: Eisenhower—The Lesson of France Ignored

President Dwight D. Eisenhower and Secretary of State John Foster Dulles were absolutely convinced that China would intervene in the Indochina war on the side of Ho Chi Minh against France, similar to the manner in which she had intervened on the side of North Korea against the United States. To forestall such an intervention, Eisenhower and Dulles had increased American military assistance to France to $500 million by 1953. By 1954 this assistance had reached the $1 billion mark. The United States was now paying over one-half the cost of the Indochinese war.[9]

The American expectation of a Chinese invasion was so powerful that it defied all evidence to the contrary. Neither the fact that the anticipated invasion failed to materialize nor the lack of evidence that it was actually planned lessened American apprehensions. Instead, the very strength of the expectation produced its own substantiation. Time and again, unfounded rumors were accepted as proof of impending intervention. The result was a recurrent pattern of false alarms. These began as early as April 11, 1951, with a headline in *The New York Times* that reported that a "Chinese Unit [was] said to join [the] Vietminh." Secretary Dulles repeatedly stated that the Chinese were directly engaged in battlefield operations. On April 5, 1954, during the siege of Dienbienphu, he claimed that Chinese troops were actually participating in the battle for the French fortress.[10] President Eisenhower, looking back upon this period in his memoirs, declared that "the struggle . . . began gradually, *with Chinese intervention,* to assume its true complexion of a struggle between Communist and non-Communist forces rather than one between a colonial power and colonists who were intent on attaining independence."[11]

Thus by 1954, largely as a result of their perceptions, the Americans were fighting a proxy war in Indochina. The battle for Dienbienphu almost changed this into a direct American war of intervention. Dienbienphu was France's last stand in Indochina. She had fought for almost a decade and had committed an army of 400,000 men. On March 20, 1954, with the fortress already under siege, General Paul Ely, commander of the French forces in Indochina, informed President Eisenhower that unless the United States intervened, Indochina would be lost. Admiral Arthur W. Radford, chairman of the Joint Chiefs of Staff, recommended military intervention, and Vice President Richard M. Nixon backed him by stating on April 16 that "if the United States cannot otherwise prevent the loss of Indochina, then the Administration must face the situation and dispatch troops."[12] President Eisenhower overruled his vice president and the chairman of the Joint Chiefs of Staff and decided not to intervene. He feared that the French had engendered too much popular antagonism to win the war and also felt that his administration would get little backing from the Congress for a military intervention in Asia so soon after the conclusion of the Korean War. Thus, on the American side the war remained a war by proxy for a little while longer, but by a narrow margin.

The facts, in all cases, were strikingly different from Eisenhower's and Dulles's perceptions. So far as Ho Chi Minh's relations with China were concerned, the North Vietnamese leader was always somewhat suspicious of China. In Bernard Fall's words, he was "probably equipped with an instinctive Vietnamese fear of Chinese domination, no matter what its political coloration, just as to a Russian, *any* Germany might be slightly suspect."[13] His policy was essentially one of balance, of maintaining the independence and integrity of his movement, vis-à-vis both China and the Soviet Union, while accepting as much aid as could safely be accepted from both.

Chinese aid to Ho Chi Minh was at times considerable, but never decisive. It consisted mostly of light weapons, trucks, and radios, largely of American manufacture, that had been captured from the Chinese Nationalists some years before.[14] In view of economic needs at home and the burdens imposed by the Korean War, China could hardly afford to become a bottomless reservoir of military assistance for the Vietminh forces. The best analysis of the Chinese relationship with Ho Chi Minh has probably been provided by Robert Guillain, the frontline correspondent for *Le Monde* in Indochina: "China adheres to a very simple principle: that the balance of power never inclines in any permanent direction toward the French side. There is no need—and this is the difference from what has happened in Korea—of direct intervention, of an invasion."[15] Thus, when France received more American aid following the outbreak of the Korean War, the Chinese stepped up their own aid program just enough to reestablish a rough equilibrium. As Melvin Gurtov put it: "The Indochina campaign eventually became a crude game in which the French could never permanently regain the high ground."[16] Thus Chinese military intervention on the side of the Vietminh never materialized. Instead, the Chinese used the Vietminh as their proxy.

The Geneva Conference of mid-1954 and the formation a few weeks later of the Southeast Asia Treaty Organization (SEATO) marked the end of French military involvement and the beginning of an American military presence in Indochina. The Geneva

Conference resulted in the signing of several agreements to cease hostilities in Indochina and to establish the three independent sovereign states of Laos, Cambodia, and Vietnam. The accords on Vietnam provided for a "provisional military demarcation line" at the seventeenth parallel. Vietminh forces were to regroup north of the line, while the forces of the French Union were to regroup to the south. The line was to have military significance only, and the political unification of Vietnam was to be brought about through a general election two years hence under the supervision of a neutral three-power International Control Commission consisting of Canada, India, and Poland.

France had little choice, but her exit was made relatively gracefully. Ho Chi Minh's Vietminh forces were dominant in more than three-quarters of Vietnam and were poised to overrun considerably more. To Ho the terms of the accords were acceptable, since he was convinced that the general election of 1956 would win him all of Vietnam. From his point of view, the certainty of a military victory was simply replaced by the certainty of a political victory. Both the Soviet Union and China, reflecting their recently adopted line of "peaceful coexistence," applied pressure on Ho to accept the terms of the accords, reassuring him that his victory at the polls was certain.

The United States never signed the Geneva Accords. But in a unilateral decision at the end of the Geneva Conference the United States government pledged to "refrain from the threat or the use of force to disturb" the settlement and added that it would view any violation of the accords with grave concern.

The general American position at the conference remained ambivalent, since on the eve of a congressional election campaign the maintenance of Eisenhower's domestic appeal as peacemaker in Asia was of great importance. Moreover, to block a peaceful settlement of the Indochina war would also have jeopardized French participation in European defense plans. These conflicting considerations led the Eisenhower administration to dissociate the United States from the Geneva Accords and to seek another solution that would prevent any further territory in Asia from falling under Communist control. The answer was the creation of SEATO. Secretary of State Dulles declared that now that the war had ended, the United States could make arrangements for collective defense against aggression and build up "the truly independent states of Cambodia, Laos, and South Vietnam." On the day the treaty was signed in Manila, its eight signatories designated in an additional protocol the states of Cambodia and Laos and "the free territory under the jurisdiction of the state of Vietnam" to be under SEATO protection. The United States thus created SEATO to offset the results of Geneva. It also decided to consider South Vietnam a separate state.

The Vietminh, on the other hand, regarded SEATO as a clear violation of the spirit of the Geneva Accords. Ho Chi Minh saw the American position as an effort to deprive the Vietminh in the political arena of what it had gained militarily on the battlefield. Nevertheless, Ho withdrew his forces from the South, assuming that he would get enough votes there in 1956 to emerge with a clear national majority at election time. His electoral strength in the North was certain, and if only a minority supported the Vietminh in the South, his election would be ensured. President Eisenhower too thought that elections, if held on the basis of the Geneva Accords, would lead to a Communist victory. As he put it in 1954: "Had elections been held as of the time of the fighting, possibly 80 percent of the population would have voted for the Communist Ho Chi Minh as their leader rather than Chief of State Bao Dai."[17]

In the meantime, Ngo Dinh Diem, an American-backed Roman Catholic from a Mandarin family, began to challenge Emperor Bao Dai in the South. The United States strongly supported Diem in his bid for power, and in October 1955 Diem proclaimed the establishment of a Republic of Vietnam, with himself as president.

Hence Geneva and the SEATO treaty meant the end of French power in Indochina and the beginnings of the American effort to enter the struggle with its own military presence. As yet there had been no significant military encounters between Vietminh and American forces. But the path had become continuous. The Vietminh saw the Americans as following the course of French imperialism, and the Americans perceived Geneva as a well-laid Communist trap to engulf all of Vietnam. The end of a colonial war merely signified the beginning of a war between Americans and Communists.

As the East-West conflict superseded the colonial war, the tenor of battle gradually intensified. A pattern of escalation emerged in which every failure at diplomatic negotiations paved the way for yet another upward step on the scale of violence.

The first such discernible moves after Geneva were the American effort between 1954 and 1956 to strengthen President Diem's military establishment, and Ho Chi Minh's visits to Moscow and Peking in 1955 to negotiate aid and friendship treaties with the two Communist powers. Diem declared in July 1955 that since South Vietnam had not signed the Geneva Accords, he was not prepared to permit elections under the conditions specified by them. He also added that there was no freedom in the North to campaign for any opposition to Ho Chi Minh. President Eisenhower supported this view, and July 1956, the date scheduled for general elections in the accords, passed without any elections being held. Ho, in retaliation, began to train Communist cadres for guerrilla warfare in the South.

During the remaining years of the Eisenhower administration the United States continued to support the increasingly unpopular President Diem with military advisers, and by 1960 almost 1,000 Americans were serving in South Vietnam in that capacity. Thus Eisenhower and Dulles, ignoring the terrible lesson of the defeat of France, nevertheless decided to take on the burden of Vietnam. "Communism" had to be stopped, even though in this particular case "Communism" was an obscure Asian peasant country that by no stretch of the imagination could have posed a threat to the United States. Once again, fear rather than facts determined policy.

Act Three: Kennedy—The Military

During his brief presidency of 1,000 days John F. Kennedy deepened the American involvement in Vietnam considerably. By the time of his death, the United States had greatly increased the number of military advisers in Vietnam; napalm and other antipersonnel weapons had been authorized for limited use against the enemy; and the United States had become identified with the highly unpopular regime of President Diem. The Vietnamese leader's violent death preceded Kennedy's own by only three weeks.

Even though Kennedy felt compelled to demonstrate his tough-

ness in the international arena, after the disaster at the Bay of
Pigs and his abrasive meeting with Nikita Khrushchev in Vienna,
he was deeply skeptical about the possibility of a decisive American victory in Vietnam. In a revealing moment, he exclaimed: "In
the last analysis, it is *their* war; it is they who must win it or lose
it." He was pressed relentlessly by the military to commit combat
troops to Vietnam, but refused to do so to the end. Yet under his
leadership the United States entered a crucial period of transi-
tion, from a marginal commitment to a fateful and direct involvement. The reason for this tragedy was that most of the men
around the president, including his secretary of defense and the
chairman of the Joint Chiefs of Staff, perceived Vietnam essentially as a military rather than as a political problem. In their
view, greater quantities of more sophisticated weapons would
guarantee victory in a relatively short period of time. Kennedy's
instincts told him that this assumption was probably wrong, but
he permitted the facts and figures of the military experts to sway
him. Shortly before his death, his doubts prevailed, but by then
it was too late. Close to 17,000 Americans were serving as advisers
in Vietnam by the end of 1963.

Kennedy's first response to stepped-up Vietcong guerrilla activity in South Vietnam was to emphasize the need for antiguerrilla
warfare training in the United States. The result was the creation
of the Special Forces, which enjoyed the president's particular
favor. In October 1961, according to David Halberstam, the entire
White House press corps was transported to Fort Bragg to watch
a demonstration put on by the Special Forces:

> It turned into a real whiz-bang day. There were ambushes, counteram-
> bushes and demonstrations in snakemeat eating, all topped off by a
> Buck Rogers show: a soldier with a rocket on his back who flew over
> water to land on the other side. It was quite a show, and it was only as
> they were leaving Fort Bragg that Francis Lara, the Agence France-
> Presse correspondent who had covered the Indochina war, sidled over
> to his friend Tom Wicker of the *New York Times.* "All this looks very
> impressive, doesn't it?" he said. Wicker allowed that it did. "Funny,"
> Lara said, "none of it worked for us when we tried it in 1951."[18]

In 1961 Walt Rostow drew the president's attention to Briga-
dier General Edward Lansdale. Lansdale had made a reputation

for himself by helping Philippine President Ramon Magsaysay defeat the Huk rebellion. He seemed to be just the man to defeat the Vietcong. Lansdale recommended that the number of American military advisers in Vietnam be increased to 3,000 men. Kennedy rejected the recommendation but authorized the dispatch of 400 men from the Special Forces to Vietnam. This would give him the opportunity to see how his favorites would acquit themselves in real action.

In March 1961 Kennedy appointed Frederick E. Nolting, Jr., ambassador to Vietnam. As head of the political section of NATO, Nolting had earned a good, solid reputation but had never been to Asia, and his ideas about Communism had been filtered through the prism of his European experience. Nolting requested as his deputy William Trueheart, another man who had never visited Asia. This was the price that Kennedy paid for the mistakes of the past. Since the days of Senator Joseph McCarthy most experts on Asia had been considered possible security risks, whereas specialists on Europe like Nolting and Trueheart were above suspicion. The fact that they were totally ignorant about Asian realities did not seem to be a serious concern.

In April 1961, in order to boost President Diem's morale, Kennedy decided to ask Vice President Lyndon Johnson to visit Vietnam on his Asian tour. Johnson was less than enthusiastic, but the president coaxed him into accepting: "Don't worry, Lyndon," he said. "If anything happens to you, Sam Rayburn and I will give you the biggest funeral Austin, Texas, ever saw."[19]

Johnson was favorably impressed with Diem. He hailed him publicly as "the Winston Churchill of Southeast Asia," though when asked by a reporter for the *Saturday Evening Post* whether he really believed that about Diem, Johnson answered: "Shit, man, he's the only boy we got out there."[20] In his official report to the president, Johnson declared that:

> The battle against Communism must be joined in Southeast Asia with strength and determination to achieve success there. Vietnam can be saved if we move quickly and wisely. . . . The most important thing is imaginative, creative American management of our military aid program.[21]

Thus, Johnson committed the president more deeply to Vietnam, and in addition committed himself personally to the war.

The most crucial single event that escalated the American commitment during the Kennedy administration was the Rostow-Taylor Report. In October 1961 the president decided to send two of his own special representatives to Vietnam for an on-site fact-finding trip. He chose Walt Rostow and Maxwell Taylor because of the interest these two men had shown in Kennedy's own favorite approach to the Vietnam problem: limited antiguerrilla warfare.

The report came as a profound shock to Kennedy. Rostow and Taylor recommended the introduction of 8,000 American combat troops into Vietnam and stated flatly that without such a commitment Vietnam could not be saved. It was their position that American air power could save Vietnam at any time, and that Hanoi and Peking would face serious logistical difficulties if they attempted to counter American power. So far as fighting conditions for the proposed American combat troops were concerned, Taylor and Rostow declared that they found South Vietnam "not an excessively difficult or unpleasant place to operate." They thought it comparable to Korea, where American troops had learned to fight efficiently and well.

Kennedy's own misgivings about this report were echoed by George Ball, the under secretary of state for economic affairs who had observed the French disaster in Indochina and noted the parallels. Ball warned the president that even a small combat commitment of 8,000 men would change the nature of the commitment and the nature of the war. Within five years, he warned, the commitment would be escalated to 300,000 men. Though Kennedy had his own doubts about the Rostow-Taylor recommendations, he nevertheless expressed his belief in the ability of rational men to control irrational commitments. He was reported to have laughed at Ball's warning and to have said: "George, you are crazier than hell."[22]

In a conversation with Arthur Schlesinger, Jr., the president expressed his own reservations very clearly:

> They want a force of American troops. They say it is necessary in order to restore confidence and maintain morale. But it will be just like Berlin. The troops will march in, the bands will play, the crowds will

cheer, and in four days everyone will have forgotten. Then we will be told we have to send in more troops. It's like taking a drink. The effect wears off and you have to take another.[23]

Finally, the president compromised. Instead of 8,000 combat troops, he authorized 15,000 military advisers and support units. In making this crucial decision, he made any future withdrawal from Vietnam that much more difficult. Yet by doing less than he was called on to do, the president maintained the illusion that he was holding the line rather than taking the United States deeper into the war. The commander of the American advisory and support team was to be Lieutenant General Paul D. Harkins, an officer described by David Halberstam as "a man of compelling mediocrity."[24]

The performance of the South Vietnamese army did not improve despite the presence of the new American advisers. The Vietcong had escalated their own guerrilla activities, and by late 1962 the situation had become desperate. Generals Taylor and Harkins persisted in transmitting overly optimistic military reports to the president. As one firsthand observer succinctly put it:

It became increasingly a policy based on appearances; Vietnamese realities did not matter, but the *appearances* of Vietnamese realities mattered because they could affect American realities. More and more effort went into public relations because it was easier to manipulate appearances and statements than it was to affect reality on the ground.[25]

Harkins argued fiercely for the unlimited use of napalm and crop defoliation. Kennedy hated these weapons because of their particularly inhumane character. Harkins persisted, however, and finally Kennedy approved the use of napalm in battles where there were no population centers and reluctantly authorized limited defoliation on lines of communications, but not on crops. Again, by authorizing less than Harkins and the military wanted, the president felt that he was limiting, rather than expanding, the use of American power.

Robert McNamara, Kennedy's secretary of defense, was also certain of an American victory. He visited Vietnam frequently, but was so much the prisoner of his own limited experience that he constantly tried to apply American production techniques to an Asian political revolution. His relentless emphasis on quantifiable data and statistics blinded him to the essential quality of his Vietcong enemy: a total commitment to the task of expelling the Americans, who by now had become identified as the successors of French colonialism.

In mid-1963 Kennedy was jarred by reports about the growing unpopularity of President Diem. Increasingly he felt that the United States would have to dissociate itself from the repressive harshness of the South Vietnamese ruling family. The new United States ambassador, Henry Cabot Lodge, advised that if a coup d'état materialized against Diem, the United States should not attempt to thwart it. During September and October the Diem regime resorted to particularly brutal measures to crush Buddhist dissidents. More and more the United States looked like the ally of a reactionary government because that government had the single virtue of being anti-Communist. In November Diem was killed, and three weeks later John Kennedy was murdered. Lyndon Johnson, who admired Diem and always opposed the planned coup against him, allegedly said, in an almost mystical way after the president's death, that "the assassination of Kennedy was a retribution for the assassination of Diem."[26]

Kennedy and his military advisers never took seriously the statement made by many Vietcong soldiers that it was the duty of their generation to die for their country. They believed that the Vietcong, in their "black pajamas," were a fake army and that the South Vietnamese had the real and legitimate army. In reality, the reverse was closer to the truth. Taylor and Rostow, in their crucial report, had equated Vietnam with Korea. They had ignored the all-important difference that Korea had been a conventional war with a classic border crossing by an enemy in uniform, whereas Vietnam was a political struggle conducted by guerrillas feeding on subversion and taking advantage of a jungle terrain where front lines became virtually meaningless.

Thus President Kennedy—essentially a man of reason with a profoundly skeptical bent—became the victim of that particularly American form of hubris that blithely assumed that technology, computerlike efficiency, production, air power, and above all, competent American management could overcome any adversary. They ignored the reality of an army of guerrillas who were quite prepared to die for their cause, who would match the American escalation man for man, if not weapon for weapon, and were prepared to fight for a generation or more. At the time of President Kennedy's death, 17,000 Americans were serving in Vietnam, but only seventy had died by the end of 1963.

Act Four: Johnson—The Catastrophe

"I can't get out. I can't finish it with what I have got. So what the hell can I do?"[27] Shortly after he made this remark to his wife in March 1965 President Johnson authorized massive combat troops to the war in Vietnam. By taking this step, he involved the United States deeply and consciously in a war that he could not win but that he also felt he could not afford to lose.

The record of the Johnson presidency in Vietnam is a story of self-delusion and misperception so vast that it turned into a national catastrophe. Despite relentless bombing raids on both North and South Vietnam and the introduction of more than half a million American troops, the enemy was not defeated. Instead, Johnson's ego, stubbornness, and pride destroyed his presidency and divided his people in a spiritual civil war.

At no single point when he made his decisions to escalate the bombing or the ground commitment did Johnson realize that he had crossed the Rubicon and unleashed a major American land war in Asia. He always hoped that a little more bombing or a few more troops would bring the enemy to the conference table. In doing this, he misperceived his enemy, misled his people, and ultimately deceived himself.

It all began in January 1964 with a memorandum to the president from the Joint Chiefs of Staff, urging him to increase the commitment in order to win the war more quickly: "The United States must be prepared to put aside many of the self-imposed restrictions which now limit our efforts, and to undertake bolder actions which may embody greater risks."[28] Specifically, the Joint Chiefs were of the opinion that aerial bombing would bring North Vietnam to its knees. Walt Rostow stated in support of this recommendation that "Ho Chi Minh has an industrial complex to protect; he is no longer a guerrilla fighter with nothing to lose."[29]

In the meantime, Robert Johnson, head of the Policy Planning

Council and deputy to Rostow, undertook a careful study of the probable effects of bombing. The study concluded that the bombing would not work and predicted, prophetically, that it would imprison the American government. Economic growth was not a major Hanoi objective, the study said, challenging one of Rostow's favorite theses; rather, it was the unfinished business of throwing the foreigners out of the country. Hanoi had two formidable pillars of strength: the nationalist component of unity and the Communist component of control, which made for an organized, unified, modern state. Bombing would not affect such a regime. On the contrary, it might even strengthen it.

This remarkable study was ignored. Rostow, who was totally committed to bombing, never brought it to the president's attention. More and more, the president's advisers, both civilian and military, moved toward a consensus on the bombing policy. Robert McNamara, McGeorge Bundy, Maxwell Taylor, and Dean Rusk—all of them perceived a chain of aggression emanating from China that urged on North Vietnam. Ho Chi Minh, in turn, was the source of the Vietcong aggression in the South. Thus, bombing would stop aggression at the source—in the North—and would convince China of American determination. No more dominoes would be permitted to fall to Communism. In a revealing "Pentagon Papers" memorandum to McNamara, John McNaughton, a former Harvard law professor and now assistant secretary of defense, set forth American goals in South Vietnam in terms of the following priorities:

70 per cent—To avoid a humiliating U.S. defeat
20 per cent—To keep South Vietnamese territory from Chinese hands
10 per cent—To permit the people of South Vietnam to enjoy a better, freer way of life.[30]

Thus the official reason given to the American people for the intervention in Vietnam with air power and ground troops made up only one-tenth of the real reason.

The specific incident that triggered the bombing of North Vietnam was the encounter of the two American warships *C. Turner Joy* and *Maddox* with North Vietnamese PT boats in the Gulf of Tonkin. The administration maintained that the ships had been fired upon in neutral waters and retaliation was mandatory. Subsequent studies have cast serious doubts on this official version. After painstaking research, one scholar reached the dramatic conclusion that there had been no attack on the *Maddox* and the *Turner Joy* at all, that the president misled Congress and the people, and through that deception was able to obtain congressional authorization for a war that he had decided on months before while promising the voters peace.[31] Whether or not one regards this conclusion as too harsh, there can be little doubt about the fact that the American retaliation was disproportionate. On August 4, 1964, American bombers destroyed twenty-five North Vietnamese PT boats and blew up the oil depot at Vinh in North Vietnam. McNamara reported to the president that, at Vinh, "the smoke was observed rising to 14,000 feet." Johnson was overheard to say to a reporter: "I didn't just screw Ho Chi Minh; I cut his pecker off."[32]

During the next few days Senator William Fulbright served as floor sponsor of the Tonkin Gulf Resolution that would give the president broad authority for military action in Indochina. When Senator John Sherman Cooper asked whether this resolution would enable the president "to use such force as could lead into war," Fulbright answered in the affirmative. Two years later, he remembered this episode with deep regret and bitterness.

During his campaign for reelection in 1964 Johnson tried to keep Vietnam out of the public eye as much as possible. When later asked why, he answered: "If you have a mother-in-law with only one eye and she has it in the center of the forehead, you don't keep her in the living room."[33] Vietnam decisions were closely guarded secrets and were made by half a dozen men. Escalation proceeded covertly, by stealth.

Only one man in Johnson's inner circle openly voiced his doubts about Vietnam: George Ball. Ball challenged the assumption made by the others that the United States necessarily controlled the scale and intensity of the war. Once on the tiger's back, one could not be sure of picking a safe place to dismount. Moreover, nothing that could be truly effective against North Vietnam could be tried without risking a much larger war. Ball did not oppose the war because he was a "dove." He simply did not believe in the dissipation of American power through misuse.

On February 7, 1965, the Vietcong attacked the American barracks at Pleiku. Eight Americans were killed and sixty were wounded. McGeorge Bundy, after a quick visit to Pleiku, recommended a reprisal policy of sustained bombing against the North that would cease only if the Vietcong would end their insurrectionist activities. An old Eisenhower aide, Emmett John Hughes, asked Bundy what he would do if the North Vietnamese retaliated by matching the American air escalation with their own ground escalation. "We can't assume what we don't believe," Bundy replied.[34]

Thus Lyndon Johnson began the relentless bombing campaign that was to devastate North Vietnam for the next three years. Though he probably had his own reservations about its effectiveness, his enormous ego and *machismo* played a considerable role. His inner circle too was supportive: McNamara considered victory through air bombardment technologically feasible; Bundy made it intellectually respectable; and Dean Rusk thought it historically necessary.

The bombing campaign, or "Operation Rolling Thunder," as it was referred to in *The Pentagon Papers,* did not produce the desired effect. Ho Chi Minh did exactly what Bundy had thought impossible: he matched the American air escalation with his own escalation, through infiltration on the ground. Hence, since withdrawal was unthinkable, there was now only one possible response: to meet the Vietcong challenge head on with American combat troops on the ground.

In March 1965 General William Westmoreland, the commander of U.S. forces in Vietnam, requested only two marine corps. By April the Joint Chiefs were recommending a commitment of 50,000 men. Some senators became a trifle uneasy, but were quickly reassured by Vice President Hubert Humphrey, who said: "There are people at State and the Pentagon who want to send three-hundred thousand men out there. But the President will never get sucked into anything like that."[35] In May the figure was revised upward to 80,000. George Ball was appalled, but could not reverse the trend. He was alone in his resistance. In June Westmoreland demanded 200,000 men. This would cross the Rubicon and turn Vietnam into a major American war. Johnson reluctantly assented, sensing the terrible trap that was closing in on him. As one reporter wrote of the occasion:

The President is a desperately troubled man resisting the awful pressures to plunge deeper into the Vietnam quagmire—resisting them as instinctively as an old horse resists being led to the knackers. The President bucks, whinnies and shies away, but always in the end the reins tighten—the pressures are too much for him.[36]

The White House gradually became a fortress. Doubters became enemies and ultimately traitors. Only unreserved and unquestioning loyalty was acceptable to the president.

Westmoreland demanded, and received, more and more men for Vietnam. Yet Hanoi met every American escalation with an escalation of its own. In November 1965 Westmoreland projected American troop levels that would reach 600,000 men by 1967. This too was to no avail. A great power of 200 million people fighting a limited war found itself stalemated by a small Asian nation of 17 million fighting a total war.

Failure took its toll. One by one the intellectuals departed. McGeorge Bundy and Robert McNamara left. Walt Rostow remained. Of him, Johnson would say: "I'm getting Walt Rostow as my intellectual. He is not Bundy's intellectual. He is not Schlesinger's intellectual; he is going to be my goddam intellectual."[37] The president refused to give in. "A bombing halt," he would say, "I'll tell you what happens when there is a bombing halt: I halt and then Ho Chi Minh shoves his trucks right up my ass. That's your bombing halt."[38] What became clear in 1967, however, even to a self-deluded Johnson, was the fact that Ho Chi Minh did not have to run for reelection in 1968.

A few months before he left the Department of Defense, Robert McNamara authorized a comprehensive study of all materials pertaining to Vietnam, going back to the 1940s. When he read the first chapters of these "Pentagon Papers," he told a friend that "they could hang people for what's in there."[39] His successor was Clark Clifford, who assumed the role thus far played unsuccessfully by George Ball. He finally succeeded in making the president face, slowly and in agony, the true dimensions of the catastrophe.

The North Vietnamese Tet offensive that began in January 1968 underscored the disaster. Americans at home were now able to see that, despite three years of bombing and a commitment of half a million men, the enemy was still able to mount offensives. It now became clear that the United States suffered much more from the war of attrition than did the enemy. The North Vietnamese manpower pool was far from depleted, and there was always the possibility of an intervention by Chinese "volunteers." There was to be no light at the end of the tunnel for Lyndon Johnson. In March 1968 he announced a bombing halt and withdrew from the presidential race. Vietnam had made the man elected by the largest landslide in American history into a one-term president.

Lyndon Johnson, totally ignorant of Asia in general and of Vietnam in particular, was governed exclusively by his own misperceptions of Asian reality. In his view, aggression had to be stopped "at the source" and the "source" was Communism in North Vietnam and China. The fact that Communism had broken up into numerous diverse political and ideological fragments seemed to have been lost on him. He never understood that this was a revolutionary war in which the other side held title to the revolution because of the colonial war that had just ended. Revolution and antirevolution were the real issues, not Communism and anti-Communism. That is why the Vietcong were willing to fight and die and the South Vietnamese were not. That is why McNamara's statistics were valueless: they overlooked the fact that even if the South Vietnamese forces outnumbered the Vietcong by a ratio of ten to one, it did no good because the one man was willing to fight and die and the ten were not.

And then there was Ho Chi Minh—a man totally unlike anyone Lyndon Johnson had ever met. The president dealt with his adversary by means of all the time-honored American political techniques; when force did not work, he tried manipulation. But neither bombs nor dollars would tempt Ho Chi Minh. Johnson, unable to understand an adversary who was unwilling to bargain, resorted to the use of military force, the only instrument of compulsion he had.

Because he believed he could not lose, Johnson dropped still more bombs and sent still more men to their deaths. He shielded himself with the belief that America was fighting in Vietnam for selfless and idealistic reasons. A credibility gap had become a reality gap: the myth of false innocence enabled the United States to wreak destruction on a grand scale in Indochina, all in the name of kindliness and helpfulness. Gradually, the means became so horrible that it became increasingly difficult to justify

the ends. The war in Vietnam finally became a lost crusade.
Ho Chi Minh the man was very different from Lyndon Johnson's image of him as Mao Tse-tung's puppet. True, the North Vietnamese leader was an old Bolshevik who had been one of the founders of the French Communist Party in 1920. But he was a more senior member of the Communist world than Mao and was a unique figure in his own right. He was as much a Vietnamese nationalist as a Communist. David Halberstam described him as "part Gandhi, part Lenin, all Vietnamese."[40] After his victory over the French at Dienbienphu in 1954, Ho not only enjoyed the veneration of his people but was also treated with a special respect throughout the Third World. Mao Tse-tung had simply defeated other Chinese, but Ho Chi Minh had defeated a powerful Western nation.

Ho Chi Minh's most distinctive quality, however, was his incorruptibility. In a country whose leaders invariably reached a certain plateau and then became more Western and less Vietnamese, corrupted by money and power, Ho Chi Minh remained a Vietnamese Everyman. The higher he rose, the less he sought the trappings of authority. He shunned monuments, marshal's uniforms, and general's stars, always preferring his simple tunic. The "black pajamas" that Lyndon Johnson mocked were in fact his source of strength, for they symbolized his closeness to the peasants, who *both* loved and obeyed him. The secret of his success was his ability to walk humbly among his own people; he was never separated from the people by police motorcades and foreign advisers.

What made Ho so effective was the contempt with which he was viewed by the West. For example, *Time* magazine once referred to him as a "goat-bearded agitator who learned his trade in Moscow." By remaining a Vietnamese, a peasant like his ancestors, he became the only leader with title to the revolution: to drive the French, and then the Americans, from Vietnam. The Soviet Communists recognized his strength; the Communist Party of Vietnam survived the Stalin years without the slightest touch of purge. The leadership of Ho Chi Minh was such that even Stalin decided not to interfere. Ho even had a sense of humor. "Come on, you will have dinner with the President of the Republic," Ho announced to Robert Isaacs, an old American friend and dinner guest in 1945, after the defeat of Japan. As they passed through a corridor, two young Vietminh guards snapped to attention and then, their revolvers showing, followed Ho to his car. Ho laughed. "How funny life is!" he exclaimed. "When I was in prison, I was let out for fifteen minutes in the morning and fifteen minutes in the evening for exercise. And while I took my exercise in the yard, there were always two armed guards standing right over me with their guns. Now I'm President of the Vietnam Republic, and whenever I leave this place, there are two armed guards right over me with their guns."[41] In his fundamental human qualities, Ho Chi Minh was the very opposite of Lyndon Johnson.

With Ho Chi Minh, Johnson followed the principle of the strong overpowering the weak. He believed that he could bend the enemy to his will and so avoid inflicting pain, death, and material destruction on the North Vietnamese. This strategy was feasible to someone who was rich, loved life, and feared pain. But in the Vietcong Johnson confronted the power of the weak. The weak defied the American president by their willingness to struggle, suffer, and die on a scale that seemed beyond reason. Interrogations of prisoners repeatedly revealed this phenomenon. When asked what would happen if more and more Americans came and bigger and bigger bombs dropped, the prisoners very often showed a fatalistic and dispassionate attitude: "Then we will all die." Such defiance brought Lyndon Johnson face-to-face with the threat of ultimate escalation—in the parlance of the time, to bomb North Vietnam into the Stone Age, or put more simply, to commit genocide. Looking into the abyss, Johnson hesitated, remembering Hitler and Hiroshima. The only alternative was withdrawal. Withdrawal meant losing, but massive escalation also meant losing, because the soul of the United States would have been lost and our social fabric completely destroyed. Thus Ho Chi Minh's strategy of weakness prevailed over Johnson's strategy of strength. Ho had less and less to lose by continuing to fight, while the stakes grew more costly for his American opponent. Time was always on the side of Ho Chi Minh.

Perhaps the essential truth about Lyndon Johnson and the men who made Vietnam policy during his presidency was that they had never experienced the kind of pain or tragedy that is the source of empathy. These men had only been successful and their vision limited to the American experience. None knew, until it was too late, that nations, like people, can die. None knew that intelligence alone, without wisdom and empathy for suffering, is hollow.

One postscript to this analysis may be of relevance. In 1988, Richard N. Goodwin, an aide to Lyndon Johnson during the 1960s, published a memoir entitled *Remembering America*. The most fascinating part of this book was Mr. Goodwin's analysis of Johnson's personality during the height of the Vietnam War. Briefly put, the author argued, the president was probably clinically paranoid.

Like many paranoids, Johnson managed to live for most of his life with this affliction. But under the increasing strain of the war, he began to be consumed by irrational resentments and fears of conspiracy. Mr. Goodwin revealed that as early as 1965 he had grown so alarmed by Johnson's erratic behavior that he consulted several psychologists about his concern that the president was experiencing "sporadic paranoid disruptions."[42] The author also reported that his fellow White House aide, William Moyers, shared many of these worries. Goodwin's belief that Johnson was becoming unbalanced helped persuade him to oppose the president publicly on the war, and finally to work for his defeat in 1968.

Goodwin's thesis is, of course, unprovable. But the fact that a thoughtful contemporary of Lyndon Johnson painted a chilling and convincing portrait of a president at war, descending into something approaching madness, is enough to give one pause and cannot be dismissed lightly. It merely deepens one's concern at the awesome power that a single individual can hold in the American democracy, for better or for worse.

Act Five: Nixon—Full Circle

The presidency of Richard Nixon brought a painful groping for extrication and "peace with honor." Nixon and Henry Kissinger, his main architect of foreign policy, devised a formula known as "Vietnamization," whereby the war would gradually be turned over to the Vietnamese as American combat troops were withdrawn. The American hope was to leave behind a viable anti-Communist South Vietnam with a friendly government firmly installed in Saigon. Thus, the central issue of the war remained the same: Who should rule in Saigon?

The withdrawal of American ground troops began in June 1969, when the peak figure of 541,500 men was reduced by 25,000. As withdrawal gathered momentum, a serious weakness became increasingly apparent in the "Vietnamization" strategy: as American strength was slowly ebbing, Communist forces became better able to attack and try to topple the South Vietnamese regime, to which American prestige remained committed. President Nixon's response to this challenge was twofold: the destruction of Communist sanctuaries by ground incursions into Laos and Cambodia, and increasing reliance on air power through bombing. Thus, as American participation in the ground fighting gradually diminished, the air war reached levels of unprecedented ferocity. This policy reflected the dilemma of a president who still believed in the essential mission of the United States in Vietnam but who wanted to attain his goal without incurring additional American casualties. Henry Kissinger, in response to a question posed by an Asian diplomat as to whether President Nixon was going to repeat the mistakes of the Johnson administration, said, half in jest: "No, we will not repeat their mistakes. We will not send 500,000 men. We will make our own mistakes and they will be completely our own."[43] Quite unintentionally, this proved to be a prophetic statement.

In July 1969 the president announced the "Nixon Doctrine," to the effect that, in the future, the United States would avoid entanglements like Vietnam by limiting its support to economic and military aid rather than active combat participation. Peace negotiations had begun in earnest in Paris, and a moratorium against the war drew huge crowds in Washington demanding a rapid withdrawal of American troops. In January 1970, however, under the euphemism of "protective reaction" to cover air reconnaissance missions over North Vietnam, the United States renewed the bombing of the North. The Vietcong once again increased infiltration on the ground.

On April 30, 1970, in a nationally televised address, President Nixon announced an American-led South Vietnamese "incursion" into Cambodia to demonstrate that the United States was "no pitiful, helpless giant." In the same speech he declared that since 1954 the United States had "respected scrupulously the neutrality of the Cambodian people," but the discovery of Vietcong supply depots and sanctuaries had made this latest incursion necessary. It would shorten the war, the president explained. Three years later, in the midst of the Watergate hearings, it was revealed that in more than 3,500 raids during 1969 and 1970 American B-52s had dropped over 100,000 tons of bombs on Cambodia and Laos. In Tom Wicker's words, the April 30 speech was "a deliberate and knowing lie broadcast in person to the American people by their president."[44] The president's spokesman at the Pentagon, Jerry Friedheim, when confronted with this contradiction, said: "I knew at the time it was wrong and I am sorry."[45]

In May 1970 President Nixon announced the end of large-scale bombing raids against the North, and in June he pronounced the Cambodian incursion a success. The Senate repealed the Tonkin Gulf Resolution and barred future military operations in Cambodia without congressional approval. American combat troops now stood at 400,000 men. The year 1971 saw protracted peace negotiations in Paris, while the fighting continued in South Vietnam between the Vietcong and the dwindling American forces and their South Vietnamese allies. By the end of the year another 200,000 Americans had returned home.

In March 1972 the North Vietnamese launched a major offensive with massed tanks and artillery in the most impressive show of force since the Tet assault of 1968. The North Vietnamese leadership had decided to make an all-out effort to seize what it could in the South at a time when it was facing the danger of a new form of diplomatic isolation. The latest American overtures to China and the Soviet Union threatened to separate North Vietnam from its two major Communist allies. The offensive began shortly after President Nixon's visit to Peking in February but before his trip to Moscow, scheduled for May.

In April and May 1972 Nixon took two gambles that escalated the war to new levels of violence. In April B-52 bombers struck Hanoi and Haiphong in saturation bombings that far surpassed the ferocity of the Johnson raids. And on May 8 the president took a step that his predecessor had always ruled out as too perilous: he ordered the mining of North Vietnam's harbors to cut off the flow of tanks, artillery, and other offensive weapons supplied to Hanoi by the Soviet Union and other Communist nations. At the same time, however, he offered a total troop withdrawal from South Vietnam four months after an Indochina-wide cease-fire and the return of prisoners of war. The risk of a Soviet-American confrontation at sea dominated world attention for several days, but only verbal denunciations emanated from Moscow and Peking. The Soviet Union by now placed a higher priority on its own vital interests, which it perceived to lie in the growing détente with the United States, than on the interests of North Vietnam. The Soviet-American summit took place on schedule, and the president's gamble paid off. North Vietnam now realized that it had been virtually abandoned by its own allies. The United States suddenly found itself in the anomalous position of having reached détente with 1 billion Communists—800 million Chinese and 200 million Russians—while it pursued a relentless war against a small peasant country precisely because it was Communist.

In July the Paris peace talks resumed and troop withdrawal continued. On October 26, in a dramatic announcement, Henry Kissinger predicted that "peace was at hand." This preelection optimism proved premature. Early in December Kissinger's "final talks" with the North Vietnamese were broken off, and he reported a stalemate.

On December 18 President Nixon ordered all-out bombing attacks on Hanoi and Haiphong. Millions of tons of explosives were dropped on the North. The fierce intensity and relentlessness of the attacks produced an outcry of protest against "terror bombings" from many parts of the world. The raids were halted on December 30, and the Paris talks once again resumed. On January 23, 1973, after almost three decades of war, a cease-fire was finally reached. The Paris Accords provided for the withdrawal of all American troops and military advisers, an exchange of prisoners, consultations between South and North Vietnam on general elections, new supervisory machinery, and the withdrawal of all foreign troops from Laos and Cambodia.

Essentially, what was achieved in Paris in 1973 was Vietnam's reversion to its status at the time of the 1954 Geneva Accords. The United States had come full circle in Vietnam, and the clock was turned back twenty years. There was an Orwellian irony to the situation. Progress was regress: 1954 by 1973.

The hope, after the withdrawal of American troops, was that South Vietnam would be able to defend itself against the North with military and financial assistance from the United States. For two years that American hope seemed justified, but then the dam broke. In the spring of 1975 the Khmer Rouge, the Communist insurgents in Cambodia, marched into the capital, Phnom Penh, and forced Marshal Lon Nol, Cambodia's American-supported president, to flee the country. Thus, the American "incursion" of 1970 finally produced the opposite of what it had intended: a Communist instead of a neutralist Cambodia. At the same time, the South Vietnamese army lost its fighting spirit and collapsed entirely. In a matter of weeks almost all of South Vietnam fell to the Communists. In the United States a test of wills took place between the administration of President Gerald R. Ford, who favored continued military aid to Cambodia and South Vietnam, and the Congress, which became increasingly reluctant to cooperate. Ultimately, the United States was left with the humanitarian responsibility of rescuing terror-stricken refugees who were fleeing the advancing North Vietnamese armies. In April Saigon surrendered to the Communists and was renamed Ho Chi Minh City. Twenty years of American effort thus ended in failure. As Dean Rusk, one of the main architects of American Vietnam policy during the 1960s, put it in April 1975:

> Personally, I made two mistakes. I underestimated the tenacity of the North Vietnamese and overestimated the patience of the American people.[46]

By the mid-1970s both the supporters and the critics of the Vietnam war in the United States tended to regard the second Indochina war as one of the most terrible episodes in the history of American foreign policy. There was a general consensus that it would take a long time for the wounds to heal, both in Indochina and in the United States.

Conclusion

The American involvement in Indochina began almost imperceptibly, rather like a mild toothache. At the end, it ran through Vietnam and America like a pestilence. Each president based his policies on exaggerated fears and, later, on exaggerated hopes. Thus, each president left the problem to his successor in worse shape than he had found it.

The United States dropped more than 7 million tons of bombs

on Indochina. This is eighty times the amount that was dropped on Britain during World War II and equal to more than three hundred of the atomic bombs that fell on Japan in 1945. The bombs left 20 million craters that ranged from 20 to 50 feet wide and 5 to 20 feet deep. After the bombardments much of Vietnam looked like a moonscape. Nothing will grow there for generations.

America too was in anguish over the war. Her leadership lost the respect of an entire generation, universities were disrupted, careers blighted, and the economy bloated by war inflation. The metal caskets in which 55,000 Americans returned from Vietnam became the symbol of the war's ultimate and only meaning.

In historical perspective, the great unanswered question about Vietnam will probably be: Which would have been less costly, an earlier Communist victory or the agony of this war? One cannot help but wonder what might have happened if not one American soldier had reached Indochina. Since history does not present alternatives, one cannot know where this road not taken might have led. Vietnam might well have gone Communist much earlier. But its form of Communism would probably have been of the Titoist variety, combining a strong dose of nationalism with a fierce tradition of independence vis-à-vis both Moscow and Peking. The United States could certainly have lived with that outcome. Its postponement was hardly worth the sacrifice of more than 55,000 American lives, hundreds of thousands of Vietnamese lives, and $150 billion.

The Khmer Rouge Communist government of Cambodia, led by Pol Pot, posed a different challenge. After this regime came to power in 1975, an estimated one million Cambodians were systematically murdered. Cities were emptied and some four million people were forced into the countryside on long marches. Survivors were herded into agricultural communes, and all vestiges of previous Cambodian society were eradicated. Money, wages, and commerce were abolished, and travel and contact with the outside world were forbidden. The slightest infraction was punishable by torture and death.

The end of this story was not without irony. In 1978 Vietnam, now a Communist nation backed by the Soviet Union, invaded and virtually dismembered Cambodia, which was receiving the support of China. The genocide of the Cambodian Khmer Rouge thus was ended not through moral pressures brought to bear by an outraged humanity, but through the power interests of the Sino-Soviet conflict. Very soon after the American withdrawal from Vietnam the only wars in Asia were fought by Communists against other Communists. Thus the reasons for the outbreak of the Vietnam war had become almost irrelevant. History had simply passed it by. When considered in this perspective, the awesome truth about Vietnam is clear: it was in vain that combatants and civilians had suffered, the land had been devastated, and the dead had died.

NOTES

1. Bernard B. Fall, *The Two Vietnams* (New York: Praeger, 1964), p. 82.

2. Victor Bator, *Vietnam: A Diplomatic Tragedy* (Dobbs Ferry, N.Y.: Oceana Publications, 1956), p. 206.

3. U.S. House Foreign Affairs Subcommittee on World Communism, *China and U.S. Far East Policy, 1946–1966,* 80th Cong., 2nd Sess. (1967), p. 45.

4. Andrew W. Green, "Are You a Middle of the Roader?" *Plain Talk* (April 1949), p. 35.

5. Policy statement by Ambassador Loy W. Henderson, *Department of State Bulletin* (April 10, 1950), p. 565.

6. Miriam S. Farley, *United States Relations with Southeast Asia with Special Reference to Indochina* (New York: Institute of Pacific Relations, 1955), p. 4.

7. U.S. Department of State, Office of Public Affairs, *Background* (Washington, D.C.: Government Printing Office, October 1951).

8. U.S. Department of State, Statement by Robert E. Hoey, officer in charge of Vietnam-Laos-Cambodia affairs, Press Release No. 178, March 8, 1952.

9. Farley, *op. cit.,* p. 4.

10. John Foster Dulles, cited in Bator, *op. cit.,* p. 210.

11. Dwight D. Eisenhower, *Mandate for Change 1953–1956* (Garden City, N.Y.: Doubleday, 1963), p. 167. Italics added.

12. Richard M. Nixon, quoted in Chalmers M. Roberts, "The Day We Didn't Go to War," *The Reporter,* September 14, 1954.

13. Fall, *op. cit.,* p. 90.

14. Melvin Gurtov, *The First Vietnam Crisis* (New York: Columbia University Press, 1967), p. 14.

15. Robert Guillain, *La Fin des Illusions: Notes d'Indochine* (Paris: Centre d'Etudes de Politique Etrangère, 1954), p. 39.

16. Gurtov, *op. cit.*, p. 15.

17. Eisenhower, *op. cit.*, p. 372.

18. David Halberstam, *The Best and the Brightest* (New York: Random House, 1972), p. 124.

19. *Ibid.*, p. 133.

20. *Ibid.*, p. 135.

21. *Ibid.*

22. *Ibid.*, p. 174.

23. Arthur Schlesinger, Jr., *A Thousand Days* (Boston: Houghton Mifflin, 1965), p. 371.

24. Halberstam, *op. cit.*, p. 183.

25. *Ibid.*, p. 207.

26. *Ibid.*, p. 292.

27. Max Frankel, "The Lessons of Vietnam," in *The Pentagon Papers* (New York: Quadrangle, 1971), p. 644.

28. Halberstam, *op. cit.*, p. 350.

29. *The Pentagon Papers, op. cit.*, p. 249.

30. *Ibid.*, p. 263.

31. Anthony Austin, *The President's War* (Philadelphia: Lippincott, 1971), *passim.*

32. Halberstam, *op. cit.*, p. 414.

33. *Ibid.*, p. 424.

34. *Ibid.*, p. 528.

35. *Ibid.*, p. 572.

36. Stewart Alsop, cited in *The Pentagon Papers, op. cit.*, p. 650.

37. Halberstam, *op. cit.*, p. 627.

38. *Ibid.*, p. 624.

39. *Ibid.*, p. 633.

40. David Halberstam, *Ho.* (New York: Random House, 1971), p. 12.

41. *Ibid.*, p. 83.

42. Richard N. Goodwin, *Remembering America* (Boston: Little, Brown & Company, 1988).

43. *The New York Times,* July 24, 1973.

44. *Ibid.*

45. *The Washington Post,* January 28, 1973.

46. Interview on ABC television, April 3, 1975.

SELECTED BIBLIOGRAPHY

BERMAN, WILLIAM C. *William Fulbright and the Vietnam War.* Kent, Ohio: Kent State University Press, 1988.

FALL, BERNARD B. *The Two Vietnams.* New York: Praeger, 1964.

FITZGERALD, FRANCES. *Fire in the Lake.* Boston: Little, Brown & Company, 1972.

GOODWIN, RICHARD N. *Remembering America.* Boston: Little, Brown & Company, 1988.

HALBERSTAM, DAVID. *The Best and the Brightest.* New York: Random House, 1972.

HANNAH, NORMAN B. *The Key to Failure: Laos and the Vietnam War.* Lanham, Md.: Madison Books, 1987.

KARNOW, STANLEY. *Vietnam.* New York: Penguin, 1984.

KISSINGER, HENRY. *White House Years.* Boston: Little, Brown & Company, 1979.

MCALISTER, JOHN T. *Vietnam: The Origins of Revolution.* New York: Knopf, 1969.

ROTTER, ANDREW J. *The Path to Vietnam: Origins of the American Commitment to Southeast Asia.* Ithaca, N.Y.: Cornell University Press, 1988.

SHEEHAN, NEIL. *A Bright Shining Lie: John Paul Vann and America in Vietnam.* New York: Random House, 1988.

STOESSINGER, JOHN G. *Henry Kissinger: The Anguish of Power.* New York: Norton, 1976.

STOESSINGER, JOHN G. *Crusaders and Pragmatists: Movers of Modern American Foreign Policy.* New York: Norton, 1985.

5

Three Battles over God: India and Pakistan in 1947, 1965, and 1971

*Man's body is so small, yet his capacity for suffering
is so immense.*   Rabindranath Tagore

The most savage religious war in history was neither the Christian Crusades against Islam nor the Thirty Years' War that pitted Catholic against Protestant. It was the war of Hindu against Moslem in the twentieth century.

So long as India remained under the British Crown, the conflict between Hindus and Moslems remained relatively dormant, although the two religions—fearing each other more than they feared their common colonial master—waged their own separate struggles for independence against Britain: the Hindus under Mahatma Gandhi and the Moslems under Mohammed Ali Jinnah. When the time for freedom approached, the Moslems insisted on their own sovereign entity, apart from the Hindu majority of colonial India. Thus, when the transfer of power took place in 1947, two new states were born: India and Pakistan.

Britain had hardly withdrawn when the two new fledgling states turned on each other with a terrible ferocity. Millions of terror-stricken Hindus in Pakistan fled for their lives to India and millions of equally frantic Moslems in India sought refuge in Pakistan. The result was the most massive population exchange in history. It had always been clear to participants and onlookers alike that these two religions agree on virtually nothing and regard each other as anathema. The Moslem believes in one god and his prophet, whereas the Hindu worships a pantheon of gods. Moslem society is not based on caste, whereas that of the Hindus has been stratified into a rigid caste system. Moslems believe in actively making converts, whereas Hindus tend to be more passive and absorptive. Moslems observe strict silence in their mosques, whereas Hindus play music in their temples. Hindus will not eat beef, and Moslems are enjoined from eating pork. Each has tended to regard the other as a peril to itself. The three wars to be examined are the outgrowth of this religious conflict. The fact that the two hostile religions were represented by sovereign states made the conflict even more ferocious. Nationalism and religion now were fatefully fused with the modern nation-state serving as a handmaiden to religious warfare. The political forces of the twentieth century were mobilized to fight the battles of an earlier age. And so three times in quick succession, India and Pakistan, each invoking its gods, met on fields of battle under empty skies from which the gods had departed.

Colonialism, Partition, and War

Ancient Hinduism was an austere doctrine subscribing to the view that the cause of all evil in the world was human desire. The path toward redemption, therefore, lay in a person's capacity to extinguish desire within himself through an act of will and thus reach a state of Nirvana. Hinduism conceived of life as a never-ending cycle, or karma. Death simply meant passage into another incarnation of life. The form this new incarnation would take depended on performance in the previous one. Hence, it was quite possible for an individual to pass into a lower or a higher form of life. The standard of excellence to which the Hindu was to aspire was Nirvana, or the renunciation of desire. Since people were by nature unequal, only a few could attain this goal. This concept of the inequality of people was expressed in the caste system, which formed the basic structure of ancient Indian society. Society consisted of four rigidly separated castes: the Brahmins, or priests, who had come closest to the Hindu ideal; the warriors, who were to defend the society; the merchants; and the laborers. Actually, the social system was even more complex since each caste had numerous subdivisions. At the bottom of the social pyramid were the outcasts, or pariahs, also known as "untouchables."

The great inroads made by Buddhism in ancient India may be explained largely in terms of the austerity of the Hindu doctrine. Though Buddhism too was directed toward the afterlife, its view of humanity was much more optimistic; under its influence the Nirvana concept gradually changed from a doctrine of extinction and renunciation to a goal not unlike the Christian paradise. The figure of the Bodhisattva gained prominence in Indian life—the priest who, though entitled to enter Nirvana, had decided to postpone his own entrance in order to show the way to others. Late Buddhism, in fact, moved further and further from the austerity of the Hindu faith. Sometimes only a few invocations would suffice to gain entrance to Nirvana, and Bodhisattvas frequently became deities who served as "social workers" assisting their less fortunate brethren. Despite this radical transformation of Hinduism, it must be remembered that Buddhism was able to grow out of Hinduism because the latter lent itself to the absorption of new forms of faith quite readily.

Islam, the third major religion of ancient India, came to India around 1000 A.D. and stands in striking contrast to the other two. Unlike Buddhism, Islam was never absorbed by the Hindus. The only attribute that Islam shared with its predecessor was its emphasis on the hereafter; there the similarity ended. When the Moslems first came to India, they destroyed all the Hindu temples and sculptures they found because they considered them idolatrous. After sections of India in the northeast and the northwest were conquered by Moslems, the Hindus tended to regard them as another caste to be kept rigidly separate. The religious conflict between Hinduism and Islam is thus at the root of the struggle between India and Pakistan. By the time the West arrived there, India was a politically divided society in which two radically different ways of life competed for the allegiance of the population: Hinduism, which was tolerant of dissension and absorptive; and Islam, which was militant, exclusive, and dogmatic.

British rule over India was established in the early seventeenth century through the instrument of the East India Company. In their campaign to gain control of the subcontinent, the British employed a strategy of "divide and conquer." The many satraps were played off against each other until, by the late eighteenth century, most of India was in British hands.

The administration of British India is a story of contradictions, harmony, and conflict. The coming of the British added yet another element to the already highly complex Indian society. Christianity was brought to India, and yet the materialism of the Christian colonizers stood in stark contrast to the spiritualism of the Hindu. The individualism of the British differed sharply from the group-centered culture of India, and the democratic ideal of equality was alien to the caste-conscious Hindu. On the whole the British tried very hard to harmonize these many conflicts, and sometimes succeeded.

In the pattern of indirect rule initiated by the British, a viceroy was put in charge of colonial administration. Local customs were left intact so long as they did not present a direct threat to the British presence or radically offend the British social ethos. Thus the British did not interfere much with the caste system, though they did insist on the abolition of the Hindu custom of suttee, or the immolation of widows on the funeral pyres of their husbands. They also outlawed infanticide and thuggee, the practice of sacrificing unsuspecting travelers in lonely mountain passes to the goddess Kali.

The British made every effort to teach British democracy to the Indians, thus planting the seeds of the Indians' demand for self-rule. British law and contractual relationships were often mingled with Indian culture, and efforts were made to use indigenous talent in the civil service, especially in the later colonial period. But the British also exhibited extreme insensitivity. For example, in 1857 a rebellion was started by the rumor that pig and cow fats were being used to grease cartridges in rifles to be employed by Hindu and Moslem recruits in the army. The Sepoy Rebellion of 1857, which was touched off by this incident, was crushed by the British with extreme cruelty.

The economic aspects of the Indian colonial experience present a similarly mixed record. The early profits made by the East India Company were enormous. By flooding India with manufactured goods, the British compelled the indigenous population to concentrate on the production of raw materials, thus causing an imbalance in the economy and a decline in Indian industry. On the other hand, the industrial development of India meant the development of modern roads, telegraphs, harbors, mails, and railroads. Some aspects of this industrialization did not conflict with traditional customs, and at times they even helped to revive them. For example, a modern network of railroads made religious pilgrimages easier for many Hindus. Another important by-product of British colonialism was the rise of a new class of professionals —bankers, traders, educators, and lawyers who were to play a major role in the rise of the new India.

It is impossible to say whether modern India has benefited or suffered more as a result of its experience with British colonialism. To be sure, colonialism had many unfortunate effects: exploitation of the labor force, overdevelopment of natural resources, and dislocation of the economy through exportation of wealth in the form of raw materials, a condition of economic colonialism that was to last much longer than its political counterpart. On the other hand, the British also did much to prepare India for the modern world: they bestowed on the country an enlightened health and education program; they provided at least the foundations for a higher standard of living; and they educated an elite of future leaders.

In sum, then, India's experience with Western colonialism was by no means entirely negative. If one considers this fact, combined with the tolerant faith of the Hindu religion, it is not surprising that when the nationalist reaction occurred in India, it followed an essentially nonviolent and democratic path.

The Indian nationalist movement was marked by the overwhelmingly powerful personality of Mahatma Gandhi. Gandhi was the spiritual father of the Indian Congress, the nationalist resistance organization under the British that, without his unifying influence, would have been destroyed by factionalism. Indeed, without the charismatic leadership of Gandhi, Indian nationalism might well have run a far more violent course.

Gandhi's nationalism was rooted in the doctrine of *ahimsa,* or noninjury to any living being. This concept was translated into the political doctrine of passive resistance, or civil disobedience, a technique of nationalist assertion that the British found very embarrassing. Gandhi lived most unpretentiously. He used a spinning wheel to produce his few garments, and his example led to a widespread boycott of foreign cloth. He denied himself all comforts and often endured long fasts in order to gain support for his causes. When the British imposed a heavy tax on salt in 1930, Gandhi walked 165 miles to the sea to make his own salt. Rather than cooperate with the British, he exhorted the population to go to jail, and he was frequently imprisoned. But he always emphasized the nonviolent character of Indian nationalism. Indeed, his rejection of bloodshed as a deplorable aberration was the movement's basic moral and political principle. The steady advance toward independence made by India between 1900 and 1947 was due in large measure to Gandhi's insistence on spiritual rather than physical power.

It was Gandhi who turned Indian nationalism from an urban, elite movement into a mass movement that reached the smaller towns and captured the popular imagination. But it was also Gandhi who unwittingly magnified the differences between Indian Hindus and Indian Moslems, through his emphasis on mass participation, majority rule, and Indian (Hindu) tradition. Moslems became apprehensive that majority rule and Hindu revivalism would undermine their faith and dim their political future.

Thus, despite his enormous influence, Gandhi was unable to forge Indian nationalism into a cohesive whole. The congress was always viewed with suspicion by the Moslems, who feared persecution at the hands of a Hindu majority once India became independent. Though he tried his utmost to do so, Gandhi never succeeded in resolving the differences between the two faiths. In the end, in 1948 he was assassinated by a Hindu fanatic who found his dogged attempts at reconciliation unbearable.

The Moslems developed their own nationalist organization, the Moslem League. Its leader, Mohammed Ali Jinnah, insisted on the creation of a separate state of Pakistan for the Moslem minority. The great chasm between Hinduism and Islam robbed the Indian nationalist movement of much of its effectiveness. Often the two antagonists feared each other more than they did the colonial rule of Britain. The depth of the conflict is illustrated by the fact that not even the unparalleled prestige of Gandhi was able to persuade his Hindu followers to make common cause with Islam. Nor did the Moslems feel any less strongly. Their view was expressed by Jinnah:

How can you even dream of Hindu-Moslem unity? Everything pulls us apart: We have no intermarriages. We have not the same calendar. The Moslems believe in a single God, and the Hindus are idolatrous. Like the Christians, the Moslems believe in an equalitarian society, whereas the Hindus maintain their iniquitous system of castes and leave heartlessly fifty million Untouchables to their tragic fate, at the bottom of the social ladder.[1]

It is quite possible that this intense communal strife would have enabled the British to maintain control over India for an indefinite period. But World War II forced the British to make their peace with the prospect of Indian sovereignty. As a condition of India's collaboration in the war, Gandhi demanded a promise of immediate independence. When the British hedged, the Indian leader stated caustically that he was unwilling to accept "a post-dated check on a bank that was obviously failing." Even a British guarantee of speedy independence did not prevent some Indian nationalist leaders, like Subhas Chandra Bose, from throwing in their lot with the Japanese. After the conclusion of the war, it fell to the British Labour government, which had always been severely critical of Conservative policy toward India, to honor Britain's pledge. But in 1947, when Indian nationalism finally triumphed, the country was a house divided. Despite Gandhi's repeated fasts and prayer meetings against it, partition seemed the only practicable solution. Hence India and Pakistan emerged from British colonial rule as two separate sovereign states.

The triumph of nationalism in India was thus distinctly marred by the tragedy of partition. Three staggering problems were the direct result of this tragedy. The first aftermath of partition saw a gigantic population exchange, probably the most massive in history. Over seven million Hindus, fearful of persecution in Pakistan, frantically sought refuge in India, and a similar number of Moslems fled India to find safety on Pakistani soil. A vast amount of violence and bloodshed generated by religious hatred accompanied this population exchange. Millions of people lost their homes in the process, and the integration of these refugees presented an almost insurmountable hurdle to both of the new states.

The second problem was economic in nature. Colonial India had been an economic unit for centuries, and now it was suddenly divided into three parts: India, East Pakistan, and West Pakistan. East Pakistan, formerly East Bengal, was separated from West Pakistan by almost 1,000 miles of Indian territory. These two Moslem enclaves, dating from the Moslem conquest, had nothing but their religion in common, not even language. Regional jealousies and economic competition between the two Pakistans immediately rose to the surface. Even worse, however, an economic war broke out between Pakistan and India. India devalued her rupee, but Pakistan refused to follow suit. Jute, an important raw material grown mostly in Bengal, now became prohibitively expensive in India. In short, the three parts of the Indian subcontinent, which for centuries had been operating as one economic entity, were now involved in a destructive economic feud.

Overshadowing all other disputes between the two new nations was the struggle over contested territory, especially the princely state of Kashmir. India demanded Kashmir on the ground that its ruler had been a Hindu, but Pakistan claimed the state on the basis that over three-fourths of the population was Moslem.

Kashmir combines extraordinary scenic beauty with great strategic importance. Since ancient times, the beautiful and fertile Kashmir Valley had been the resting place for caravans traveling between the plains of India and the highlands of Central Asia. Both India and Pakistan considered Kashmir absolutely vital to their strategic and defense requirements. India's Prime minister Jawaharlal Nehru asserted that:

India without Kashmir would cease to occupy a pivotal position on the political map of Central Asia. Strategically, Kashmir is vital to the security of India; it has been so since the dawn of history.[2]

But Pakistan's prime minister Liaquat Ali Khan justified his claim with similar emphasis:

Kashmir is very important, is vital to Pakistan. Kashmir, as you will see from the map is like a cap on the head of Pakistan. If I allow India to have this cap on our head, then I am always at the mercy of India.[3]

To make matters even more complicated, the British left three choices to the so-called princely states after their departure: accession to India, accession to Pakistan, or independence. Lord Mountbatten, as representative of the British Crown, advised the leaders of the 565 princely states that they were free "to accede to one or the other of the two new Dominions as the effective successive Powers to the British Raj, at their discretion, with due consideration to be given to geographical contiguity and communal composition."[4] If neither choice was acceptable, they could form independent states. Of the 565, whose sizes ranged from that of a European country to that of a small village, only three opted for independence: Junagadh, Hyderabad, and Kashmir. Of these, the first two did not present insuperable obstacles. But Kashmir, larger than England, with an area of almost 85,000 square miles, now became a vital object of competition, coveted with equal fervor by both new states.

The Maharajah of Kashmir, Hari Singh, offered to enter into a "standstill agreement" with both states in order to buy time and ensure Kashmir a measure of autonomy. By now, however, communal strife had engulfed much of the subcontinent, and Kashmir was drawn in. Moslem tribesmen from the northwest, enraged by alleged atrocities against the Moslems of nearby Jammu, invaded Kashmir. They came close to overpowering Kashmir's defenses and carried out mass killing, looting, and arson. Pakistan described the situation as a popular revolt by the Moslem majority of Kashmir against the Hindu ruler's autocratic rule. The Maharajah, in desperation, asked India for military aid. India, seizing the opportunity, made military intervention contingent on Kashmir's formal accession to India. The hard-pressed Maharajah signed the Instrument of Accession to India on October 26, 1947. On the following day, Lord Mountbatten accepted the accession, but transmitted an accompanying letter in which he stated:

> It is my Government's wish that as soon as law and order have been restored in Kashmir and her soil cleared of the invaders, the question of the State's accession should be settled by reference to the people.[5]

Indian forces were rushed to Kashmir, just in time to stop the Moslem invaders a few miles from Srinagar, the capital. Pakistan immediately dispatched troops so as to forestall the collapse of the Moslem invasion. Thus, by late 1947, the two nations found themselves locked in deadly combat over Kashmir. The war continued inconclusively with neither side able to win a decisive military victory.

Charging Pakistan with aggression, India brought the dispute before the United Nations Security Council in early January 1948. Pakistan in turn accused India of genocide and illegal occupation of Kashmir. The Security Council called on both states to refrain from doing anything "which might aggravate the situation." It also established a UN Commission for India and Pakistan that was to investigate the facts and mediate between the contending parties. In August 1948 the commission recommended a cease-fire, which went into effect on January 1, 1949.

Thus ended the first phase of a modern religious war that erupted in the aftermath of colonial rule. The human tragedy surrounding the partition of the subcontinent was a grim reminder that turbulence and war had not ended with the passing of the European order in India. On the contrary, with the colonial lid off, Hindus and Moslems were free to turn on each other with the pent-up ferocity of centuries.

The Kashmir War of 1965

The political structures of Hindu and Moslem nationalism diverged sharply after partition. India, under the leadership of Jawaharlal Nehru, Gandhi's successor, immediately embarked on the ambitious and unprecedented experiment of shaping an overwhelmingly illiterate country into an advanced democracy. The Indian national elections of 1951–1952 were indeed an impressive performance. The new Indian government spared no effort to make this election truly democratic, and, on the whole, succeeded admirably. The Congress party, now pursuing a policy of gradual socialism patterned after the example of the British Labour party, became the dominant political power, with Nehru its undisputed leader. Pakistan set out on a totally different road and fashioned its political system along authoritarian lines. After a succession of politicians had demonstrated their inability to govern, the army seized power in 1951. Under the leadership of General Ayub Khan, Pakistan instituted its first effective government and embarked on an ambitious economic development program. Pakistan developed a formidable power base, but at the expense of the democratic process.

Far from resolving the Kashmir dispute, the 1949 cease-fire had provided merely a breathing spell. India and Pakistan now continued the struggle by diplomatic means. Their initial involvement in international affairs was determined by their overriding search for security vis-à-vis each other. In fact, their quest for friends and allies may be interpreted quite accurately as an outgrowth, first and foremost, of their fear of one another. All other considerations were secondary.

During the 1950s the military leadership of Pakistan committed the Moslem nation to the Western alliance system. Believing that meaningful negotiations with India over Kashmir could be undertaken only by making Pakistan a strong military state, General Ayub Khan led Pakistan into two American-sponsored regional alliances: the Southeast Asia Treaty Organization (SEATO) and the Central Treaty Organization (CENTO). But in 1962, when war erupted between China and India over disputed border territory, Pakistan quickly gravitated toward India's enemy. Relations between China and Pakistan grew increasingly cordial. By the mid-1960s Pakistan was in the unique position of being a member of two Western military alliances and at the same time enjoying the friendship of the People's Republic of China.

In India Prime Minister Jawaharlal Nehru labored hard and long during the 1950s to develop a policy of nonalignment and economic advancement for his country. Nehru's policy was handed a severe setback in the decisive defeat India suffered in the 1962 border war with China. The Soviet Union, increasingly estranged from China, attempted to exploit the situation by consolidating its ties with India, while the American leadership, fearful of Communist expansion, extended large quantities of military aid to both India and Pakistan, ostensibly for purposes of defense against Communism. In reality, however, both India and Pakistan used the American military equipment to bolster their strength vis-à-vis each other. It was against this complex background of multidimensional maneuverings that the conflict between Hindus and Moslems erupted once again into open warfare.

The war began in an unlikely spot, the so-called Rann of Kutch, an uninhabited piece of territory of little value that was a virtual desert during the dry season but became a flooded marsh during the monsoon. In the spring of 1965 both India and Pakistan stepped up patrolling activity in that area, and soon serious clashes occurred. Pakistani forces quickly outmaneuvered Indian troops, winning an easy victory. Although a cease-fire was achieved through the mediation efforts of British prime minister Harold Wilson, and both parties agreed to a mutual withdrawal of forces, the Rann of Kutch encounter "left Pakistan dangerously overconfident and India dangerously frustrated."[6]

The Pakistani leadership began to feel that the Kutch strategy should be tried in Kashmir. A prominent Urdu newspaper openly recommended that "the Rann of Kutch prescription should be applied on the Kashmir front,"[7] and *The Pakistan Times,* in a burst of euphoria, predicted that, "In the event of war with India, Pakistani troops would march up to Delhi, would occupy the Red Fort, and hoist the Pakistani flag on it."[8]

In India, on the other hand, resentment was rampant. To be defeated by China was one thing; to be outfought by Pakistan was something that most Indians were unwilling to accept. Lal Bahadur Shastri, Nehru's successor, came under increasing pressure to redress the Kutch defeat. *The Times of India* warned that "Pakistan has put the fish into the water to measure the temperature and one fine morning Pakistan will present the world with a *fait accompli*—the occupation of Kashmir."[9]

Thus, Pakistan's overconfidence and India's humiliation brought the two nations to the brink of war:

> It was barely credible in 1962 that two great countries should be at the brink of full-scale war, as China and India were, over an almost inaccessible stretch of barren and snow-bound track. It is no more credible today that India and Pakistan should fight over a piece of barren land that spends half its life under water; yet it has happened.[10]

In August 1965 Ayub Khan, convinced that his policy of "leaning on India" was working, made the fateful decision of sending Pakistani-trained guerrillas into Kashmir. The infiltrators blew up bridges, disrupted lines of communication, and raided army convoys and military installations. Not surprisingly, Indian forces in Kashmir rounded up the guerrillas and then proceeded to occupy the three main mountain passes that had served as supply routes for the Pakistanis. Ayub Khan now faced a difficult dilemma. He could hardly sustain a guerrilla campaign in Kashmir with the key mountain passes in Indian hands. He either had to back down or raise the stakes. Calculating that Indian fear of China would deter her from a vigorous response against Pakistan and confident of his own military superiority, the Pakistani leader decided to escalate the conflict.

On September 1 Pakistani forces, supported by ninety Patton tanks, crossed the cease-fire line into southern Kashmir and advanced so rapidly that they threatened the vital road over the mountains linking Srinagar with the plains of India. If Pakistan captured this road, Indian forces in Kashmir would be encircled. Thus India was now left with the choice of yielding or expanding the war.

On September 5 India opened a new front and invaded West Pakistan in a massive attack. The two armies were now locked in large-scale combat over a wide area. Despite superior weapons and greater mobility, the Pakistani forces were unable to break through Indian lines and advance on India's cities as their leaders had so confidently predicted. In several encounters the Indians even managed to outmaneuver and outfight their opponents, thus reversing the situation that had prevailed in the Rann of Kutch. The Pakistani leadership was badly shaken and resorted to desperate fighting to hold the line. After several weeks of war, the battlelines became relatively stationary, with both sides having fought each other to a virtual standstill.

The war finally ended through the efforts of Soviet premier Aleksei Kosygin, who invited both parties to the negotiating table at Tashkent to settle their differences. Reasoning that a continued conflict between India and Pakistan would probably benefit China, the Soviet leader decided to act the role of peacemaker. Edward Crankshaw, who was in Tashkent during the Soviet-sponsored negotiations, commented as follows:

> Mr. Kosygin, whose ideology demands the fostering of chaos and disruption in non-Communist lands, finds himself doing his level best to calm down a Hindu under direct threat from China and a Moslem supposed to be on friendly terms with Peking, embroiled in a quarrel over the possession of the mountain playground of the late British Raj. And, except for China, nobody minds.[11]

And so the world was treated to the strange spectacle of a Communist state successfully fashioning a truce between two bourgeois nations. The Kashmir problem was not resolved, of course. Both sides merely agreed to set forth their "respective positions" on the issue. Nor were the deeper animosities removed, or even mitigated. Tashkent merely signified a pause in a protracted conflict that thus far had proved inconclusive. The decisive encounter was to come half a decade later, when the flames of war erupted once again with terrible ferocity.

The Bloody Dawn of Bangladesh

New nations are seldom born without great pain. The scale of human suffering that marked the birth of Bangladesh, however, was so vast that it stands out starkly even against the grim and melancholy canvas of the twentieth century. First, a natural disaster of titanic proportions, followed by a fratricidal war, then a flood of refugees, and finally another war—these were the four horsemen of the apocalypse that ushered into the world the state of Bangladesh in 1971.

To understand the outbreak of the war between Moslem and Moslem, one must appreciate that, first and foremost, the two Pakistans had nothing whatsoever in common *but* Islam. For almost a quarter century, the two wings of Pakistan stood more than 1,000 miles apart—with Indian territory in between. Aside from this physical, and consequently psychological, distance, the two peoples spoke different languages, had different racial characteristics, and prided themselves on different cultural achievements. As one observer put it rather bluntly: "The only bonds between the diverse and distant wings of their Moslem nation were the Islamic faith and Pakistan International Airlines."[12]

As if this condition were not enough to weaken the union, a sequence of developments aggravated the situation and eventually plunged the two Pakistans into all-out war. First, the founder of Pakistan, Mohammed Ali Jinnah, died one year after the creation of the state, and his successor, Liaquat Ali Khan, was felled by an assassin's bullet two years later. The loss of these two charismatic leaders left a serious void and contributed to the declining popularity of the Moslem League, which had provided a semblance of unity throughout Pakistan. Second, and even more serious, was the flagrantly unequal distribution of economic resources between the two Pakistans. From the very beginning, the West Pakistanis were far more generously endowed than their coreligionists in Bengal. As well, West Pakistan, six times the size of East Pakistan, had to support only 40 percent of Pakistan's entire population. Third, and perhaps most important, was the tendency of the West Pakistani leadership to treat the Bengalis as poor relations. The nation's capital was established in the West, first in Karachi and later in Islamabad. As Pakistan became a major recipient of American military and economic aid, the West remained the main beneficiary. Westerners were always richer than easterners, and between 1950 and 1970 this income gap more than doubled. The Bengali jute and tea supplied between 50 and 70 percent of the nation's revenue, but the Bengalis received only 25 to 30 percent of Pakistan's total income. Thus, there was a parasitic quality to the West's relationship to the East. As a leading Bengali spokesman put it:

> We are only a colony and a market. If the only reason for our ties with West Pakistan is that we are both Moslem, why shouldn't we join some other state, like Kuwait, from which we might get more money?[13]

Finally, the West had a virtual monopoly on Pakistan's power elite: 85 percent of all government positions were held by westerners; two-thirds of the nation's industry and four-fifths of its banking and insurance assets were controlled by the West; and only 5 percent of Pakistan's 275,000-man army were Bengalis.

East Pakistanis tried hard to compensate for this disparity with cultural arrogance. They were lovers of art and literature and regarded the westerners' respect for the martial virtues with contempt. But gradually, under the growing pressures of deprivation, pride gave way to a Bengal nationalism that demanded its case be heard. Still, violence might have been avoided had not nature visited upon Bengal one of the most terrible calamities of the century. In November 1970 a devastating cyclone struck the coast of Bengal and claimed the lives of almost half a million people. Those who survived suffered starvation and disease. The catastrophe was so awesome that it was described as "a second Hiroshima."

At the time of the disaster the president of Pakistan was Yahya Khan, a general who had assumed power in 1969 by virtue of his military status. Yahya had promised free elections by the end of 1970. Two weeks elapsed, however, before the president even managed to visit the scene of the catastrophe, and most Bengalis perceived this delay as an example of West Pakistan's callousness and indifference to the calamity that had befallen them. The Bengalis' outrage now vented itself at the ballot box.

The election results turned out to be a bitter surprise for the military leadership as well as for the People's Party, headed by Zulfikar Ali Bhutto, a westerner. To their dismay, Sheik Mujibur Rahaman's Awami League won a sweeping victory in East Pakistan. Whereas Sheik Mujibur had always favored Bengali civil liberties, Yahya Khan's apathy in the wake of the cyclone provoked the Sheik's followers into a genuine nationalist movement. The league's platform of complete regional autonomy for East Pakistan would have given control of only foreign affairs and defense matters to the central government. On the basis of the election returns in December 1970, East Pakistan, with its large Bengali population, was allotted 169 seats in the National Assembly, while Bhutto's People's Party won only 90 seats. The results left no doubt that the next prime minister of Pakistan would not be Bhutto but the Bengali leader Sheik Mujibur Rahaman.

The western leadership found this outcome simply unacceptable. It feared that the Awami League, with its absolute majority in the National Assembly, would vote itself a program for virtual self-government, thus removing East Pakistan from the control of the central government. The weeks following the election were marked by a feverish contest for power that finally erupted into bloody conflict.

President Yahya Khan triggered the crisis when he announced the postponement of the assembly session to a later, unspecified date. The Awami League, perceiving this as a deliberate attempt to disregard a popular mandate for Bengali autonomy, launched a campaign of civil disobedience. The Bengalis, in turn, defied the central government by calling a massive strike and managed to bring government operations to a virtual standstill. In response to this pressure, Yahya Khan scheduled the date of the assembly session for March 26, but at the same time made arrangements for a massive airlift of West Pakistani troops to East Pakistan.

In such a climate, negotiations were doomed from the start. On March 25 private talks between Yahya and Sheik Mujibur broke down, and on his return to Islamabad the president denounced the Sheik's activities as "acts of treason." He ordered the immediate arrest of Awami League leaders and directed the army to crush the secessionist movement and restore full authority to the central government. This decision directly precipitated the civil war and led to the end of a united Pakistan. In view of its crucial importance in the sequence of events, it is worth examining in some detail.

Yahya's plan was to destroy all Bengali resistance centers in one massive strike, thereby crushing the rebellion once and for all. West Pakistan leaders never doubted their own military superiority nor expected the Bengalis to put up more than token resistance. As one high-ranking army officer put it: "Those little brown buggers won't fight," and another predicted confidently: "A good beating and these chaps will come around."[14]

This attitude was deeply rooted in the culture of West Pakistan. The light-skinned westerners had always extolled martial virtues and looked down on the dark-skinned Bengalis, who preferred the pen to the sword. Thus, Yahya crucially underestimated the appeal of Sheik Mujibur, whom he never regarded as a legitimate spokesman for Bengali aspirations; instead, he imprisoned the sheik as a traitor. The sheik's statement in March that the Bengalis were "prepared to sacrifice one million people to gain independence"[15] was dismissed as empty rhetoric. Yahya, in fact, was reported to have referred to the Bengalis as "mosquitoes" who could be killed with one determined slap of the hand. He ignored the possibility that the "mosquitoes" might soon become guerrillas. Moreover, he never recognized the charisma of the Bengali leader, whom he dismissed as a saboteur and mischief maker. And finally, he never took into account the enormous logistical difficulties of supplying an occupation army from bases that were a thousand miles away. Instead, Yahya Khan preferred a military solution of the most brutal kind that not only alienated the Bengalis from West Pakistan forever but plunged the entire subcontinent into open conflict.

The western crackdown on Bengal was marked by extreme brutality. Pillage, murder, and rape were so pervasive that by April a powerful guerrilla movement had sprung up that fought the West Pakistanis with a courage born of desperation. On April 17 the Bengali resistance fighters, or Mukti Bahini, as they quickly came to be known, established a provisional government of their own in a mango grove just inside the East Pakistan border. They gave their embryonic state the name of Bangladesh.

In terror millions of Bengalis fled for their lives from the pitilessness of the West Pakistanis. They chose as their haven the neighboring province of West Bengal, which was a part of India. Thus it came about that Moslems, in order to save themselves from other Moslems, sought refuge in India, the country of their former archenemy. The growing influx of these panic-stricken people began to create a terrible burden on the overpopulated and impoverished neighboring Hindu nation. India had to draw upon its meager resources in order to provide food, medical assistance, and shelter for the refugees, and as a result, had to suspend its own economic development plans. To make matters worse, West Bengal also happened to be one of India's politically most volatile and unstable states, and the flood of refugees naturally exacerbated this instability.

In view of these developments, India could not remain a passive observer of the civil war in Pakistan for very long. On April 16 the government, under Prime Minister Indira Gandhi, accused the West Pakistan army of "planned carnage and systematic genocide."[16] By May Pakistani troops were chasing Bengali guerrillas across the Indian border, and armed clashes between Indian and Pakistani border patrols were becoming commonplace.

As the flood of Bengali refugees gathered momentum, the Indian government became increasingly alarmed. Its treasury was being drained of $2.5 million a day. In the spring Gandhi warned the parliament that the refugee problem was "going to be hell for us; we are not going to allow them to stay here."[17] By November the Indian estimate of Bengali refugees had reached the 10 million mark. If this figure is correct, then "the mass movement of humanity over eight months of 1971 was the most intensive, regionally concentrated large-scale migration in the history of man."[18]

By mid-July Gandhi had evidence that a war with Pakistan would be cheaper than the economic burden of coping with the refugee problem for a single year. This evidence was supplied by the Institute for Defense Studies and Analysis in New Delhi. The Indians concluded that the refugees would cost their country $900 million within a year, or more than thirteen times the cost of the entire Kashmir war with Pakistan in 1965. This report was widely circulated and resulted in a wave of popular emotion in favor of war. The Indian leadership had to respond forcefully to alleviate the pressure.

On August 9 Gandhi, with an eye toward Pakistan's friendship with China, abandoned India's traditional policy of nonalignment and signed a treaty of friendship with the Soviet Union. This twenty-five-year treaty had all the earmarks of a military alliance. Reflecting the popular mood, the Indian Parliament hailed the new "realism" in India's foreign policy and praised Gandhi for having "put some meat in our vegetarian diet of non-alignment."[19] The pact was intended as a clear warning to Pakistan and as a deterrent against the possibility of Chinese intervention. Several weeks later, Gandhi embarked on a tour of the United States, Britain, and Western Europe to underline the gravity of the situation and the need for a political solution. Specifically, she demanded the release of Sheik Mujibur, which she hoped would result in Bengali autonomy and the return of the refugees to their former homes.

On the home front Gandhi quietly took measures to prepare the Indian army for action in case her diplomatic efforts failed. During the months of October and November 1971 Indian forces began to help the Mukti Bahini more actively. Gandhi was still hopeful that a major war could be averted and that the Indians, as discreetly as possible, could secure enough territory within East Pakistan to establish a Bangladesh regime. However, this clandestine support for the Bengali guerrillas turned out to be insufficient. Moreover, another natural calamity forced the Indian government to become even more actively involved.

In early November another cyclone struck, this time spending its fury on Indian soil. The death of 20,000 Indians sharply increased public pressures on Gandhi. The parliament now demanded that priority be given to the Indian victims and that forceful measures be taken to effect the repatriation of the Bengalis. In response to these pressures, Gandhi made a crucial military commitment. She authorized Indian forces to engage Pakistani troops on the East Pakistan border. Her strategy was to hit the West Pakistanis with quick, limited strikes that would tie down the occupation troops and give the Bengali guerrillas more freedom to maneuver. This "hit and run" strategy was greeted with a chorus of approval in the parliament. The commander of the Indian forces in the area, General Jagjit Singh Aurora, was happy that his troops could now challenge the Pakistanis in open combat. As he put it:

I had finished building up my force in September, and I really began to retaliate in mid-October, but it wasn't until the third week of November that I got permission to go in and silence their guns by pushing them back and giving them a bloody nose.[20]

Gandhi had confidence in her strategy for another reason. She was convinced that China would be deterred from intervening, not only because of India's new alliance with the Soviet Union, but also because the Himalayan passes were already blocked by snow. Her assumption proved to be correct.

On November 30 Gandhi ordered a blackout of Calcutta, and on the following day Indian troops penetrated 5 miles into Pakistan as a "defensive measure." On that day the United States began its "tilt" toward Pakistan by canceling an arms shipment to India, and Gandhi exploded:

If any country thinks that by calling us aggressors it can pressure us to forget our national interests, then that country is living in its own paradise and is welcome to it. The times have passed when any nation sitting three or four thousand miles away could give orders to Indians on the basis of their color superiority. India has changed, and she is no more a country of natives.[21]

Tension also ran high in Pakistan. By late November it had become public knowledge that President Yahya Khan had taken to heavy drinking. On November 25, while entertaining a delegation of visiting Chinese, he exclaimed to a reporter:

If that woman thinks she can cow me down, I refuse to take it. If she wants a war, I'll fight her! In ten days, I might not be here. There might be a war. I'll be off fighting a war![22]

Indira Gandhi's demand that Yahya Khan release Sheik Mujibur enraged the Pakistani leader so much that he sentenced the Bengali nationalist to death. Not only did he resist all appeals and efforts to change his mind, but on November 26 he outlawed the entire Awami League on grounds of conspiracy against the government. The death sentence against Sheik Mujibur, however, was never carried out.

Yahya Khan also displayed an increasing tendency to reduce the conflict between India and Pakistan to a personal test of strength between himself and Gandhi. In an interview with a *Time* correspondent, his vanity broke through. Proud of his thick black hair, he exclaimed to the reporter: "My strength lies in it—like Samson's."[23] And to a *Newsweek* correspondent, who questioned him about the possibility of war with India, he confided: "The worst losers will be the Indians themselves. I hope to God that woman understands."[24] A week later, the same reporter interviewed Gandhi, who promptly returned the compliment:

"That woman!" I am not concerned with the remark, but it shows the mentality of the person. He is one man who could not get elected in his own country if there were a fair election. I would say he would not even get elected in his province if there were a fair election. What weight has his judgment on India? It is a world which is quite outside his ken.[25]

On December 1 Gandhi issued an ultimatum in which she demanded that Yahya Khan withdraw all his forces from East Pakistan. This was a hard blow under any circumstances, but for a man with Yahya Khan's fragile ego, such an ultimatum from a woman was psychologically unacceptable. Thus, even though he knew that the Indian forces outnumbered his own by a ratio of five to one, the president of Pakistan authorized a massive air strike against India on December 3. The decision was greeted with a chorus of approval. Bhutto, who had just assumed the post of deputy prime minister, exclaimed that "Pakistan is faced with a predatory aggressor who never reconciled itself to the establishment of this country."[26] And Lieutenant General Niazi, commander of Pakistan's forces in the east, got right to the heart of the matter: "We are Moslems and we don't like Hindus. One Moslem soldier is worth five Hindus."[27]

Yahya Khan's military strategy was based on the example of the Israeli surprise attack of June 1967. He hoped to cripple the Indian Air Force with a single devastating blow and then move with impunity into Kashmir, which he could use as a trump card in postwar bargaining.

The execution of the December 3 air attack, however, turned out to be a military disaster. Indian jet planes, unlike Egyptian planes in 1967, were well protected in concrete revetments and thus were virtually immune to the Pakistani assault. As well, since only thirty-two Pakistani planes participated in the attack, the offensive strike was very feeble indeed. India's air marshal claimed that India was hardly bruised, let alone hurt, by the attack, and another military expert commented that "In military terms, no one in his right mind would have attacked with three or four planes at each airfield. It was sheer madness."[28]

The failure of the air attack, far from forcing the Pakistanis to face reality, had precisely the opposite effect. Fervent appeals for a holy war against India increased in frequency. *The Pakistan Times* editorialized:

> Plainly Islam is the issue between India and Pakistan. . . . Only those qualify to fight the battle of Pakistan who are prepared to fight the battle of Islam. . . . For us there is no choice but to fight, if need be to the last man.[29]

As the conflict intensified in early December, the elements of a fierce religious war made their appearance. Gradually all restraint was lost, and the religious basis of the struggle was revealed in all its fanaticism and ferocity. As a Pakistani pilot put it: "Our one god makes our victory certain. The Indians are worshippers of idols, of many gods. Ours is the true strength."[30] And an army colonel took strength from the concept of *jihad,* or holy war, when he asserted confidently that there would be no Pakistani casualties on the field of battle since, "in the pursuit of jihad, nobody dies; he lives forever."[31]

When Pakistan was confronted with dismemberment and defeat in mid-December, the truth was so appalling that it was unacceptable. Even the conquering Indian generals were moved to compassion when they saw their former colleagues from the British colonial army under siege in Dacca. Major General Gandharv Nagra's appeal to General Niazi, the defender of Dacca, makes poignant reading: "My dear Abdullah, I am here. The game is up. I suggest you give yourself up to me and I'll look after you."[32]

Gandhi thus emerged as the undisputed victor. India agreed to a cease-fire at her own convenience, acquired 2,500 square miles of territory in West Pakistan, and detained some 93,000 prisoners of war for almost two years. Pakistan was dismembered and Ben-

gal East emerged as Bangladesh. A bitter political divorce and a
bloody war had led to the emergence of a new state in the family
of nations.

Strife between Hindus and Moslems still erupts periodically. In
1984, for example, major riots took place in several Indian cities.
In addition, the Sikhs, followers of a monotheistic blending of
Hinduism and Islam that began about 1500, waged a campaign for
national self-determination against the Indian government.
Prime Minister Gandhi ordered the military suppression of the
Sikh insurrection. In November, 1984, however, she was assas-
sinated by Sikhs who resented her strong-arm methods. Her
death, in turn, triggered violence against the Sikh community in
India.

When one surveys the histories of India and Pakistan since the
end of British colonial rule, it is difficult to avoid the conclusion
that a high price in human suffering had been paid for independence.

Conclusion

The elements that produced the three armed conflicts between
India and Pakistan constituted a veritable witches' brew. When
one sorts out these elements, it seems difficult indeed to conceive
of a more explosive mixture. The awesome list includes religious
conflict, territorial claims, economic imbalance, natural calamity,
nationalist aspirations, refugee migration, and personality clas-
shes.

The most basic conflict, of course, was religious in nature. Had
it not been for the long-standing and bitter enmity between Hindus and Moslems, a single state, rather than two hostile ones,
would have emerged out of the British colony. The ambiguous
status of Kashmir, whose ruler had been a Hindu but whose
population had been predominantly Moslem, injected the element
of territorial conflict into the picture. To make matters even more
complicated, Pakistan was not really one state but two, with the
eastern part suffering deprivation while the western part enjoyed
relative affluence. A natural disaster in the shape of a cyclone that
devastated Bengal with the fury of an atomic bomb highlighted
the economic imbalance between the two Pakistans even further

and precipitated demands for equality. When these demands for equal rights were denied, they grew into a virulent nationalism that turned the two Pakistans against each other in a ferocious civil war. The result was a gigantic exodus of refugees from Bengal into India that probably constituted the largest single mass migration in human history. When India decided that war with Pakistan was cheaper than the support of 10 million refugees, armed conflict became a distinct possibility. And when personal antagonisms and a leader's fragile ego were added to the mixture, war became a certainty. The dreadful circle was closed, with Hindu once more pitted against Moslem.

It is not easy, of course, to assess the relative weight of each link in this fateful chain. Yet the evidence suggests that of all the chapters in this tragic story, the religious one is the most awful and most desperate. It is not an accident that the conflict began and ended as a religious war; this was always its most basic and most irreconcilable feature. When the situation is viewed from this perspective, one must question the confident assertion made so often in Western history books: that the age of religious warfare came to an end in 1648, when Catholics and Protestants made peace and signed the Treaty of Westphalia. In our secular age, more than three centuries later, the battle over God continues unabated, though with more awesome weapons and under bleaker skies.

NOTES

1. Quoted in George McT. Kahin, *Major Governments of Asia* (Ithaca; Cornell University Press, 1958), p. 268.

2. Jawaharlal Nehru, *Independence and After* (New Delhi: Government of India Publication Division, 1949), p. 95.

3. M. Gopal, "Considerations of Defence," *Caravan* (New Delhi: February 1967), p. 67.

4. Alan Campbell-Johnson, *Mission with Mountbatten* (London: Robert Hale, 1952), pp. 357–358.

5. P. L. Lakhanpal, *Essential Documents and Notes on the Kashmir Dispute* (New Delhi: Council on World Affairs, 1965), p. 57.

6. William J. Barnds, *India, Pakistan, and the Great Powers* (New York: Praeger, 1972), p. 200.

7. *Nava-I-Waqt* (Lahore), May 9, 1965, p. 4.

8. *The Pakistan Times* (Lahore), July 11, 1965, p. 7.

9. *The Times of India* (New Delhi), July 18, 1965, p. 7.

10. *The Economist* (May 1, 1965), pp. 502–503.

11. *The London Observer,* January 9, 1966, p. 11.

12. Dan Coggin *et al.,* "Pakistan: The Ravaging of Golden Bengal," *Time* (August 2, 1971), p. 26.

13. Khushwant Singh, "Why They Fled Pakistan and Won't Go Back," *The New York Times Magazine,* August 1, 1971.

14. Wayne Wilcox, "Conflict in South Asia," Paper presented at the University of London Institute of Commonwealth Studies, February 1972.

15. "Another War in Asia: Who's to Blame?" *Newsweek* (December 20, 1971).

16. "Bangladesh Is Over the Border," *The Economist* (April 24, 1971).

17. Singh, *op. cit.*

18. Louis Dupree, "Bangladesh" (Part I), *American Universities Fieldstaff Reports,* South Asia Series, Vol. 16, No. 5, p. 2, 1972.

19. Quoted by Sydney H. Schanberg, "Pact Said to Bury India's Non-Alignment," *The New York Times,* August 14, 1971.

20. Robert Shaplen, "The Birth of Bangladesh" (Part I), *The New Yorker* (February 12, 1972), p. 55.

21. *The London Times,* December 3, 1971.

22. Shaplen, *loc. cit.*

23. "Good Soldier Yahya Khan," *Time* (August 2, 1971).

24. "A Talk with Pakistan's President Yahya Khan," *Newsweek* (November 8, 1971).

25. "A Talk with India's Prime Minister Indira Gandhi," *Newsweek* (November 15, 1971).

26. Radio Pakistan Broadcast, December 3, 1971.

27. Shaplen, *loc. cit.*

28. "Another War in Asia: Who's to Blame?" *op. cit.*

29. *The Pakistan Times,* December 4, 1971.

30. Rosanne Klass, "Pakistan's Costly Delusion," *Saturday Review* (February 5, 1972).

31. "Bangladesh: Out of War, a Nation Is Born," *Time* (December 27, 1971).

32. "India: Easy Victory, Uneasy Peace," *Time* (December 27, 1971).

SELECTED BIBLIOGRAPHY

BARNDS, WILLIAM J. *India, Pakistan, and the Great Powers,* New York: Praeger, 1972.

BHATIA, KRISHNAN. *Indira: A Biography of Prime Minister Gandhi.* New York: Praeger, 1974.

ERIKSON, ERIK. *Gandhi's Truth.* New York: Norton, 1969.

JACKSON, ROBERT. *South Asian Crisis: India, Pakistan, and Bangladesh.* New York: Praeger, 1975.

LALL, ARTHUR. *The Emergence of Modern India.* New York: Columbia University Press, 1981.

LAMB, ALASTAIR. *The Kashmir Problem.* New York: Praeger, 1967.

SHAPLEN, ROBERT. "The Birth of Bangladesh," *The New Yorker,* February 12, 1972.

6

The Forty Years' War in the
Holy Land: Israel and the Arabs

War can protect; it cannot create.
Alfred North Whitehead

Historical tragedies do not arise from encounters in which right clashes with wrong. Rather, they occur when right clashes with right. This is the heart of the conflict between Israel and the Arab states in Palestine. A large number of Jews, responding to the horror of Hitler's systematic extermination of the Jews of Western Europe attempted to save themselves by creating a state of their own. They established it in a land that had been occupied by Arabs for centuries, at the precise moment when the Arab peoples were emerging from the crucible of Western colonialism and were rediscovering their own national destinies. Thus Jewish nationalism clashed head-on with Arab nationalism in Palestine.

The four wars between Israel and her Arab neighbors have been the result of this collision. The modern Middle East has been the scene of both irreconcilable hopes and aspirations and bitter hatreds and violent passions. The wars were fought with the deepest emotion. Each contestant regarded his rights as self-evident and firmly based on the will of God, morality, reason, and law. As passions rose, irrationality became commonplace. Desperate deed was heaped on desperate deed until right and wrong, responsibility and guilt could no longer be distinguished. Each side had done things that the other could neither forgive nor forget.

This tragic clash between two valid claims and two appeals for justice has not abated much with time. Nor has it been possible to break the impasse through a lasting peace settlement.

All this suggests that there is perhaps no solution to the Arab-Israeli problem outside the course of history. In the meantime, it is the scholar's duty to offer a diagnosis, even though it may not be possible to prescribe a cure for a "sickness unto death." The four Palestine wars were merely massive eruptions of a historical encounter that is nothing less than a protracted war spanning an entire generation. As such they offer us insight into, but not liberation from, some of the darkest recesses of the souls of nations and men.

The Palestine War of 1948

The Zionist movement was founded in 1897 with the publication of a book entitled *The Jewish State,* by Dr. Theodore Herzl, an Austrian journalist who urged the settlement of Jewish agriculturists and artisans in Palestine. These pioneers, Herzl hoped, would realize an ancient Jewish dream—the reestablishment of a Jewish homeland in the Promised Land and the gathering together of the Jewish people from their Diaspora of 2,000 years. Responding to Herzl's vision and reacting to anti-Semitic pogroms in Russia and Poland, 60,000 Jews emigrated to Palestine between 1881 and 1914. The land that was used for the Jewish settlements was purchased from absentee Arab landlords by wealthy philanthropists like Baron de Rothschild of Paris or through funds collected by the Zionists abroad. By 1914 almost 100,000 acres of Palestinian land had been purchased by the Jews.

In 1917 Chaim Weizmann, a scientist of world renown and a fervent Zionist, persuaded British foreign minister Lord Arthur James Balfour to issue a proclamation that would convert Herzl's dream into a British pledge:

His Majesty's Government views with favor the establishment in Palestine of a national home for the Jewish people, and will use their best endeavours to facilitate the achievement of this object, it being clearly understood that nothing shall be done which may prejudice the civil rights of existing non-Jewish communities in Palestine, or the rights and political status enjoyed by Jews in any other country.

In 1922 Britain was given a League of Nations mandate over Palestine.

The Palestinian Arabs, understandably enough, objected to the Balfour Declaration and became increasingly uneasy about the large influx of Jewish immigrants. During the 1930s, when Hitler's persecution of European Jews gathered momentum, Jewish immigration soared dramatically. By 1937 the Jews constituted almost one-third of the total population of Palestine. Between 1928 and 1937 their number had risen from 150,000 to 400,000. As the Zionist movement looked toward Palestine as the last refuge from the impending Nazi holocaust, Arab alarm grew accordingly. It was no longer a question of land purchased by individual settlers but the threat of an alien state in a land that had been inhabited by Arabs for over 1,000 years. The British, caught in a vise between their pledge to the Jews on the one hand and to Arab oil and strategic interests on the other, tried to temporize, but finally placated the Arabs by imposing a ceiling on Jewish immigration. The Jews, in their plight, tried to run the British blockade. In most cases, the British intercepted the immigrant vessels and shipped the passengers to internment camps in Cyprus. In the particularly tragic case of the immigrant ship *Exodus,* the British sent the helpless Jews back to Germany. As one survivor put it, "The Germans killed us, and the British don't let us live."[1]

Despite the British blockade, tens of thousands of Jewish immigrants landed in Palestine illegally. The Arabs became increasingly restive, and bitter fighting erupted. The British, caught in the lines of fire, were unable to restore the peace. In 1947, in total frustration, Britain announced her intention to relinquish the mandate over Palestine and decided to place the entire problem before the United Nations.

The undisputed leader of the more than a half million Jewish settlers in Palestine in 1947 was David Ben-Gurion. Ben-Gurion's commitment to the Zionist ideal was total and unswerving. He had come to Palestine in 1906, had been a leading delegate to the World Zionist Congress, and by 1935 had become chairman of the Jewish Agency, which represented the World Zionist Movement. No single leader represented the Arab cause, but the most influential men were Haj Amin el-Husseini, the Grand Mufti of Jerusa-

lem, Azzam Pasha, the secretary-general of the Arab League,
King Abdullah of Transjordan, and Glubb Pasha, the commander
of the British-trained Arab Legion. The Grand Mufti had been in
Germany during the war and had helped the Nazis plan their
"final solution" to the Jewish problem. He had designs to rule all
Palestine and for this reason was distrusted by the other Arab
leaders. Azzam Pasha was an Egyptian diplomat with relatively
moderate views. King Abdullah of Transjordan, who had a reputation for compassion and humanity, met secretly once with Golda
Meir to explore the possibility of an Arab-Jewish compromise.
And Glubb Pasha's Arab Legion was the only Arab military force
that was truly feared by the Zionists.

In early 1947 a specially constituted United Nations Committee on Palestine (UNSCOP) visited the area and examined the
alternatives. After several months of highly charged debate, the
committee finally recommended that Palestine, with its population of 1.2 million Arabs and 570,000 Jews, be partitioned into two
states—one Arab and one Jewish—with Jerusalem held as
trustee of the UN. The Jewish state would include 55 percent of
the land and its population would be 58 percent Jewish, while the
Arab state would encompass 45 percent of the land and have a 99
percent Arab population. This partition plan was eagerly welcomed by the Jews and denounced with equal fervor by the Arabs.

A number of meetings on the partition plan took place between
Arab and Jewish leaders. In one such encounter Abba Eban, then
an official of the Jewish Agency, met with Azzam Pasha to discuss
the possibility of a compromise. Eban stated that "the Jews [were]
a *fait accompli* in the Middle East and that the Arabs [would]
have to reconcile themselves to that fact."[2] He then went on to
propose an economic program for joint development of the Middle
East. Azzam Pasha conceded that the plan was "rational and
logical" but added that "the fate of nations [was] not decided by
rational logic." "We shall try to defeat you," he said. "I am not
sure we will succeed, but we will try. We were able to drive out
the Crusaders, but on the other hand, we lost Spain and Persia.
It may be that we shall lose Palestine. But it is too late for peaceful
solutions."[3] When Abba Eban interrupted by pointing out that
this left no alternative but a test of strength through force of
arms, Azzam Pasha replied:

It is in the nature of peoples to aspire to expansion and to fight for what they think is vital. It is possible that I don't represent, in the full sense of the word, the new spirit which animates my people. My young son who yearns to fight, undoubtedly represents it better than I do. He no longer believes in the old generation. . . . The forces which motivate peoples are not subject to our control. They are objective forces. Nationalism, that is a greater force than any which drives us. We don't need economic development with your assistance. We have only one test, the test of strength.[4]

An eyewitness to this encounter detected no hatred in Azzam Pasha's tone. He referred to the Jews over and over as "cousins." Not once during the two-hour conversation did he express an unkind thought or use a hostile expression about the Jews. But he did confirm the character of the position of the Arab majority—a position based not on logic but "on a blind fatalism, ungovernable as the wind."[5] Sadly and without hatred the two leaders took their leave of one another.

The lobbying for and against the partition resolution was the most intense that the United Nations had experienced in its short history. A two-thirds majority was required for passage of the resolution by the General Assembly. To offset the votes of just the Arab and Moslem nations, the Zionists needed twenty-two votes, and for each additional vote against partition they needed two in favor. While the Zionists were by no means certain that they could muster a two-thirds majority, they were encouraged by the fact that the two main antagonists in the Cold War, the United States and the Soviet Union, both supported them. In the United States President Truman was deeply sympathetic to the Jewish cause. Moreover, his political instincts told him that the Jewish vote might well be crucial to the presidential election of 1948. Overruling the objections of leading State Department officials over the Soviet threat and American access to military bases, Truman personally warned the United States delegate to the United Nations, Herschel Johnson, to "damn well deliver the partition vote or there will be hell to pay."[6] From the Soviet point of view partition seemed the easiest way to oust Britain from the Middle East and to keep the United States at arm's length while playing the Arabs off against the Jews. Two days before the vote it became clear that the fate of Zionism was in the hands of a few small, remote nations, in particular Liberia, Haiti, the Philippines, and Ethiopia. The Zionists persuaded the United States to apply strong pressure to these countries. Nevertheless, on November 29, 1947, the outcome was very much in doubt. Moshe Sharett, the Jewish Agency's "foreign minister," solemnly warned the assembly that the Jewish people would never submit to any attempt to subjugate them to an Arab majority. On the other hand, Jamal Husseini, the acting secretary-general of the Arab League, declared that if the assembly did vote for partition, the Arabs of Palestine would go to war against the Jews as soon as the British left: "the partition line will be drawn in fire and blood."[7]

Two eyewitnesses have left a poignant account of that fateful vote on November 29:

An aide set a basket before Aranha (the President of the General Assembly). In it were fifty-six slips of paper, each bearing the name of one of the nations represented in the hall. Aranha extended his hand and slowly drew from the basket the name of the nation whose vote would begin the poll. He unfolded the piece of paper and stared an instant at the men ranged before him.

"Guatemala," he announced. At his words, a terrible silence settled over the Assembly. Even the press gallery fell quiet. For an instant, the three hundred delegates, the spectators, the newsmen, seemed united in awe of the moment before them, in their awareness of the grave and solemn decision about to be taken.

The delegate of Guatemala rose. As he did, suddenly, from the spectators' gallery, a piercing cry sundered the silence of the Assembly hall, a Hebrew cry as old as time and the suffering of men: "Ana Ad Hoshiya. O Lord, save us."[8]

With a vote of thirty-three votes in favor, thirteen against, and ten abstentions, the partition resolution was adopted. The Zionists were ecstatic, but the Arab delegates walked out of the General Assembly, declaring that their governments would not be bound by the United Nations decision.

Both Ben-Gurion, who had heard of the Zionist victory 6,000 miles away from the UN, and the Grand Mufti of Jerusalem, who had followed every word of the Palestine debate in New York, knew that the vote was no guarantee that the Jewish state would actually come into being. Between the vote on that late November afternoon and the expiration of the British mandate in Palestine, scheduled for May of the following year, lay a span of time that might well be decisive. Both men immediately set out to strengthen their forces for the battle that loomed ahead. Violent Arab-Jewish clashes occurred in Jerusalem and other parts of the country the day after the United Nations vote. The Jews were fearful that Arab resistance would deprive them of the fruits of the partition vote. The Arabs were enraged at a decision that, in their view, deprived them of their patrimony. On both sides, there seemed to be no time to lose.

The search for arms now dominated the minds of Arab and Jewish leaders alike. In this vital quest, the Zionists were at a disadvantage. The right to buy arms openly on the international arms market was the prerogative of sovereign states. Lebanon and Syria, which had won their independence in 1943 and 1946, respectively, were legally free to purchase arms for the Arab cause. Syria's defense minister, for example, was able to place an order for 10,000 rifles with a leading arms manufacturer in Czechoslovakia. The Jews, on the other hand, had to resort to clandestine means. The Haganah, the underground Zionist army, bought up American surplus arms and machine tools that were destined to be converted into scrap metal. To bypass the British arms embargo, most of the equipment was broken down into its component parts, classified by code, and then shipped to Palestine in random bits and pieces under official import permits for such items as textile machinery. Another technique used by Ben-Gurion's men was to place an order on the stationery of a sovereign state. One such order, from "Ethiopia," reached the same Czechoslovak arms manufacturer who had served the Syrians. That order too was filled. Thus by late 1947 a jostling for territory between Arabs and Jews was threatening to erupt into organized warfare between two desperate peoples.

In December 1947 the seven members of the Arab League met in Cairo to discuss the threat of a Jewish state in their midst. The states that were represented at this historic meeting were Egypt, Iraq, Saudi Arabia, Syria, Yemen, Lebanon, and Transjordan. Together, their leaders ruled some 45 million people and had at their command five regular armies. Azzam Pasha, the secretary-general of the Arab League, had labored patiently to reach a consensus among the seven Arab leaders, whose only common bond was their hostility to Zionism but who were otherwise deeply divided by historic rivalries and future ambitions. After protracted debate, the leaders resolved to "prevent the creation of a Jewish state in Palestine and to conserve Palestine as a united independent state."[9] To that end they pledged to furnish the league with 10,000 rifles, 3,000 volunteers, and £1 million sterling to provide an immediate beginning for guerrilla operations against the Zionists in Palestine.

At the same time David Ben-Gurion summoned his Haganah leaders to an emergency meeting in Jerusalem. "It is time," he told the men before him, "to start planning for a war against five Arab armies."[10] Ben-Gurion perceived the threat of war with the Arabs as a terrible menace that could strangle the Jewish state before it was born. On the other hand, he felt that if the Arabs insisted on going to war, the frontiers of the Jewish state would not be the boundaries assigned to it by the United Nations but those that the Jews could seize and hold by force of arms. If the Arabs rejected the United Nations decision and went to war, Ben-Gurion thought, that would give his people "the right to get what we could."[11] Thus, paradoxically, the Jewish leader turned the Arab cause into a handmaiden of Zionist aspirations.

As the two hostile armies engaged in strikes and counterstrikes that mounted in frequency and ferocity during the final months of the British mandate, events were taking place in Washington that once again placed the birth of the Jewish state in serious doubt. Shaken by the violence of Arab resistance and skeptical of Jewish military strength, President Truman was extremely reluctant to enforce the United Nations partition resolution with American troops even if such troops were part of a United Nations force. Moreover, the State Department continued to be deeply critical of partition and considered it to be legally unenforceable. In December 1947 the department prevailed upon the president to declare an arms embargo to the Middle East. Since under various agreements Britain was still free to ship arms to the Arabs, this embargo amounted to a ban on arms to the Jews. Perhaps most damaging to the Zionist cause was the fact that President Truman had become resentful of certain Zionist leaders, particularly Rabbi Abba Hillel Silver, who, in the president's opinion, had exerted improper pressure to support the Jewish cause. Thus, the United States abandoned its support of the partition plan and now proposed an international trusteeship over Palestine. In desperation the Zionists appealed to the aging, almost blind, Chaim Weizmann, who had enjoyed a close relationship with the American president over many years. On February 10, 1948, Weizmann wrote Truman a letter asking "for a few minutes of [his] precious time."[12] The request was refused.

Sitting at Weizmann's bedside, Frank Goldman, president of B'nai B'rith, came up with a last-ditch plan to change Truman's mind. He offered to telephone Eddie Jacobson, who was once a partner with Harry Truman in a haberdashery store and who, Goldman thought, might persuade the president to receive Dr. Weizmann. Jacobson responded favorably and was granted an interview with the president on March 12. Truman at first was not receptive to the overtures of his former business partner, but Jacobson persisted. His appeal to the president made a crucial difference in Zionist fortunes:

> Chaim Weizmann is a very sick man, almost broken in health, but he travelled thousands and thousands of miles just to see you and plead the cause of my people. Now you refuse to see him because you were insulted by some of our American Jewish leaders, even though you know that Weizmann had absolutely nothing to do with these insults and would be the last man to be a party to them. It doesn't sound like you, Harry.[13]

According to the same account, President Truman, after a long silence, looked Jacobson straight in the eye and said: "You win, you baldheaded son-of-a-bitch! I will see him."[14] One week later Truman met with Weizmann and promised the Jewish leader that he would work for the establishment and recognition of a Jewish state.

The battle was not yet won by the Zionists, however. On March 19 United States Ambassador Warren Austin announced in the Security Council that the United States would propose the suspension of the partition plan and the establishment of a temporary trusteeship in Palestine in its place. When a shocked and angry Truman wanted to know how such a thing could have happened, he discovered that Secretary of State George Marshall, who had not been privy to the president's personal pledge to Dr. Weizmann, had directed Austin on March 16 to make the trusteeship speech at the earliest appropriate moment. The Zionists were in despair, the Arabs were jubilant, Secretary-General Trygve Lie of the United Nations briefly considered resigning, and President Truman, according to his counsel, Clark Clifford, was "boiling mad."[15] He now had to go along with the trusteeship idea, at least for the time being, since yet another reversal would have deprived the United States of all credibility.

As the British mandate drew rapidly to a close, the fighting in Palestine became increasingly desperate. In April 1948 Jewish extremists of the Irgun and Stern groups massacred the inhabitants of Deir Yassin, a small village near Jerusalem. Even though Ben-Gurion personally cabled his shock at the slaughter and the Chief Rabbi of Jerusalem excommunicated the Jews who had participated in it, Deir Yassin became a stain on the conscience of the Jewish state. Not only did it elicit demands for vengeance and retribution, but in the years ahead it was to become a symbol of the homelessness of hundreds of thousands of Arab refugees. The mass exodus of terrified Arabs from Jewish-controlled areas began in earnest after this event. The Arab decision to encourage the refugees to leave and to broadcast the massacre in all its horror contributed to the growing panic. Thus Deir Yassin marked the beginning of the Palestinian problem that was to haunt the Middle East for decades to come.

Several days after the carnage of Deir Yassin, Ben-Gurion sent Golda Meir on a final peace mission. Disguised as an Arab woman, Meir traveled to Amman for a secret meeting with King Abdullah of Transjordan to discuss the possibility of preventing a collision. The king proposed that the proclamation of the Jewish state be postponed and that Palestine be kept united with the Jews autonomous in their areas. He also suggested a parliament composed equally of Arab and Jewish deputies. He desired peace, he told his visitor, but if his proposals were not accepted, war, he feared, would be inevitable. Meir replied that the postponement of the birth of a Jewish state was unacceptable and added that the Jews would fight as long as their strength lasted. Abdullah said that he realized that the Jews would have to repel any attack and that it was probably no longer in his power to act as mediator between his fellow Arabs and the Zionists. "Deir Yassin has inflamed the

Arab masses," he said. "Before then I was alone. Now I am one of five and have discovered that I cannot make any decisions alone."[16] Thus, this last effort to stave off the catastrophe ended in failure.

In May, with the days of the British mandate numbered, the Jews faced a crucial dilemma. Should they proclaim the Jewish state immediately, or, in light of the erosion of American support and the massing of Arab armies, should they wait? On May 12 Ben-Gurion called a secret meeting of the provisional National Council to make a decision. Opinion was sharply divided. Some council members felt that it would be wise to wait since the United States would probably not come to the aid of a self-proclaimed state but might do so if the Arabs acted first and invaded a United Nations-declared state. Others felt that the Jewish state would have to stand alone under any conditions, and so statehood should be proclaimed without delay. Ben-Gurion was for immediate statehood, even though he gave the Jews only a 50-50 chance for survival. When the vote was taken, six of the eleven council members voted to go ahead. By a margin of one vote the council decided to proclaim the new state on May 14, a few hours before the British mandate was to expire.

At 4 P.M. on May 14, 1948, two hours before the termination of the British mandate, David Ben-Gurion announced the birth of Israel. The news triggered a frantic debate in the United Nations General Assembly in New York, but the world body was unable to reach a decision. A short time after Ben-Gurion's proclamation, Warren Austin, on the personal instruction of President Truman, announced that the United States had recognized the new state of Israel. Shortly thereafter, the Soviet delegate followed suit. "We have been duped," said Charles Malik of Lebanon in an assault of fury on the American and Soviet delegations. It was now 6:15 P.M. and the mandate had ended. Ben-Gurion broadcast a personal message of thanks from Tel Aviv to the American people. As he spoke, the building shook from the impact of an Arab bomb. "The explosions you can hear," he told his audience across the Atlantic, "are Arab planes bombing Tel Aviv."[17] The war for Palestine had broken out.

At dawn on May 15 Israel was simultaneously invaded by the Egyptian army from the south, the Transjordanian Arab Legion from the east, and the forces of Syria and Lebanon from the north.

The total strength of the invading Arab armies was approximately 23,500 men, equipped with tanks, airplanes, heavy artillery, spare parts, and ammunition. The Israelis had approximately 3,000 regulars under arms plus 14,000 recruits. They also had 10,000 rifles, 3,600 submachine guns, four ancient cannons smuggled in from Mexico; they had no tanks. The United States and the Soviet Union both disapproved of the invasion. Andrei Gromyko, speaking for the Soviet Union in the Security Council on May 29, 1948, stated: "This is not the first time that the Arab states, which organized the invasion of Palestine, have ignored a decision of the Security Council or of the General Assembly."

At the end of several months' fierce fighting, interspersed by periods of truce, Israel was left in possession of the whole of Galilee, a section of central Palestine connecting the coastal area with Jerusalem, and the whole of the Negev. Jerusalem became a divided city. The entire area controlled by Israel in 1949 was somewhat larger than the area that had been allotted to the Zionists in the partition resolution of 1947. Thus the Arab invasion had played into the hands of the Jews. Almost 1 million Arabs were rendered homeless by the conflict and entered Syria, Transjordan, and the Egyptian-controlled Gaza Strip as refugees. From their midst would rise the fedayeen and the Palestinian resistance fighters who would hold Israel responsible for depriving them of their homeland. Thus the bloody birth of Israel set the stage for a mortal conflict between two nationalisms—one Arab, the other Jewish—both equally desperate and determined to secure what to each was holy ground.

The Sinai Campaign and the Suez Crisis of 1956

Time did not appease feelings even after the armistice agreements were concluded in 1949. On the Arab side, the plight of almost 1 million refugees was a constant reminder of the alien Zionist presence. No matter how defensive or conciliatory Israel's policy would be, this massive displacement would make the Jewish state into a standing provocation in the eyes of the entire Arab world. The Jews, of course, were fearful of allowing the refugees to return to their former homes. How could 700,000 Jews permit nearly 1 million Arabs to return to their land without also risking the destruction of the Jewish state? And yet how could they refuse it without inflicting on innocent people the very injustice they had themselves suffered in the Diaspora? Thus the Jews took back a few, compensated some, but most continued to linger in refugee camps in Jordan, Lebanon, Syria, and Egyptian-controlled Gaza. At the same time large numbers of Jews were driven out of Iraq, Yemen, Egypt, and Morocco.

During the early 1950s Palestinian Arab fedayeen from the refugee population mounted raids on Israeli territory that steadily increased in ferocity and frequency. The Israelis in turn engaged in massive and powerful reprisals. Thus, despite the military armistice, a state of belligerency continued to exist.

In 1952 Gamal Abdel Nasser, who had distinguished himself in the Palestine war, became president of Egypt and was soon the unrivaled champion of Arab nationalism. He instituted a blockade on Israeli shipping through the Suez Canal and in 1953 extended this blockade to include all goods being shipped to Israel. This left the Israelis with only the port of Elath, at the head of the Gulf of Aqaba in the Straits of Tiran. In late 1953 Nasser began to restrict Israeli commerce through the straits by making its ships subject to inspection by Egyptian coastguards. In 1955 he broadened the blockade and imposed a ban on overflights by Israeli aircraft. In Israel Prime Minister Ben-Gurion, who considered the port of Elath vital to Israel's survival, wanted to strike at Egypt immediately but was restrained by his colleagues. By 1956 relations between Egypt and Israel had reached the boiling point.

At this juncture the Arab-Israeli conflict blended into a broader confrontation between Arab nationalism and the remnants of the Anglo-French postcolonial presence in the Arab world. This confrontation was brought to a head by two huge engineering structures, one long in existence and the other about to be constructed: the Suez Canal and the High Dam at Aswan. President Nasser viewed the former as a leftover from colonial times and the latter as a modern pyramid to be built as a symbol of a resurgent Arab nationalism.

The United States had initially agreed to help finance the Aswan High Dam through the World Bank, but Secretary of State John Foster Dulles was irked by President Nasser's decision to purchase arms from Czechoslovakia in 1955 and his recognition a year later of Communist China. As a result, the United States reneged on its pledge to finance the dam, ostensibly because the Egyptian economy was deemed unsound, and Nasser became incensed. In his rage, he declared that the United States "should drop dead of fury, but [it would] never be able to dictate to Egypt."[18] Two days later, in an emotional "declaration of independence from imperialism," he announced the nationalization of the Suez Canal, which was partially owned by British and French financial interests. Thus Britain and France were made to pay for Dulles's policy reversal, and fatefully the two Western European powers now perceived a common interest with Israel: the removal of Gamal Abdel Nasser from power.

The perceptions of the British and French leaders now began to play a crucial role in the gathering crisis. In Britain Prime Minister Anthony Eden's memories of Hitler at Munich were still fresh, and he now compared Nasser's actions to those of the German dictator in the 1930s. In the words of one thoughtful student of British policy at the time, the prime minister "saw Egypt through a forest of Flanders poppies and gleaming jackboots."[19] French premier Guy Mollet shared this perception. He had been an anti-Nazi resistance chief at Arras during World War II and now "saw Nasser as Hitler more plainly than anyone."[20] The two men became so obsessed with Nasser's action that "Lady Eden is believed to have complained that the Suez Canal was running through her drawing room."[21]

There was, of course, good reason for consternation in Britain and France. The International Convention of Constantinople of 1888 had provided that "The Suez Maritime Canal shall always be free and open, in time of war and in time of peace, to every vessel of commerce or of war without distinction of flag." Thus the two Western powers considered Nasser's action as a violation of their legal rights. Moreover, to Britain, control of the canal symbolized her status as an empire and as a world power. To the French, who blamed Egypt for supporting the Algerian rebellion against France, seizure of the canal served as a kind of last straw. For both, the issue at stake was not merely safeguarding the economic rights of their shareholders in the Suez Canal Company; far more important was their emotional reaction to the seemingly insolent and Hitler-like nationalism represented by the Egyptian leader.

To Nasser, on the other hand, the Suez Canal had become the

symbol of a shameful colonial past. Its architect, Ferdinand de Lesseps, had become an Egyptian folk ogre. Under his brutal direction, as Nasser saw it, more than 100,000 Egyptian workers had died to build a canal that was to belong not to them or their country but to a foreign company that profited for its own enrichment and never for Egypt's benefit. "Instead of the Canal being dug for Egypt," Nasser declaimed, "Egypt became the property of the Canal and the Canal Company became a state within a state. But now the days of alien exploitation [were] over; the Canal and its revenues [would] belong entirely to Egypt. We shall build the High Dam and we shall gain our usurped rights."[22]

These sharply divergent perceptions set the stage for a violent encounter. During the weeks that followed Nasser's action, the conflict broadened. Eden and Mollet privately sounded out American reactions to the situation. They were partially reassured by the fact that Secretary of State Dulles also appeared outraged by Egypt's action. In their conversations with Dulles the British and French leaders again compared Nasser's action to Hitler's behavior at Munich and stated in the strongest terms that this type of Western appeasement must not be allowed to occur again. Secretary Dulles replied that "force was the last method to be tried, but the United States did not exclude the use of force if all other methods failed."[23] From this statement, Eden and Mollet inferred that at best the United States would present a united front with Britain and France in a show of force against Nasser and at worst remain benevolently neutral.

Britain and France now prepared for military action. They hoped to mount a lightning attack against Egypt, occupy the canal, depose Nasser, and then negotiate with his successor from a position of strength. In the course of these preparations, highly secret meetings took place with Israeli leaders for the purpose of coordinating the attack. Prime Minister Ben-Gurion and his chief of staff, General Moshe Dayan, were intent on seizing Gaza, the main base of fedayeen activities, and Sharm-el-Sheik on the Tiran Straits, from where the Egyptians maintained their blockade of the Gulf of Aqaba against ships bound for the port of Elath. Mollet pledged that if the Israelis would thrust into Sinai, French forces would join them, and Israel could seize Sinai and end the Egyptian blockade. Ben-Gurion hesitated; he feared that Egyptian bombers might attack Tel Aviv while Israeli forces were advancing into Sinai.[24] But when Eden pledged to use British air power to prevent Egyptian air attacks on Israel, Ben-Gurion agreed to move into Sinai.

The final plans worked out among the three prime ministers were the following: Israel was to launch her attack on October 29. As soon as Dayan's troops began their advance into Sinai, Britain and France were to issue an ultimatum to Israel and Egypt, requiring them to cease fire, to withdraw their forces 10 miles on either side of the canal, and to "accept the temporary occupation by Anglo-French forces of key positions at Port Said, Ismailia and Suez."[25] As soon as Israel had agreed to these terms and Egypt had rejected them, British bombers were to destroy the Egyptian air force and disrupt Egypt's communications and military capabilities in preparation for an Anglo-French invasion by paratroops from Cyprus and seaborne forces from Malta. Then, when these forces had occupied the canal from Port Said to Suez, a further attack was contemplated, aimed at the occupation of Cairo, if necessary, to depose Nasser. As these arrangements were being concluded, by a fateful coincidence in time, thousands of miles away Russian tanks rolled into Budapest to crush the two-day-old Hungarian revolt against Soviet domination.

On the afternoon of October 29 Israel's army launched its four-pronged advance against Egypt. Two thrusts were aimed at the canal while the third and fourth were to seal off the Gaza Strip and seize Sharm-el-Sheik. On the following day, while Israeli forces were advancing rapidly across the Sinai Peninsula, Britain and France issued their prearranged ultimatum, which in effect told the Egyptians to retreat and the Israelis to advance. Caught by complete surprise, Nasser rejected the ultimatum but was unable to put up much military resistance. He was convinced, however, that world opinion in the United Nations would come to his rescue.

On October 31 British and French bombers began air attacks against Egyptian targets, including Cairo. In retaliation, Nasser sank ships in order to block the canal. Within six days, Israel overran the greater part of the Sinai Peninsula and achieved its main military objective, the occupation of Sharm-el-Sheik.

The United Nations entered the picture on October 30. The American delegation called for a meeting of the Security Council and, to the consternation of Britain and France, introduced a resolution calling on Israel to leave Egypt without delay and asking all member states to "refrain from the use of force or threat of force."[26] The resolution was immediately vetoed by Britain and France. As the Security Council stood paralyzed and the Anglo-French-Israeli action continued, Soviet premier Nikolai Bulganin, in a news conference in Moscow, warned of the possibility of a third world war and declared that Soviet "volunteers" were ready to aid the Egyptian forces. He proposed that the United States and the Soviet Union restore the peace through a joint show of force. This suggestion was rejected as "unthinkable" by President Eisenhower. The United States was eager to see the Anglo-French action ended, but it was equally eager to prevent the establishment of a Soviet presence in the Middle East.

On November 2, in an emergency session of the General Assembly, the United States took a leading role in calling for a cessation of the fighting and the immediate withdrawal of the Anglo-French-Israeli forces from Egypt. The United States found support for this action from a not particularly welcome source—the Soviet Union. Thus the United States found itself in the paradoxical position of being allied in the United Nations with its great antagonist in the Cold War and at odds with its closest friends and allies, Britain and France.

By November 6 Britain had to yield. Confronted by United Nations resolutions charging her with aggression, dismayed by the action of the United States, and troubled by an increasingly hostile opposition at home, Prime Minister Eden terminated his abortive venture. As one critical British analyst summed it up: "The spectacle of over one hundred thousand men setting off for a war which lasted barely a day and then returning has few parallels in the long gallery of military imbecility."[27] France had no choice but to follow suit, but Israel still clutched tenaciously what her army had conquered in the six days of the war.

The role of the American leadership, of course, was crucial in the evolution of the crisis, and personalities played an important part. Both President Eisenhower and Secretary Dulles felt a sense of outrage because Eden and Mollet had not bothered to consult them on a matter as important as military action in the Middle East at a time when a national election was imminent in the United States. From a purely military standpoint, only the Israelis were attaining their objectives. The Anglo-French punitive expedition seemed to be foundering and thus could not be presented to the General Assembly as a fait accompli. The United States, by supporting the Anglo-French venture, or even by taking a neutral view of it, would have risked the ill will of a large majority of the United Nations membership and, in addition, might have had to look on helplessly while the military action failed or bogged down. Moreover, such an American response might have persuaded many neutralists that the United States, by countenancing aggression in the Middle East, differed little from the Soviet Union, which was aggressively crushing a rebellion in Hungary with military force. Most important, the United States feared the possibility of Soviet intervention in the Middle East through "volunteers" and the risk of sparking a major war through direct superpower confrontation in the contested area.

From the Soviet point of view, the Suez crisis was a windfall: the British and French appeared to be digging their own graves in the Middle East, and the United States seemed to be doing its best to help them. Thus, by appealing to the cause of Arab nationalism, the Soviet Union saw its opportunity to eject all Western influence from the Middle East and gain a foothold of its own. The fact that Israel was allied with the two colonial powers also played into Soviet hands.

Britain and France were clearly the main losers in the Suez affair. In humiliation, they had to watch Nasser snatch a political victory from a military defeat. Abandoned by their closest and oldest ally, they had to admit that they could no longer act like great powers and that, in the last analysis, their initiative in world politics depended on the decisions of the United States. The very issue that they had set out to rectify by force of arms—the internationalization of the Suez Canal—now seemed beyond redemption. For all practical purposes, the Suez crisis terminated Anglo-French authority in the Middle East. Suez had become another Dienbienphu.

The greatest victory in the Suez crisis was won by Arab nationalism. Nasser was now clearly master of the Suez Canal. The two great superpowers had supported him. Not only did he triumph in the showdown with Britain and France, but his other great foe, Israel, now came under increasing pressure to withdraw. Dag Hammarskjöld, secretary-general of the United Nations, had been successful in dispatching to the Middle East a special peace force, the United Nations Emergency Force (UNEF). Under strong American pressure Israel agreed to evacuate most of the territories it had conquered from Egypt, and beginning on November 15 the UNEF soldiers replaced the Israeli troops. Only an explicit American guarantee, however, that Israel's right to free and innocent passage in the Gulf of Aqaba would not be infringed upon persuaded the Israelis to evacuate the last fruits of their Sinai campaign—the Gaza Strip and the east coast of the Sinai Peninsula down to the Straits of Tiran. By March 1957 Israel had given up all the territories it had conquered, on the understanding that UNEF would prevent fedayeen raids from Jordan and the Gaza Strip. Hence, Israel emerged from the Sinai campaign with a marginal gain.

President Nasser was now at the zenith of his power. Among the Egyptian people he enjoyed the title of *rais,* or captain of the ship of state. With deep satisfaction he watched Eden and Mollet resign their posts. Thus encouraged, he now planned to turn on his archenemy, the Zionist state. In March 1957 he appointed an Egyptian civil governor of Gaza, a move that was viewed with indignation and misgivings in Israel. At the same time Radio Cairo declared that "the Gulf of Aqaba will be closed to Israeli ships and our commandos will continue to sow terror in Israel."[28] Thus the seeds of the next war, which was to erupt a decade later, were sown.

The Six-Day War of 1967

Once again, time did not heal but exacerbated the tensions between the Arab states and Israel. Within the Arab world, deep rifts had appeared on the overriding question of policy vis-à-vis Israel. By early 1967 three basic positions had crystallized.

First, the Syrians, who were the most radical and whose country was a major base for border raids against Israel, had created an organization named El Fatah, or "conquest." Its commando units carried out attacks against Israel in the tradition of the earlier fedayeen raids. In addition, Syria's president Al Atassi demanded a war of liberation against Israel similar to the one being fought against the United States in Vietnam. Second, and at the other end of the spectrum, was King Faisal of Saudi Arabia, who was relatively friendly toward the West and who regarded the violent temper of the Syrians with considerable distrust. While the huge oil deposits of Saudi Arabia provided the king with a formidable economic weapon, they also made him dependent to some extent on the Western nations for his revenue. President Nasser of Egypt found himself caught between these two rival factions. Eager to maintain his role as the embodiment of Arab nationalism, his ear was more sensitive to the gravitational pull of the Arab radicals than to the more conservative and traditional Arab leaders, such as King Faisal of Saudi Arabia and King Hussein of Jordan. This made him vulnerable to Syrian efforts to involve him in a larger war with Israel.

In April 1967, a major clash took place on the Israeli-Syrian border. Six Syrian MIG fighters were shot down by Israel in the course of the battle. El Fatah raids continued to mount in ferocity, and on May 14 Israeli prime minister Levi Eshkol declared that a serious confrontation with Syria would be inevitable if the attacks continued. The Syrians responded by declaring that Israel was concentrating huge armed forces on her border in preparation for an attack against Syria. Eshkol denied this charge and invited the Soviet ambassador to visit the areas in question. The Soviet diplomat refused. The pressure on President Nasser to help the Syrians was mounting rapidly. On May 16, Nasser proclaimed a state of emergency for the Egyptian armed forces and took measures to work out a joint Syrian-Egyptian defense agreement. The Syrian leadership, however, continued to taunt the Egyptian president by accusing him of "hiding behind the sheltering skirts of the United Nations Emergency Force."[29] A wave of emotion now spread throughout the Arab world from Casablanca to Baghdad. Demonstrations against Zionism took place in virtually every Arab country. On May 16, the Palestine Service of Radio Cairo declared:

> The menace and challenge of Israel have persisted far too long. The very existence of Israel in our usurped land has endured beyond all expectation. An end must be put to the challenge of Israel and to its very existence. Welcome to aggression by Israel which will send us into action to destroy it! Welcome to the battle for which we have long waited! The hour of battle is imminent. In fact, this is the hour of battle.[30]

President Nasser chose to ride the emotional tide of Arab nationalism rather than to resist it. This meant, however, that he had to take an active part in escalating the crisis, and so he decided to terminate the presence of the United Nations Emergency Force in Egypt and the Gaza Strip. On May 18 Foreign Minister Mahmoud Riad asked United Nations secretary-general U Thant to withdraw UNEF "as soon as possible." He reminded the secretary-general that the force had been stationed on Egyptian soil at the invitation of the Egyptian government and that its continued presence depended on Egyptian approval.

The United Nations Emergency Force had patrolled the hundred-mile-long Egyptian-Israeli frontier for ten years. It had been stationed on the Egyptian side of the border but not on the Israeli side. During the decade the force had been in effect, border eruptions had been kept to a minimum, and so the demand for its withdrawal caused considerable dismay at the United Nations. While U Thant never questioned Egypt's legal right to demand the withdrawal of the force, he expressed "serious misgivings" about its termination. He immediately referred the matter to the UNEF Advisory Committee. The Indian and Yugoslav representatives made it clear that their contingents were likely to be withdrawn in any case. Since they made up almost half of the 3,300-man force, additional pressure for withdrawal was thus applied. Furthermore, UN forces were already being jostled out of their positions by Egyptian troops. So the secretary-general complied with the Egyptian demand, reasoning that UNEF could no longer remain in the area if the consent of the host government were withdrawn.

Few actions have been discussed more heatedly by governments, the world press, and public opinion than U Thant's withdrawal of the United Nations Emergency Force. Criticism was particularly sharp in the United States, the United Kingdom, Canada, and, of course, in Israel. The Israeli ambassador to the United Nations, Abba Eban, stated caustically that "the umbrella was removed at the precise moment it began to rain." U Thant answered these charges by stating that he had no alternative by law but to accede to a request that was rooted in Egypt's sovereign rights. He also reasoned that if he did not comply with the request of a sovereign government, then consent for the admission of a United Nations peacekeeping force in a future crisis might be infinitely more difficult to obtain. Given all these conflicting considerations, the secretary-general made his difficult and fateful choice.

The withdrawal of UNEF brought the crisis to a new and much graver stage. Israeli and Egyptian forces now confronted each other directly across the border. Israel ordered a limited mobilization of reserves to which Egypt, on May 21, responded in kind. Encouraged by the ease with which he had accomplished the removal of the United Nations buffer force, and spurred by the groundswell of emotions in the Arab world, President Nasser, on May 22, announced the decision that was to become the direct cause of the Six-Day War: closure of the Straits of Tiran at the entrance of the Gulf of Aqaba to Israeli shipping, thereby blockading once again the port of Elath. In an emotional speech at the Egyptian Air Force Headquarters in Sinai he declared:

> The armed forces yesterday occupied Sharm-el-Sheik. What does this mean? It is affirmation of our rights and our sovereignty over the Gulf of Aqaba which constitutes territorial waters. Under no circumstances will we allow the Israeli flag to pass through the Gulf of Aqaba. The Jews threaten war. We tell them you are welcome, we are ready for war, but under no circumstances will we abandon any of our rights. This water is ours.[31]

The imposition of the blockade catapulted the crisis into the international realm. Israel had withdrawn from the Straits of Tiran only after she had received explicit assurances that the Western powers would guarantee freedom of passage for her ships. On May 23 Prime Minister Eshkol reminded the Western powers of their obligations, and Abba Eban, Israel's foreign minister, was dispatched to Paris, London, and Washington to secure the necessary assurances.

The responses of the Western powers to Israel's appeal for help were sympathetic but did not amount to guarantees. President Lyndon Johnson described the blockade as "illegal and potentially dangerous to peace." It was unlikely, however, that in the light of the American experience in Vietnam, the United States would be prepared to risk military intervention in the Middle East. In fact, President Johnson emphatically urged Israel not to take unilateral action. Little support came from anyone else. The

British too were sympathetic but did not offer a definite commitment to keep the waterway open, and President de Gaulle of France, observing a glacial neutrality, stated: "France is committed in no sense or on any subject to any of the states involved."[32]

These responses were not reassuring to Israel. Prime Minister Eshkol was under increasing pressure to assume a more belligerent position. On May 24 the United Nations Security Council convened but was unable to take any action whatsoever to lift the blockade. The sense of foreboding in Israel increased. On May 26, when President Nasser asserted that the Gulf of Aqaba was only part of the major problem that was caused by Israel's aggression in simply existing, the response in Israel was electric. Pressure now became intense to appoint General Moshe Dayan, the hero of the 1956 Sinai campaign, to the ministry of defense. On the same day that Nasser delivered his belligerent address, his friend Mohammed Hasanein Haikal, the editor of the leading Egyptian newspaper *Al-Ahram,* wrote a remarkably frank and perceptive article:

> The closure of the Gulf of Aqaba means, first and last, that the Arab nation, represented by the UAR, has succeeded for the first time vis-a-vis Israel in changing by force a fait accompli imposed on it by force. To Israel this is the most dangerous aspect of the current situation, not who can impose the accomplished fact and who possesses the power to safeguard it. Therefore, it is not a matter of the Gulf of Aqaba but of something bigger. It is the whole philosophy of Israeli security. Hence, I say that Israel must attack.[33]

This was a fair assessment of Israel's predicament. On June 1 it was announced that General Dayan was appointed minister of defense. This move was widely interpreted as a sign that Israel had decided that she could not depend on outside help and would therefore have to resort to a preemptive attack to break her hostile encirclement. On June 2 Ahmed Shukairy, leader of the Palestine Liberation Organization, called for a holy war for the liberation of Palestine. Addressing a large congregation in the Old City of Jerusalem, he declared that the Arabs wanted "fighters, not Beatles" and called on Arab women to don battle dress, adding that "this is no time for lipstick and mini-skirts." Meanwhile, on June 3 General Dayan stated at a press conference that, while

Israel welcomed all the help she could get on the diplomatic front, she wished to fight her own battles with her own troops. He added that he did "not want British or American boys to get killed" in the defense of Israel. Asked whether Israel had lost the military initiative, General Dayan replied: "If you mean to say we stand no chance in battle, then I cannot agree with you."[34] The brink was reached.

At 7:45 A.M. Monday, June 5, the Six-Day War began. The Israeli air force attacked Egyptian airfields in a series of lightning strikes. By the end of the week, the armed forces of Israel occupied the Sinai Peninsula, the Gaza Strip, the whole West Bank of the Jordan, the entire city of Jerusalem, and the Golan Heights. The armies of Egypt, Jordan, and Syria had been completely routed.

Israel had destroyed or captured 430 aircraft and 800 tanks and had inflicted 15,000 fatal casualties on Arab troops. It had taken 5,500 officers and men as prisoners. Its own losses were 40 aircraft and 676 dead.

A study made by the Institute for Strategic Studies in London by Michael Howard and Robert Hunter summarizes the campaign:

> The third Arab-Israeli war is likely to be studied in Staff Colleges for many years to come. Like the campaigns of the younger Napoleon, the performance of the Israeli Defence Force provided a textbook illustration for all the classical principles of war: speed, surprise, concentration, security, information, the offensive—above all, training and morale. Airmen will note with professional approval how the Israeli air-force was employed first to gain command of the air by destruction of the enemy air-force, then to take part in the ground battle by interdiction of enemy communications, direct support of ground attacks and, finally, pursuit. The flexibility of the administrative and staff system will be examined and the attention of young officers drawn to the part played by leadership at all levels. Military radicals will observe how the Israelis attained this peak of excellence without the aid of drill sergeants and the barrack square. Tacticians will stress the importance they attached in this, as in previous campaigns, to being able to move and fight by night as effectively as they did by day. Above all, it will be seen how Israel observed a principle which appears in few military textbooks, but which armed forces neglect at their peril: the Clausewitzian principle of political context which the British ignored so disastrously in 1956. The Israeli High Command

knew that it was not operating in a political vacuum. It worked on the assumption that it would have three days to complete its task before outside pressures compelled a cease-fire.[35]

On the deepest level, the secret of Israel's military success probably lay in the realization of every one of her citizens that losing would have meant the end of the nation's existence. In that light, the comparison, offered by the Soviet delegate to the United Nations Security Council, of Israel's offensive with Hitler's attack on the Soviet Union was hardly persuasive. In a sense, Israel's military system was the very opposite of that of nineteenth-century Prussia, which had resulted in the militarization of society. The Israeli approach led to the civilianization of the army; officers maintained their authority not by orthodox discipline but by personal example. Thus the Israelis got the utmost from their men and their machines.

President Nasser was so shocked by the swiftness and efficiency of Israel's offensive that he believed, or purported to believe, that the United States and the United Kingdom had given assistance to the Zionists by maintaining an "air umbrella" over Israel. The truth was that in the Arab countries political fanaticism simply was no substitute for military expertise, and fantasies of victory could no longer mask the totality of the disaster.

Israel's leaders knew that they had to achieve their victory quickly to make it stick. They operated on the assumption that they had three days to defeat the Arabs before outside pressures compelled a cease-fire. In fact, they had four and needed five. The chorus of disapproval that arose even in the West when Israel ignored a United Nations cease-fire call and, on the fifth day of the war, opened its offensive against Syria showed how narrow was the time margin in which Israel had to work. Israel knew that there was a tacit agreement between the two superpowers not to permit the Arab-Israeli war to escalate into a larger conflict, provided that the war was quickly brought to an end. Once it had ended, the great powers were reluctant to risk a second conflict in order to undo the victory that had been achieved in the first. Thus a premium was placed on preemption and the lightning speed of Israeli arms.

An analysis of the changes in power constellations after the Six-Day War reveals some interesting comparisons and contrasts with the crisis of 1956. First, the Soviet Union had backed a loser this time, whereas she had been on the winning side a decade earlier. Most of the military hardware that the USSR had shipped to the Arab states was destroyed or captured by the Israelis. The United States, on the other hand, was on the winning side, and superficially her policy seemed successful. But on a deeper level it was clear that the swiftness of Israel's victory had saved the United States from having to make some difficult decisions. Had the war gone badly for Israel or remained inconclusive, the United States might have been forced to intervene and risk a confrontation with the Soviet Union.

Israel, which had to withdraw in 1956, was determined this time not to yield its military gains except in exchange for an end to belligerency. Within six days Israel had exchanged its vulnerability for a position of unprecedented military domination in the Middle East. Within two brief decades, a fledgling Jewish state in Palestine had become a formidable power.

The October War of 1973

Israel's swift and decisive victory in 1967 had left a legacy of shame and bitterness on the Arab side. Diplomacy had not been able to dislodge the Israelis from the five territories that they had captured from three Arab countries in June 1967: Sinai and the Gaza Strip from Egypt; Old Jerusalem and the West Bank from Jordan; and the Golan Heights from Syria. The UN Security Council had been able to adopt only a single resolution on the Middle East over a period of six years. That resolution, which was passed on November 22, 1967, linked a promise of secure and recognized boundaries to Israel with a promise of withdrawal from occupied territories to the Arabs. But neither side was willing to take the first step, and so the entire situation remained frozen. No face-to-face negotiations between Arabs and Israelis ever took place. The Arabs gazed across the cease-fire line with increasing fury and frustration as Israel made plans to populate the territories with Jewish settlers. Israel seemed bent on de facto annexation, and the Arabs seemed equally determined to prevent it.

Anwar Sadat, who became Egypt's new president after

Nasser's death in 1970, gradually and without much fanfare prepared the ground for an Arab counterattack. Unlike Nasser, the less flamboyant Sadat did not divide the Arab world but doggedly worked toward a consensus. The Soviet Union, though not prepared to give the Arabs offensive weapons for use against Israel, did replace the military hardware that had been captured or destroyed by Israel in 1967. The Soviets also trained Egyptian and Syrian commanders in Soviet military strategy and tactics in order to prevent a repetition of the debacle of the Six-Day War. By 1973 the Arabs were encouraged to believe that at least some of the lost territories could be regained by force of arms. Thus the stage was set for yet another violent encounter.

On Yom Kippur, the Jewish Day of Atonement, Syria and Egypt launched a well-coordinated surprise attack. In the north, Syria attacked the vital Golan Heights in an effort to regain the vantage point over Israeli settlements in the valley below. In the Sinai, Egypt threw a major military force across the Suez Canal, capturing Israeli positions on the eastern bank and sending Israel's defenders backward into the desert.

The Arab attack had not come as a complete surprise to the Israeli leadership. Defense Minister Moshe Dayan claimed several days later that he had had advance information that some sort of attack was imminent but had decided against a preemptive strike. The reason for this decision, according to Mr. Dayan, was to "have the political advantage of not having attacked first, even at the expense of the military advantage."[36] Israel's image abroad would thus be improved with resultant long-term political benefits.

The price that Israel paid for this apparent self-restraint was heavy. On the Suez front, the Egyptians swarmed across the canal in large numbers, laid down bridges, and landed hundreds of tanks and other war matériel. They managed to overrun the famous Israeli defense installation, the Bar-Lev line, with heavy air and artillery assaults. The lightly defended Israeli positions had to be abandoned. On the Golan Heights an enormous Syrian force equipped with 800 tanks plunged across the cease-fire line at four points. Commando units landed by helicopter on Mount Hermon and seized a major Israeli position. Overwhelmed by the force of the attack, Israeli defenders had to evacuate several outposts.

One explanation of these early Arab successes may be found in

Israel's perception of its own military superiority and of the Arabs as notoriously poor, bumbling soldiers. The Israeli leadership had convinced itself of its own superiority to such an extent that it believed that any Arab attack would be suicidal. Israel, in short, was suffering from a case of military hubris.

By the end of the first week of war, Israel had stemmed the Arab onslaught, but the myth of its invincibility had nevertheless been shattered. Egypt had managed to install almost 100,000 men on the East Bank of the Suez Canal and the fiercest tank battles since World War II were raging in the Sinai desert and the Golan Heights. Casualties were heavy on both sides, and new Soviet ground-to-air missiles presented a grave threat to the Israeli air force. Buoyed by the successes of Syria and Egypt, other Arab countries joined in the battle. Iraq and Jordan supplied troops for the Syrian front, and Saudi Arabia and other oil-rich Arab sheikdoms applied increasing pressure on the United States to abandon its support of Israel.

As casualties mounted and both sides suffered staggering losses in war matériel, the superpowers entered the arena. The Soviet Union began to resupply the Arab states with ammunition and light weapons. When the United States decided to do the same for Israel, the Soviet Union escalated its supply operations to tanks and planes. This too was matched by the United States. Thus, by the end of the first week, the war had reached a new and dangerous plateau. Not only was the armor of both sides locked in a death struggle, but the fragile détente between the Soviet Union and the United States hung in the balance.

During the second week of war Israel gradually gained the upper hand on both the Syrian and Egyptian fronts. After fierce tank battles in the Golan Heights, the Israelis not only threw back the Syrians but embarked on the road to Damascus. In the words of General Dayan: "We have to show them [the Syrians] that the road leads not only from Damascus to Tel Aviv, but from Tel Aviv to Damascus."[37] The Israeli advance into Syria came to a standstill at the village of Sasa, twenty miles from the Syrian capital.

On the Egyptian front, Israeli troops, in a daring tactical maneuver, entered the West Bank of the Suez Canal on Egyptian territory. Their aim was to encircle the Egyptian troops on the East Bank in Sinai and to cut off their retreat across the canal back to Egypt. After massive air and tank battles, the Israeli objectives were attained. The Egyptian troops were trapped in two large pockets in Sinai, and the Third Army was at Israel's mercy for its supply of food and water. At this juncture, with the balance shifting rapidly in Israel's favor, the superpowers once more intervened.

On October 21, acting with great urgency to protect its Egyptian ally, the Soviet leadership agreed with Secretary of State Henry Kissinger on a formula for a cease-fire resolution. This resolution, which was rushed through the UN Security Council on the following morning under joint Soviet-American sponsorship, provided for a cease-fire in place and called on all parties to start immediate negotiations toward implementing the 1967 Security Council plan for peace in the Middle East. The cease-fire began shakily, with the Egyptian forces trapped behind Israeli lines trying to break out and Israel seeking to destroy the Egyptian forces once and for all. A second cease-fire call still did not end the fighting. As a result, the Soviet Union proposed that a joint Soviet-American peace force be dispatched to the Middle East. This proposal was rejected by the United States, which feared the possibility of a military confrontation in the area. The Soviet Union then declared that it would introduce its own troops into the area unilaterally. To this Soviet threat, President Nixon responded by placing the armed forces of the United States on military alert.

During the "alert" crisis, a compromise was worked out. The UN Security Council approved a third resolution sponsored by the nonaligned countries that authorized the secretary-general to send a UN buffer force to the area. This 7,000-man emergency force would be patterned after the old UN Emergency Force that had been created by Dag Hammarskjöld in 1956. It was to exclude the permanent members of the Security Council from active participation. To save face, however, the two superpowers insisted on sending a small number of observers into the cease-fire area. The first UN troops began to arrive from Cyprus on October 27. By then, all fronts were quiet. The precarious Soviet-American détente had held after all.

As the "October war" drew to a close after seventeen days of violent fighting, Israel had won another victory, but a costly one in blood and treasure. Although it had managed to roll back the initial Arab advance and had assumed a commanding military position on both fronts, the price paid in human lives for this achievement was far higher than the toll that had been taken in the war of 1967. The heavy losses made the victory somewhat joyless. Moreover, the immediate postwar Israeli attitude on the question of the occupied territories hardened. If an Arab surprise attack had been launched along the pre-1967 armistice lines, then Tel Aviv and Jerusalem—not the Golan Heights and the Bar-Lev line—would have had to absorb the initial shock. Thus, in the Israeli view, tens of thousands of their people could be killed if such a surprise attack were only slightly more successful than the one launched in October 1973. In Abba Eban's words:

> If we had been mad enough to abandon the Golan Heights and Sharm el Sheikh and all the Sinai and the whole West Bank, would not the massive attack launched on October 6 have murdered thousands of our civilians, devastated our population centers and brought us to catastrophe? I tell you, a massacre more hideous than Auschwitz would have been a real prospect and Israel's survival would be in doubt. To suggest a restoration of the pre-1967 lines is sheer irresponsibility in the light of what has been revealed.[38]

Just as the setbacks of the first few days of war were deeply etched on Israeli minds, so the Arabs cherished and glorified their short-lived victory. Despite his ultimate defeat, President Sadat proclaimed that "Egyptian forces had performed a miracle by any military standard" and had thus "restored the honor of the nation." Egypt and Syria had been able to break out of the frustration and futility of unending diplomatic stalemate. They had placed Israel on notice that it could not hold on indefinitely to occupied territory unless it was prepared to accept the risk of yet another war with the odds against it. As Egypt's foreign minister, Mohamed El Zayyat, put it:

> The Israeli attitude had been to assume that they were invincible and that we were meek and weak. They pictured Egyptians as people who would never fight. The argument that this occupied territory serves as a protective buffer for Israel—that was the argument of Hitler. What we are asking for is very simple: that our territorial integrity and the rights of the Palestinians be respected. These two elements are the *sine qua non* conditions for peace in the Middle East.[39]

Thus the fourth round ended with positions hardened on both sides and passions unallayed. The Israelis were embittered by the

Yom Kippur surprise attack and, in their bitterness, tended to forget that the attack was launched in order to regain lost territories. The Arabs were so intent on restoring their dignity and regaining lost ground that they believed that they had won even though actually they had lost. Neither side was able any longer to understand the fears of the other. All empathy was lost. For two weeks the superpowers had made the desert a proving ground for new destructive weapons. Kings played chess while pawns bled on the battlefield. Only when the kings were fearful that the battle might engulf them too did they stop the bloodshed. Once again the United Nations was used as a rescue operation at the edge of the abyss. Frantic cease-fire resolutions had to take the place of preventive diplomacy. And only a fragile superpower détente prevented yet another fateful escalation with dire consequences for humankind.

The October War of 1973 had one positive result. Under superpower pressure, Israelis and Arabs did agree to meet in a peace conference in Geneva in December 1973, their first face-to-face diplomatic encounter in a quarter of a century. As Abba Eban put it: "For something to be born, the parents have to meet at least once." Chastened by four wars, Arabs and Jews alike began to feel that unless wisdom and reason ultimately prevailed, the only alternative would be mutual annihilation.

The role of the United States during and after the October War was primarily defined by Secretary of State Henry Kissinger. For the next three years, the Middle Eastern scene was dominated by the tireless peacemaking efforts of this extraordinary statesman.

Kissinger's role in the October War can be described as neither pro-Israeli nor pro-Arab but as essentially pro-equilibrium. Before the war erupted, Kissinger perceived Israel as the stronger side and thus warned the Jewish leaders "not to preempt." But when he turned out to have been mistaken and Syria and Egypt launched their coordinated surprise attack, Kissinger switched sides and provided American military aid to Israel in order to restore the military balance. And when the Israelis, with this American assistance, gained the upper hand, Kissinger switched sides again and insisted on the rescue of 100,000 trapped Egyptian soldiers. When a cease-fire was finally proclaimed by the United Nations, both sides were exhausted and roughly even—exactly what Kissinger had wanted. It had always been his firm belief that only a war without victory or defeat could contain the seeds of peace.

As Kissinger surveyed the ravages of the October War, he conceived his plan for peace in the Middle East. He decided to subdivide the problem into manageable segments instead of addressing it in its totality. He would approach it step by step, beginning with the least forbidding obstacle, and then, after having built a basis of trust between the rivals, he would try to negotiate the more formidable hurdles. A first tentative step had already been taken. Egypt had agreed to talk to Israel. If Kissinger could achieve a military disengagement between Israel and Egypt, a momentum toward peace might then be set in motion. It would perhaps then be possible to leap over yet another hurdle and effect a military disengagement between Syria and Israel. If such military interim agreements were possible, perhaps one might be able to move the rivals toward political accommodation. Once Egypt and Syria had entered into negotiations with Israel, Saudi Arabia might be persuaded to lift her oil embargo, and if luck held, it might even be conceivable to think about a compromise between Israel and the Palestinians and a Jerusalem settlement. Such was Kissinger's train of thought. The peacemaking process would be like a steeplechase, with each successive hurdle higher and more treacherous. But Kissinger believed that the step-by-step approach would yield at least some limited successes and should not be a total failure.

The objective that Kissinger had in mind, of course, was equilibrium. Israel would have to withdraw from some of the conquered territories, but in the context of her national security. The diplomatic reemergence of the Arabs would be encouraged, but in a context of realism and responsibility. An effort would be made to woo the Arabs away from the Soviet Union. They would come to the United States because, in Kissinger's judgment, "they could get weapons from the Russians, but territory only from the United States." Thus by delivering some real estate to the Arabs, Soviet power in the Middle East would be diminished and American influence strengthened. To achieve this objective, however, pressure would have to be applied to Israel. She would have to be encouraged to trade territory for security. And if Kissinger's reasoning was wrong, he would have to protect Israel by always being generous with arms.

Kissinger's step-by-step approach to peace was not greeted with universal acclaim. The Soviet Union was highly critical and pushed for a general peace conference to be held in Geneva. There was also criticism in the United States. Numerous Middle East experts asserted that Kissinger's approach was that of a doctor who planned to stitch up one wound while permitting an infection to rage unattended elsewhere.

According to these critics, Kissinger, by concentrating on Egypt, intended to woo the moderate Sadat away from the Arab camp. This would not only remove the most conciliatory voice from Arab councils, but it would postpone and ultimately make more difficult the moment of truth. The heart of the matter, Kissinger's critics declared, was neither Egypt nor Syria, but the problem of the Palestinians, which Kissinger had chosen to postpone indefinitely, in addition to Jerusalem, which he had chosen to ignore completely. Thus, as George Ball, one of Kissinger's most trenchant critics, put it, "the step-by-step approach was the work of a tactician when the times called for a strategist."

Kissinger was undaunted by these attacks. He believed that the aftermath of an inconclusive war was the best time for a concentrated peace effort. Shortly after the last shot had been fired, he decided to commit his skill, energy, and reputation to a highly personal diplomatic peace offensive in the Middle East. During the next few months he would visit virtually every Arab capital, shuttle between Aswan and Jerusalem, and later between Damascus and Jerusalem. Sadat would call him "brother"; Faisal would welcome him even though he was a Jew; Hussein would pilot him in the royal helicopter; even Assad would learn to like him; and Golda Meir would have endless conversations with him in her kitchen. The end result of this extraordinary diplomatic tour de force was the successful negotiation of the first two hurdles. In January 1974 Kissinger was able to produce a military disengagement accord between Israel and Egypt, and four months later, after immense effort, he was able to achieve a similar accord between Israel and Syria.

The high point of Kissinger's "shuttle diplomacy" was the Sinai agreement between Israel and Egypt, signed in Geneva in September 1975. The Sinai agreement bore the imprimatur of a Kissinger settlement. Neither side was happy with it, but neither side could offer a better alternative that was acceptable to both. The Israelis promised to return two mountain passes and an oil field. In exchange they received pledges from President Sadat to the effect that Egypt would refrain from the threat or use of force against the Jewish state. Sadat also agreed to continue negotiations toward a final peace agreement and to extend the mandate of the UN buffer force annually for at least three years.

What finally made it possible, however, for Israel to conclude the agreement was a specific American commitment that Kissinger had not made before. Kissinger offered to station 200 American civilian technicians in the Sinai *between* the contending parties. They would serve as a kind of early warning system in case either side planned an attack on the other, and they would report to both Israel and Egypt. In addition, Kissinger pledged to recommend an American aid commitment of $2.3 billion to Israel. Israel, which did not trust the UN buffer force, found the pledge of a small symbolic American presence reassuring. The aid package too was attractive, and furthermore, Prime Minister Rabin could tell the opposition that Israel still retained over 85 percent of the Sinai and the entire Gaza Strip. Sadat received his coveted mountain passes and oil fields plus an American commitment of $700 million needed for the impoverished Egyptian economy. The 200 Americans were welcome too, since their presence only underscored Sadat's growing independence from the Soviet Union. Thus Egypt gained some territorial allowances, and Israel received political concessions. What could not be bridged between the parties directly was bridged by American commitments. Some senators grumbled that the 200 Americans in the Sinai reminded them of the beginning of Vietnam, but Kissinger was quick to point out that the Americans in the Sinai were civilians who were to aid both sides in keeping the peace, not soldiers who were to help one side to win a war.

On the whole, Kissinger was pleased with the second Sinai interim agreement. It was, after all, the first accord between Israel and an Arab nation that was not the immediate consequence of war. He knew that it was far from a genuine peace treaty, but he was convinced that his step-by-step approach was still the best way to proceed. In his judgment, most Americans were still willing to take great risks to preserve the state of Israel, but were *not* willing to take such risks to preserve Israel's conquests.

During most of 1976 a deus ex machina postponed the moment of truth for Israel. Syria and the Palestine Liberation Organization, Israel's two bitterest adversaries, turned on each other in a murderous war in Lebanon. While it lasted Israel was in no mood to make concessions. By 1977, however, when Jimmy Carter assumed the presidency of the United States and Menachem Begin became prime minister of Israel, the Lebanese war had tapered off and a renewed Arab alliance confronted the Jewish state.

Thus by 1977 it had become clear that the step-by-step approach had reached a dead end. The heart of the matter was now the problem of the Palestinians. Israel was confronted with a dreadful choice. If she agreed to negotiate with the PLO and return some territories to be used for the creation of a Palestinian state, such a state would clearly be a dagger pointed at the heart of Israel. If, on the other hand, she refused to negotiate, she risked another war or another oil embargo, as well as slow economic strangulation and increasing isolation. Despite the risks involved, President Carter believed that ultimately Israel would have to face the Palestinians as a reality that would not go away, just as America after more than two decades had been forced to adjust to the reality of a China that was Communist. There were now three million Israelis and three million Palestinians. Both were permanent realities, and sooner or later a compromise solution would have to be discovered. The alternative was yet another war.

In November 1977 the world held its breath when, in a spectacular and unprecedented move, President Sadat visited the Jewish state and addressed the Israeli Knesset. Though neither Sadat nor Prime Minister Begin made any substantive concessions during that first face-to-face encounter in Jerusalem, both leaders made a solemn pledge never again to go to war with one another. Whereas peace, unlike war, does not break out, the Sadat mission was widely heralded as a major turning point in the thirty-year-old conflict between Arab and Jew. At last an Arab statesman had openly recognized the Jewish state. Two old enemies had suddenly become friends.

In September 1978 President Carter, in an all-out effort to forge a peace settlement between Begin and Sadat, invited the two leaders to a summit meeting at Camp David. After two weeks of intense and secret deliberations, two important agreements were hammered out. First, Begin and Sadat agreed on a "Framework for Peace between Egypt and Israel" that provided for the phased withdrawal of Israeli forces from the Sinai and the signing of a full-fledged peace treaty. Second, the two leaders agreed on a broader "Framework for Peace in the Middle East" that was designed to enable the Palestinian issue and the West Bank problem to be resolved progressively over a five-year period.

But at the very moment these agreements were being made, the Shah of Iran was deposed and driven into exile by the fundamentalist Islamic forces loyal to the Ayatollah Ruhollah Khomeini. As Iranian oil exports plummeted, the United States became increasingly dependent on Saudi Arabian oil. Recognizing their advantage, the Saudis insisted on a linkage between the separate Egyptian-Israeli peace treaty and progress toward the far more difficult issues of the West Bank, the Palestinians, and the status of Jerusalem. Motivated by American energy needs, Carter in turn exerted pressure on Israel to be more flexible. Finally, in March 1979 Begin and Sadat, after yet another Carter visit to the Middle East, signed a separate peace treaty. The president's tenacity and faith had finally borne fruit. After thirty years of war the Middle East had taken a large step toward peace.

Many vexing issues remained unresolved, of course. The fate of Jewish settlements on the West Bank continued to torment the Israelis, who also worried about the very real possibility of the ultimate creation of a Palestinian state. In 1981, Israel, using American-made planes, destroyed an Iraqi nuclear reactor that had been constructed with French and Italian help. This preemptive strike precipitated a diplomatic crisis between the United States and Israel. On the Arab side, Jordan and Saudi Arabia were dubious about the Israeli-Egyptian treaty; Syria and the PLO were bitterly opposed and regarded Sadat as a traitor. And perhaps most important, all Arabs insisted that Israel withdraw from Jerusalem and renounce the city as its capital. Israel in turn declared in 1980 that Jerusalem would remain its capital for "all eternity." In 1981, President Sadat was assassinated by Moslem fanatics. Under his successor, Hosni Mubarak, Egypt's relations with Israel cooled considerably. Worst of all, Israel launched an invasion of Lebanon which not only raised levels of violence in the region to new ferocity, but upset the entire balance of power in the Middle East.

The Lebanese Tragedy

There was a time when Lebanon was a peaceful, happy land, a kind of Middle Eastern Switzerland, with its graceful seaport capital, Beirut, a major tourist attraction. This tranquillity depended on a fine balance between the Moslem and Christian populations of the country. Without that balance, Lebanon gradually descended into an abyss of devastation. Jealous factions fighting for turf dismembered Lebanon piece by bloody piece until it became a country without an effective government. Unable to control its own destiny, Lebanon was drawn into the vortex of the major power struggles in world politics. It became a bitterly divided country, with Beirut a divided city.

After Israel occupied the West Bank in 1967, hundreds of thousands of Palestinians moved to Lebanon over the years, gradually upsetting the fragile balance between Moslems and Christians. In 1975 the country erupted in civil war, triggered by a round of local murders, which were to become typical of the Lebanese scene. Beirut was devastated for the first time. Syria's President Assad, seeing an opportunity for expansion, sent a "peacekeeping" force into Lebanon, which signaled the beginning of the Syrian occupation of central Lebanon. Israel's Premier Begin, apprehensive about Syrian intervention, carved out for Israel a "security strip" in southern Lebanon in 1978. Four years later, in June 1982, Israeli forces invaded Lebanon in full force, all the way to Beirut. Their goal was to drive the Palestinian guerrillas out of southern Lebanon and to counter Syria's growing influence in that war-torn country.

At this juncture, the United States, fearful that the apparent disintegration of Lebanon might play into Soviet hands, decided to become involved. The Reagan administration worked out an agreement with three of its allies—Great Britain, France, and Italy—to send about five thousand marines into Lebanon. The objective of this "multinational peacekeeping force" was to monitor the withdrawal of PLO forces from Lebanon and eventually to persuade Israel to pull out so that Syria too might withdraw. The

United States hoped, in short, that it might be helpful in returning Lebanon to the Lebanese. Unfortunately this was not to be. As the Palestinians were evacuated and the Israelis returned West Beirut to President Amin Gemayel's forces, the mission of the four-power peacekeeping force became somewhat unclear. Gradually it was redefined as providing support for the Gemayel government. But the young president acted more like the head of the Christian faction than the leader of the entire country, and the force quickly became identified as pro-Christian and anti-Moslem. A new tragedy was in the making.

In October 1983 a Moslem fanatic, kamikazelike, drove a truck loaded with explosives into the sleeping quarters of the American marines in Beirut. The vehicle exploded with such force that the structure collapsed in seconds, killing 241 American servicemen. Simultaneously another suicide mission killed 58 French soldiers, also asleep in their compounds. For the United States, this was the highest death toll since the Vietnam War; for France, it was the heaviest since the Algerian War.

When observed in the cold light of political analysis, this dreadful tragedy had all the overtones of a neocolonial conflict. The Moslem fundamentalists who committed these murders probably perceived the American, British, French, and Italian soldiers not only as partial to the Christian cause in Lebanon, but also as the vanguard of a new Western imperialism. After all, these were the very four nations that had engaged in colonial adventures not many years before. Lebanon had been a French colony, Libya had belonged to Italy, much of the Middle East had belonged to Britain, and the United States was, of course, the main instigator of this renewed colonial intrusion. Islam, especially Shi'ite Islam inspired by Iran, perceived itself as the main bulwark against Western aggression. The murderers were thus not really murderers. They were freedom fighters, and their reward would be immediate entry into paradise.

After the Beirut catastrophe, the days of the multinational peacekeeping force were numbered. Senator Ernest Hollings of South Carolina put it well when he called on President Ronald Reagan to withdraw the marines within sixty days: "If they've been put there to fight, then there are far too few," he said, "but if they've been put there to be killed, there are far too many." Accordingly, after some fruitless shellings by the USS *New Jersey*, the American soldiers were withdrawn from Lebanon in February 1984. Shortly thereafter, their French, British, and Italian fellow marines were removed. Lebanon by now was a carcass, and a dismembered one at that. For all practical purposes, by mid-1984 Lebanon was a divided country. Within its divisions there were further factions that made the country look like a crazy quilt. Nevertheless, these factions tended to fall, either directly or indirectly, along East-West lines. On the Western side were the Israeli forces stationed in southern Lebanon, now left to fend for themselves after the American withdrawal. The Maronite Christians and, to a lesser extent, the Sunni Moslems, were not unfriendly to Israel and the Western cause. On the other side, Druze and Shi'ite Moslems supported the Syrian presence, which in turn was backed by the Soviet Union. President Gemayel, virtually powerless after the pullout of the Western forces, had to accept the indefinite presence of the Syrians and even felt compelled to host a Soviet delegation in Beirut. When in early 1985 Israel began a phased withdrawal of its troops from Lebanon, Gemayel's hold on power became even more precarious. In historical perspective, Israel's incursion into Lebanon seemed like an ominous portent: Israel had to withdraw after three years of war, with its mission unaccomplished. And worse was yet to come.

By the late 1980s, Lebanon had become a disaster area, a place of war of all against all and each for himself. Not only were Moslems pitted against Christians once again, but several outside powers continued to aggravate the conflict: Syria, which had 25,000 troops stationed on 60 percent of Lebanon's territory; Iran, which wielded influence through Shi'ite Moslems and Revolutionary Guards in the east of the country; Israel, through the continued occupation of an enclave in southern Lebanon that it called its security zone; and 400,000 Palestinians, including a guerrilla force of 10,000. Lebanon itself was virtually without a government and had a regular army of only 37,000 men. Among these men, Moslems were in the majority in the ranks, but Christians controlled the officer corps. The prime minister was a Sunni Moslem, the speaker of parliament a Shi'ite, and the president, Amin Gemayel, a Christian.

It appeared that, with all these factions, military strength would continue to dictate who controlled the country or, more accurately, who would keep it out of someone else's hands. No end appeared in sight to the destructive civil war that had erupted in 1975. Lebanon remained a tragic and dismembered land.

The Palestinian Uprising

Israel celebrated its fortieth birthday in May 1988, during a time that was marred, as Israel's birth had been, by the sound of gunfire. But this time the violence did not emanate from invading armies, but erupted instead in two areas conquered by Israel in the Six-Day War of 1967: the West Bank and Gaza. Two decades of Israeli occupation had finally inflamed the passions of almost two million Palestinians yearning for an independent state.

By 1988, more than half of the Palestinian population of Gaza and the West Bank had lived all their lives under Israeli rule. These younger Palestinians were among the best-educated groups in the Middle East yet had only limited opportunities to apply their skills. Most made a meager livelihood in teeming villages, towns, and refugee camps. The rage and frustration of these young people finally boiled over into the West Bank. Thousands of young Palestinians began to throw rocks, iron bars, and an occasional Molotov cocktail at Israeli security forces and insisted on flying the colors—red, white, green, and black—of the banned Palestinian flag.

What began as occasional protests by groups of embittered youths quickly developed into an organized resistance movement with an underground leadership and a well-planned strategy. By the spring of 1988, the movement had gone far beyond rock throwing to an economic boycott of many Israeli products, nonpayment of taxes to Israel, mass resignations of Israeli-appointed Arab police and local government officials, and strikes that closed down trade, transport, education, and other essential public services. The movement also had a name: Intifadeh, the Palestinian Uprising. It had grown into something quite new in the context of the Arab-Israeli conflict: a massive civil-resistance movement, demanding self-determination and an end to military occupation. Israel suddenly faced an entirely new kind of challenge: war from within.

Israel's efforts to quell the uprising through thousands of arrests, imprisonments, and beatings brought no real respite. The larger the number of arrests, the wider the Intifadeh. Gradually, even though the Palestinians were no military match for the Israelis, they gained an important political advantage: the uprising raised Palestinian national consciousness and once again focused world attention on the Palestine problem. By the summer of 1988, much of the outside world regarded Israel as an occupation power and the Palestinians as the underdog. To the dismay of the Israeli authorities, some of the Western media even began to compare Israel's occupation policies to those of South Africa. Sympathies had begun to shift. In an age of national self-determination, it had become counterproductive for a country of three million people to keep two million under permanent subjugation.

The uprising further deepened the profound rifts within Israel over the occupied territories. The Likud party of Prime Minister Itzhak Shamir perceived the uprising as a conspiracy to end Israel's very existence. In the Likud's view, the Palestinians were not after a Palestinian state in Gaza and the West Bank; they were out to destroy Israel altogether. Hence, a tough policy was the only appropriate response. The Labour party under its leader, Shimon Peres, on the other hand, advocated a more flexible policy. Believing that ultimately the Jews would be outnumbered in their own country if Israel held on to the territories, the Labour party was in favor of negotiations. The peace initiative of United States secretary of state George Shultz, for example, was welcomed by Labour, but foundered on the rock of Likud's refusal to compromise.

In a sense, the uprising redivided Israel. Many Israeli civilians became reluctant to enter the territories, and Israel's 700,000 Arab citizens became increasingly "Palestinianized." Even Jerusalem, enthusiastically described by its mayor, Teddy Kollek, as a united city of Arabs and Jews, became de facto divided once again. Very few Jews ventured into the increasingly hostile Arab sector of the city. Nor did many Palestinians cross over into the new predominantly Jewish sector. The clock had been turned back.

By late 1988, the Arab-Israeli conflict was at a complete impasse. The Palestinians demanded complete self-determination, which the Israelis were totally unprepared to grant. The Palestinians asserted that the PLO was their only legitimate representative, a premise rejected by the Israelis. Efforts by the Americans to search for mediators such as King Hussein of Jordan also came to naught when the Jordanian king, in August 1988, removed himself from the scene by relinquishing his claim to the West Bank to the PLO. A contest of wills had taken shape in which Israel remained militarily the stronger but was losing the political initiative to the Palestinians. The Arabs, after five unsuccessful wars, had at long last discovered a formula that worked.

Events now began to move more quickly. In November 1988 the PLO met in Algiers and a jubilant Yassir Arafat proclaimed national independence for a state of Palestine. He then applied for a visa to the United States to address the United Nations General Assembly. When the State Department denied the visa on the grounds that Arafat had been an accessory to terrorism, the United Nations decided to reconvene in Geneva where it decided by an overwhelming vote to recognize Palestinian independence and to place the Israeli-occupied West Bank and Gaza under UN supervision. Arafat, in a shrewd political move, also declared in Geneva that he recognized "the right of all parties in the Middle East conflict to exist in peace and security," implying the recognition of Israel. Moreover, he renounced "all forms of terrorism, including individual, group, and state terrorism." Secretary of State Henry Kissinger had declared in 1975 that if the PLO ever recognized Israel and gave up terrorism, the United States would be prepared to open a dialogue with the Palestinians. According to his successor, George Shultz, these conditions had now been fulfilled, and hence the United States decided to hold its first meeting with PLO representatives in December 1988 in Tunisia. The Israeli government, in considerable dismay, reiterated that it would not negotiate with the PLO under any conditions. Arafat had clearly succeeded in driving a large wedge between Israel and its American ally and, moreover, had won a considerable propaganda victory. He could now claim that the United Nations had created Israel by majority vote in 1947. Now, more than forty years later, the United Nations had passed an even more overwhelming vote on behalf of the Palestinian people. Hence, the time for the creation of a Palestinian state had finally arrived.

What of the future? More than likely, Israel will let the Palestinians rise to their feet only if the Jewish state's survival is an absolute certainty. The memory of the Holocaust will not permit the Jews to place their state at risk. And deep in their bones, most

Jews believe that the Palestinians want to do away with Israel. It will take a Palestinian Sadat to convince them otherwise. In the meantime, the Palestinians will not go away. On the contrary, they will grow politically stronger and ever more resourceful. Like the Jews, they will continue to insist on a sovereign state of their own. Israel's ambivalence over Gaza and the West Bank will probably continue too. Israel does not really want the territories but is afraid to give them up. In that sense, Israel's greatest military victory in 1967 might have sown the seeds of a political disaster, a kind of Israeli Versailles.

David Ben-Gurion, Israel's first prime minister, believed that sooner or later, the territories would have to be traded for security. And indeed, Israel did make peace with Egypt for the price of Sinai. Sooner or later, similar compromises will have to be worked out so that *both* Jews and Palestinians will enjoy their right to nationhood. That is the fundamental message of the Palestinian Uprising.

Conclusion

When people of goodwill despair of finding a solution, they often take solace in time as the great healer of wounds. But the experience of the six wars between the Arab states and Israel has not inspired such confidence in the curative power of time. The shock inflicted on the Arab consciousness by the establishment of Israel and the resulting homelessness of a million native Palestinians grew more, rather than less, acute as Arab nationalism gathered momentum. This trauma was accentuated by the fact that Israel—four times its original size—was seen as an ever-growing menace by the Arab world. Many Arabs feared that if expansion continued at this rate, Israel would soon dominate the whole of Palestine.

On the Jewish side, time has turned Israel into virtually a garrison state. How strange it is to contemplate the fact that the Jews, who lived homeless in the Diaspora for two millennia, should within the span of only four decades create a state with such fearsome military capability. Who would have guessed that the Jews, to whom things military were anathema, should now make them their first priority? Yet this is exactly what time has done.

Four times the Arabs made fatal mistakes that the Zionists used to their advantage. In 1948, five Arab armies invaded a Jewish state whose modest boundaries had been assigned to it by the United Nations. The Jews repelled the invaders and engaged in some annexation of their own, managing to enlarge their territory. The Sinai campaign of 1956 demonstrated vividly what Israeli arms could do, even though the territorial gains had to be given up. In 1967, Nasser's blunder, the blockade of Aqaba, led directly to his humiliation and to Israel's spectacular victory. In October 1973, the Israelis turned an initial setback into yet another costly victory. But in 1982, Israel's invasion of Lebanon involved the Jewish state in a long and divisive war. And the Palestinian Uprising confronted the Jewish state with the real possibility of civil war. The question, by 1990, was whether Israel and her Arab neighbors, involved in six wars in a generation, would finally settle for permanent coexistence without victory or defeat.

There is one ultimate and final paradox that emerges from Israel's victories. The six wars with the Arabs created a situation in which 3 million Jews came to control territories that contained nearly 2 million Arabs. It is difficult to see how Israel can keep the fruits of victory and yet remain a Zionist state.

Perhaps this is the form that destiny assumes on earth. For the Jews, Zionism was a response to the threats to their national survival. In their own need and plight, they drove more than a million other human beings to despair. Of the two nationalisms that clashed in Palestine, the Jewish was militarily superior but not politically stronger. The vanquished are yearning for redress. Zionism, to endure, will have to find the courage not to inflict on others what has been inflicted on the Jews throughout history. This will take a generosity of spirit that had seldom been extended to the Jews in their diaspora. According to their faith, they had been chosen to have a great capacity for suffering. Now, at long last, they are no longer chosen; they themselves must choose.

NOTES

1. John Neary, "The Bloody Dawn of Israel," *Life* (May 1973), p. 28.
2. Dan Kurzman, *Genesis 1948* (New York: Signet, 1972), p. 26.
3. *Ibid.*, p. 27.

4. David Horowitz, *State in the Making* (New York: Knopf, 1953), p. 140.

5. *Ibid.*, p. 141.

6. Larry Collins and Dominique Lapierre, *O Jerusalem* (New York: Simon & Schuster, 1972), p. 27.

7. Kurzman, *op. cit.*, p. 38.

8. Collins and Lapierre, *op. cit.*, p. 30.

9. *Ibid.*, p. 78.

10. *Ibid.*, p. 80.

11. *Ibid.*, p. 81.

12. Kurzman, *op. cit.*, p. 120.

13. *Ibid.*, p. 123.

14. *Ibid.*, p. 124.

15. *Ibid.*, p. 126.

16. Collins and Lapierre, *op. cit.*, p. 345.

17. *Ibid.*, p. 300.

18. Anthony Nutting, *Nasser* (New York: Dutton, 1972), p. 143.

19. Hugh Thomas, *Suez* (New York: Harper & Row, 1966), p. 163.

20. *Ibid.*

21. *Ibid.*

22. Nutting, *op. cit.*, p. 145.

23. Anthony Eden, *Full Circle,* quoted by Herbert Feis in *Foreign Affairs* (July 1960), p. 600.

24. Nutting, *op. cit.*, p. 163.

25. *Ibid.*

26. United Nations Document 5/3712, October 29, 1956.

27. Thomas, *op. cit.*, p. 164.

28. Keesing's Research Report, *The Arab-Israeli Conflict* (New York: Scribner's, 1968), p. 8.

29. Michael Howard and Robert Hunter, *Israel and the Arab World: The Crisis of 1967* (London: Institute for Strategic Studies, 1967), p. 17.

30. *Ibid.*

31. *Ibid.*, p. 20.

32. *Ibid.*, p. 22.

33. Cited in *Ibid.*, p. 24.

34. Keesing's Research Report, *op. cit.*, p. 25.

35. Howard and Hunter, *op. cit.*, p. 39.

36. *The New York Times,* October 14, 1973.

37. *The New York Times,* October 21, 1973.

38. *Time* (October 29, 1973), p. 44.

39. *Ibid.*, p. 45.

SELECTED BIBLIOGRAPHY

ARONSON, GEOFFREY. *Creating Facts: Israel, Palestinians, and the West Bank.* Washington: Institute for Palestine Studies, 1987.

EVRON, YAIR. *War and Intervention in Lebanon.* Baltimore: Johns Hopkins University Press, 1987.

FEINTUCH, YOSSI. *U.S. Policy on Jerusalem.* Westport, Conn.: Greenwood Press, 1987.

GILMOUR, DAVID. *Lebanon: The Fractured Country.* New York: St. Martin's Press, 1983.

HARKABI, YEHOSHAFAT. *Israel's Fateful Hour.* New York: Harper & Row, 1988.

HOWARD, MICHAEL, and ROBERT HUNTER. *Israel and the Arab World: The Crisis of 1967.* London: Institute for Strategic Studies, 1967.

ISSAWI, CHARLES. *The Arab World's Legacy.* Princeton: Darwin Press, 1981.

KURZMAN, DAN. *Genesis 1948.* New York: Signet, 1972.

MORRIS, BENNY. *The Birth of the Palestinian Refugee Problem.* New York: Cambridge University Press, 1988.

NUTTING, ANTHONY. *Nasser.* New York: Dutton, 1972.

POLK, WILLIAM R. *The Arab World.* Cambridge: Harvard University Press, 1980.

SAHLIYEH, EMILE. *In Search of Leadership: West Bank Politics Since 1967.* Washington: Brookings, 1988.

SHEPHERD, NAOMI. *Teddy Kollek: Mayor of Jerusalem.* New York: Harper & Row, 1988.

ST. JOHN, BRUCE RONALD. *Qaddafi's World Design: Libyan Foreign Policy.* London: Sagi Books, 1987.

STOESSINGER, JOHN G. *Henry Kissinger: The Anguish of Power.* New York: Norton, 1976.

STUDY GROUP. *Toward Arab-Israeli Peace.* Washington: Brookings, 1988.

THOMAS, HUGH. *Suez.* New York: Harper & Row, 1966.

7

The Price of Martyrdom: The Persian Gulf

Things fall apart; the centre cannot hold
Mere anarchy is loosed upon the world,
The blood-dimmed tide is loosed, and everywhere
The ceremony of innocence is drowned;
The best lack all conviction, while the worst
Are full of passionate intensity . . .
somewhere in sands of the desert . . .
The darkness drops again; but now I know
That twenty centuries of stony sleep
Were vexed to nightmare by a rocking cradle,
And what rough beast, its hour come round at last
Slouches towards Bethlehem to be born?
William Butler Yeats, *The Second Coming*

The Shah, the Ayatollah Khomeini, and America

On January 16, 1979, after thirty-seven years of autocratic rule, Muhammad Reza Pahlevi, the shah of Iran, left his country never to return. From exile he watched his mortal enemy, the Ayatollah Khomeini, establish an Islamic theocracy that demanded the shah's execution, called Iran's old ally, the United States, the "Great Satan," and turned more than fifty American embassy personnel into hostages in their own embassy. The shah's death in Egypt in July 1980 unleashed a frenzied orgy of jubilation in Teheran, capped by executions of "enemies of the Islamic Revolution." Khomeini, now leader of Iran "for life," predicted the destruction of "satanical" America. A tyrant friendly to the West has been replaced by a fanatical adversary. How did these shattering events come about?

The shah of Iran had been a complex man. Austere and remote in his demeanor, he had nonetheless been a man of vision. For thirty-seven years, he had pursued a grand design with single-minded zeal: under his tutelage, Iran was to become a powerful industrial state. This modern Persian renaissance was to be achieved through the shah's "White Revolution," a "shock program that would allow Iran to overcome in 25 years its centuries of suppression."[1] In the shah's own words, this march toward a "Great Civilization" would turn Iran into "one vast workshop in which all the elements indispensable to modernization would spring up: universities, school groups, professional institutes, hospitals, roads, railroads, dams, electric plants, pipelines for gas and oil, factories, industrial, cultural, artistic, and sports complexes, cooperatives, metropolitan areas, and new villages."[2] Within a single generation, Iran would wrest its oil resources from foreign ownership and use its newfound wealth in the service of modernity and power. In this quest, the shah had found a natural ally: the United States. For decades, American firms supplied the shah's Iran with the technology and weapons that were the instruments of his "White Revolution." And the shah, in return, supplied the United States with badly needed oil and an unconditional fidelity in the struggle against Communism. Friendship and foreign policy thus went hand in hand.

Unfortunately, the shah exacted a high price for his modernization program. In the first place, he had created a secret police, the Savak, to deal with enemies of the state. The Savak's net was wide and its techniques ruthless. Torture and abuse were commonplace in Savak prisons. It is estimated that over 100,000 Iranians died in the Savak's dungeons. Even the shah himself admitted that "there were people arrested and abused," and that his country "fell victim to excesses."[3] "To let saboteurs act freely," the shah explained, "would not have permitted the program's realization."[4] In other words, terror was essential for the attainment of the "Great Civilization." Who, then, were the saboteurs?

Khomeini and his Islamic fundamentalists considered the shah an archtraitor to his country. According to the Moslem Shi'ite clergy, the shah had sold Iran out to the West and stolen its resources, all for the sake of personal wealth and glory. Islam, in the fundamentalists' opinion, had to cut loose from the United States and return to its historical tradition. The shah's program led only to sinfulness and atheism. Women would have to wear the veil again, as they did before the shah's emancipation program. Justice would be meted out according to the Koran, including the stoning of adulterous women. Secular government officials would be subject to "spiritual leadership" by members of the Shi'ite clergy. These "mullahs" were the shah's bitterest enemies, and together with victims of Savak, Communists, and "student" militants, they prepared the ground for the Iranian monarch's fall.

Until the advent of Jimmy Carter in 1977, the alliance between Iran and the United States had continued relatively undisturbed. The new president, however, deeply committed to the cause of human rights, criticized the shah and pressed him to institute reforms. Political prisoners, the president demanded, should be given a fair trial and set free if found not guilty. Human rights abuses, President Carter declared in the United Nations, would no longer be the offending nation's exclusive domestic business. The United States would punish the offenders by cooling off relations. Iran was one of many nations that Amnesty International had described as "serious violators of human rights." The shah, shaken by these criticisms emanating from his ally, embarked on a program of liberalization. By November 1977, "the police-state atmosphere had altered drastically to a mood of vastly greater individual freedom and relaxation."[5] This very loosening of controls, however, emboldened the shah's enemies and prepared the ground for revolution.

President Carter did not seem to be aware of the coming revolution in Iran. No one in Washington, including the Central Intelligence Agency, expected the shah to fall. It was generally assumed that the liberalization moves would save and strengthen the regime. Besides, Carter had begun to realize the shah's importance as an ally. Muhammad Reza Pahlevi had been an unconditional friend of the United States for thirty-seven years. He had sold the United States oil during the Arab embargo of 1973; he had even sold Israel oil; he had provided the United States with a listening post on the Soviet border; he had refueled the American fleet without question; he had bought aircraft and technology from the American firms and paid cash; and he had been a staunch anti-Communist. Accordingly, Jimmy Carter, on New Year's Eve 1978, visited the shah in Teheran and made the following statement:

"Iran, because of the great leadership of the shah, is an island of stability in a turbulent sea."[6] He also spoke effusively about the "love and admiration" that the Iranian people apparently gave to their leader. A week later, on January 7, 1978, the first riots erupted that, one year later, were to seal the doom of the Pahlevi dynasty.

During most of 1978, the year of the shah's slide to oblivion, Jimmy Carter temporized. Had he remained consistent and continued to press on for human rights, the new revolutionary government might have been more friendly when it came to power. Alternatively, a show of force by the United States including military aid might just possibly have saved the shah. As it turned out, Carter's policy of vacillation got him the worst of both worlds. It did not save the shah, nor did it save his victims while he ruled Iran. Henry Kissinger, in early 1979, added the final touch: "A foreign policy that makes human rights its cornerstone, invites revolution." Jimmy Carter did not have an answer. The Iranian tragedy, more starkly perhaps than any other case, showed up the dilemma of human rights and naked power. By year's end, desperate emotions had swept events beyond the possibility of compromise.

On November 4, 1979, with the shah mortally ill in a New York hospital, the United States endured one of the worst humiliations in its history. Iranian militants seized the American embassy in Teheran and held ninety-eight persons hostage, demanding that the United States return the deposed shah and make restitution on the wealth that he had "stolen" from Iran. The seizure of embassy personnel in their own compound had few precedents in the annals of diplomacy and was in clear violation of all established norms of international law. As anti-American fervor rose to a fever pitch in Teheran, with President Carter burnt in effigy as the "Great Satan," the Ayatollah Khomeini gave his blessing to the seizure of the hostages. Under the new Islamic constitution, Khomeini had just been given "supreme power for life" over Iran. The eyes of the world now were on the United States.

President Carter responded cautiously. Unwilling to risk the lives of the hostages, he took no military action. Instead, he halted oil imports from Iran, froze Iranian assets in the United States, and called on the United Nations for assistance. Khomeini decided to release women and blacks, leaving fifty-three Americans held captive. In January 1980 the UN Security Council, by a vote of 11 to 0, demanded the release of the hostages without delay. One of the four abstaining nations was the Soviet Union, which complained that the tone of the resolution was "too belligerent." The Soviet delegate failed to note that, while he spoke, Russian tanks were rolling into Afghanistan.

The geopolitical effects of the shah's demise were now becoming evident. The loss of Iran as a reliable Western ally had no doubt emboldened the Soviet Union when contemplating the possible costs of the invasion of Afghanistan. If the United States would not move to save a valuable friend, why should it move to save a neutral country? The conviction of the shah that the United States would not permit events in Iran to run out of control had been shared widely by friends and enemies alike. Now that this assumption had proved to be completely wrong, the Soviet Union drew the logical conclusion. It began to lean toward Iran in its test of wills with the United States. In short, it began to support nationalism—even Moslem fundamentalism—against the "imperialism" of America. When, in late January 1980, the United States asked for economic sanctions against Iran by the UN, the Soviet Union cast a veto, thus preventing any forceful action. The shah, before his fall, had predicted an "unholy alliance" between the mullahs and the Communists.[7] It seemed that, by 1980, he was not altogether wrong.

The year 1980 was dominated by the hostage crisis. Hopes were in turn raised and dashed. United Nations secretary-general Kurt Waldheim went to Teheran only to return empty-handed. "I do not trust this man," Khomeini had said about the secretary-general. Nor did the ayatollah agree to see a UN commission of five men who had flown to Teheran. The United States brought its complaint against Iran to the International Court of Justice at The Hague. The Court ordered the captors to release the hostages, but Iran ignored the ruling. Finally, in April 1980 President Carter ordered a helicopter rescue mission, which ended in a debacle in the Iranian desert. The Soviet Union, eager to exploit American discomfort, accused the president of an "abortive provocation" that could have caused "mass bloodshed and the death of the hostages," lives the Soviets claimed "the president was willing to sacrifice for his election interests." Carter's misadventure not only lowered the United States' esteem throughout the world, but also shifted international attention away from the Soviet Union's invasion of Afghanistan.[8] Once again, the Soviet Union had exploited the struggle between Iran and the United States for its own purposes.

The shah's death in July 1980 had no effect upon the situation. One of the hostages had been released by Khomeini for reasons of health, leaving fifty-two captives. Economic sanctions had no impact, nor did the war between Iraq and Iran that broke out in the fall. In October there seemed to be some progress. Khomeini announced four conditions for the release of the hostages who, since the rescue attempt, had been dispersed throughout Iran: an American pledge not to interfere, "either directly or indirectly, politically or militarily, in the affairs of the Islamic Republic of Iran"; return of the fortune of "the cursed Shah"; unfreezing of Iranian assets in American banks; and cancellation of United States legal and financial claims against Iran.

On November 4, 1980, Jimmy Carter lost the presidential election to Ronald Reagan. An Iranian offer, made shortly afterward via Algeria, to release the hostages for a payment of $24 billion did little to alleviate the situation. President Carter turned the offer down, and Ronald Reagan, the president-elect, declared that "the United States would not pay ransom to barbarians."[9] Finally, after a frenzy of negotiations, a deal was struck: the Iranians were to receive their money, and the Americans were to get their people back. After $3 billion of Iran's assets were transferred to that nation's central bank, the fifty-two hostages made their flight to freedom on January 20, 1981, Ronald Reagan's inauguration day as president. Apparently, the Iranians did not wish to deal with a new United States administration that might have taken a much tougher line than that of President Carter.

In retrospect, it became clear how deep the chasm of misunderstanding had been between the United States and Khomeini's Iran. The Americans, basing their claim on the sanctity of embassies and international law, had forgotten that these concepts had their origin in the Judeo-Christian tradition and that revolutionary Iran had not participated in their formulation. Moreover, the Americans had tended to negotiate with their Western-educated counterparts in Iran, overlooking the fact that the real power rested with the Islamic clergy. They had also underestimated the Iranians' fury when the United States admitted the deposed shah

into the country. The Iranians in turn had failed to appreciate the
United States' commitment to principles of Western diplomacy.
Their leaders had little understanding of the way the American
government worked. The prime minister, for example, believed
that Jimmy Carter's power in the United States was as absolute
as that of Khomeini in Iran. Finally, it took several months before
the Iranians believed that the United States had not instigated
the Iraqi invasion of Iran. Thus, misperception and ignorance of
each other's cultures were the real villains in the tragedy of the
encounter between Iran and the United States.

In 1980, the conflict between the United States and Iran was
eclipsed by what was to become one of the most ferocious conflicts
of the century: the war between Iran and Iraq.

The Iran-Iraq War:
The Price of Martyrdom

In the fall of 1980 Iraqi infantry punched across five hundred
miles of desert front, and Iraqi pilots flying Soviet-built MIGs
bombed military targets and oil facilities. Caught by surprise at
first, the Iranians soon responded with attacks of their own, and
American-made Phantom F-11 fighter bombers streaked toward
Iraqi cities and military installations. A nightmare had become
reality. An area that was crucial to the Western world's oil supply
was aflame. Moreover, there was the dire possibility that the
Strait of Hormuz might be closed by the Iranians. Forty percent
of the West's oil passed through this vital shipping lane, and
hence the war quickly assumed global implications. The United
States and the Soviet Union had contributed to the problem by
heavily arming Iran and Iraq in the 1970s, when Washington had
close relations with the shah, and Moscow had equal influence in
Baghdad.

There were several reasons for the outbreak of this dangerous
conflict. In the first place, the war between Iraq and Iran had the
earmarks of a religious conflict between two major sects of Islam.
The Shi'ite Moslems, under the leadership of the Ayatollah
Khomeini of Iran, believed that there were intermediaries between Allah and human beings. These deputies of God were *aya-*

tollahs, an Arabic term signifying "reflection of Allah." The Sunni Moslems, who were dominant in the Iraqi leadership of President Saddam Hussein, believed that there should be no such intermediaries, and that each person had a personal relationship with Allah. To some degree, the conflict was reminiscent of the religious wars in seventeenth-century Europe between Catholics, who believed in a papacy, and Protestants, who did not. It may be significant in this connection that when Christianity was torn apart by these internal struggles, it was fifteen hundred years old, which is the age of Islam today. So fierce was the religious nature of the struggle that the Iraqi president, in a national broadcast in November 1980, declared the conflict a *jihad,* a holy war to defend the ideals of the prophet Mohammed. Khomeini reciprocated by pronouncing the Iraqis enemies of God and Islam. Iraqis and Iranians alike believed that, if they died in battle, they would go directly to paradise. Death in a *jihad* assured the Moslem warrior of immortality.

Nationalism was at least as strong a force as religious fanaticism. Although more than half of Iraq's population was Shi'ite, the Iranians were unable to incite them against the Sunni leadership of Saddam Hussein. However, Iraq's appeals to Arabs in Iran's embattled Khuzistan province provoked an uprising there against Persian rule. Territorial ambitions further fueled nationalism. The Iraqi war plan apparently hinged on seizing enough territory in an initial strike to use as a bargaining counter to regain sovereignty over the Shatt-al-Arab waterway, which Iraq had agreed to share with Iran in a 1975 agreement with the shah. Iran, however, rebounded from the Iraq attack and, fighting with fanatical zeal, turned the war into a prolonged and bloody stalemate.

Personal ambitions also played a role. The Ayatollah Khomeini, the self-appointed prophet of Islam, had spent thirteen years in exile in Iraq, preparing for the uprising that eventually ousted his enemy, the shah. But in 1978, Iraq's government asked him to leave the country, thereby obliging him to spend the final months of his exile in France. The ayatollah never forgave nor forgot that insult. Saddam Hussein, on the other hand, eager to replace Anwar Sadat of Egypt as the most powerful leader in the Arab world, was convinced that a *Blitzkrieg*-type victory over Iran would vastly enhance his status and prestige. He was eulogized in the Iraqi press as "the awaited, the promised one" to destroy the Persian tyrant. His portrait was prominently displayed all over Iraq, from coffeehouses to supermarket checkout counters. Both leaders thus had exalted perceptions of themselves while entertaining devil images of one another.

The course of the war itself resembled that of World War I. In an era when military thinking was dominated by nuclear weapons or guerrilla warfare, the Iran-Iraq War was reminiscent of the trench battles of an earlier age. The Iranians mounted costly human-wave assaults against Iraq: troops were entrenched behind tanks and artillery. Iraq even resorted to the use of poison gas, banned by international conventions after World War I. And again, as in 1914, neither side could make a decisive breakthrough. After eight years of maneuvers and confrontations up and down the winding 700-mile boundary between the two countries, the battle lines returned almost exactly to their original borders. Like Britain, France, and Germany in 1918, Iran and Iraq lost a generation of their best young men.

On the Iranian side, an obsession with martyrdom helped sustain the war's popularity despite enormous casualties. In the martyrs' cemetery outside Teheran, a fountain of blood reminded visitors of the fallen heroes. Though only colored water, it was chillingly realistic. The visitors stood among row upon row, acre after acre, of graves. People came in cars, on bicycles, or on foot, the women wrapped in black *chadors.* "My country, my country is like Karbala now," they chanted. Karbala, in the deserts of Iraq, was the place where the seventeenth-century religious leader Hussein, son of Ali, the successor to the prophet Mohammed, met his death at the hands of a rival caliph. As new victims of the war were laid to rest in the martyrs' cemetery, young men in black shirts carried bundles of chains, which they whipped across the backs of their shoulders. *"Allah akhbar,"* they chanted. *God is great.*

Later in the war, when the Iranian army began to run out of men, thousands of teenagers were recruited by the Shi'ite clergy to clear battlefields of mines and barbed wire. Their tickets to paradise were blood red headbands reading "Warrior of God" and small metal keys signifying that the ayatollah had given them special permission to enter heaven. In some battles, the Iranian reinforcements arrived proudly, carrying their own coffins.

In Iraq too the coffins of the dead were borne home on the roofs of taxis. These victims were also called martyrs.

In 1986 Iranian troops captured the Fao peninsula and mounted an offensive against Basra, Iraq's second-largest city. It appeared, for the moment, that Iran might be victorious. But then the fortunes of war began to tilt against the ayatollah.

In 1987 the United States made the decision to commit its navy to patrol the Persian Gulf. This was done for three reasons. The first was to ensure freedom of navigation for oil-carrying tankers since an interruption of such shipping would threaten the industrial democracies with a recurrence of the oil shock of the 1970s, which had produced inflation, recession, and unemployment. The United States also wanted to prevent Soviet domination of the area. After all, Iran shared a 1,500-mile border with the Soviet Union. Finally, the United States hoped to protect the safety of friendly Arab states such as Kuwait and the oil-rich United Arab Emirates from the Iranian threat. The United States even decided to reflag Kuwaiti tankers with the American flag, thus placing them under the direct protection of its navy.

This policy suffered from an element of inconsistency, to put it mildly, since at that very time the Reagan administration was engaged in selling arms to Iran in the hope of freeing American hostages held captive in Lebanon. Not surprisingly, an accident was now merely waiting to happen. In May 1987, an Iraqi aircraft accidentally hit an American warship, the USS *Stark,* with a missile, killing 37 men. A year later, in July 1988, a second, even more tragic mistake occurred. An American warship, the *Vincennes,* shot down a civilian Iranian airliner, killing all 290 passengers. Captain Will Rogers of the *Vincennes* had only a few seconds to decide whether the blip on his radar screen was a civilian aircraft or a hostile fighter plane. Remembering the fate of the *Stark,* he took no chances, precipating yet another unintended disaster.

In the meantime, in the land war, the Iranian offensive against Basra collapsed, and the Iraqis quickly recaptured the Fao peninsula and recrossed the Iranian border. Exhausted after eight years of war with Iraq and checkmated by the United States Navy in the Gulf, the Iranians finally had enough. In July 1988, the Ayatollah Khomeini personally endorsed a cease-fire, declaring that his decision was more painful than taking poison. United

Nations secretary-general Javier Perez de Cuellar dispatched missions to Teheran and Baghdad to make arrangements for a formal end to the war.

What can be said of this conflict in historical perspective? First, it took over one million lives and may thus claim the dubious distinction of being one of the most vicious wars of this century. Second, like most theological conflicts, it ended inconclusively, very near the borders where it had erupted in the first place. And finally, it devastated the resources of both combatants, leaving their economies destroyed and deeply in debt. Stated bluntly, the war accomplished absolutely nothing. The ambitions of two ruthless men had created a wasteland.

In larger historical perspective, perhaps the Thirty Years' War within Christendom in the seventeenth century may serve as the best analogy. Neither Catholics nor Protestants came out as winners after thirty years and several million casualties. Both had to settle for compromise and coexistence. Similarly, it appears that neither Israelis nor Palestinians will be able to make each other disappear from the Middle Eastern map and will ultimately have to find a way to live together without victory or defeat. Iraqis and Iranians will have to learn this terrible and costly lesson from history. Today, wars over God and land are fought with more awesome weapons, and under bleaker skies, than hundreds of years ago. But in one sense they remain the same: all they do is kill for nothing.

Terrorism and the Twilight of Diplomacy

The new era of Third World instability contains yet another feature: the rise of terrorism and the decline of diplomacy. By the late 1980s the world's diplomats had become very much concerned. Since 1971, there had been hundreds of terrorist assaults on embassies and diplomatic missions, and almost half of these had taken place during the 1980s. Twenty-five countries had been victimized, with the Americans held captive in Iran and Lebanon only the most widely publicized examples. A diplomat's job, formerly considered sacrosanct, had become as dangerous as that of a police officer in an angry crowd. Seldom before in modern history had diplomacy been so dangerous a calling. Some career diplomats expressed the fear that terrorism had struck at the very heart of diplomacy itself.

By far the largest number of these terrorist attacks took place in the Persian Gulf, further highlighting the explosive character of that region. A survey of the most significant of these makes melancholy reading.

On December 28, 1972, four Palestinian "Black September" terrorists seized the Israeli embassy in Bangkok, Thailand. After negotiations with the Thai government, they surrendered the hostages and fled to Egypt. On March 1, 1973, "Black September" terrorists seized the Saudi embassy in Khartoum, Sudan, and killed several American and Belgian diplomats. After three days the terrorists surrendered to Sudanese authorities. On September 13, 1974, three Japanese Red Army terrorists seized the French embassy in The Hague, Netherlands. They demanded—and got—a ransom of $1 million, flew to Damascus on a French plane, and surrendered to the Palestine Liberation Organization. On December 21, 1975, three people were killed and seven wounded when six pro-Palestinian terrorists seized eighty-one persons attending an Organization of Petroleum Exporting Countries (OPEC) conference in Vienna, Austria. The terrorists fled to Tripoli, Libya. On March 26, 1979, Palestinians stormed the Egyptian embassy in Kuwait to protest the conclusion of a peace treaty between Egypt and Israel. On July 13, 1979, Palestinian terrorists attacked the Egyptian embassy in Ankara, Turkey, killed two security guards, and took nineteen hostages. On March 2, 1981, Pakistani terrorists hijacked a Pakistani airliner and flew it to Damascus, demanding the freeing of fifty-five Pakistani political prisoners in exchange for 102 passenger hostages. After eleven days of negotiations—the longest hijacking on record—the government of Pakistan bowed to the hijackers' demands. Terrorism had chalked up another victory in its assault on the civilized world. In May 1981 a Moslem terrorist shot and severely wounded Pope John Paul II in St. Peter's Square in Rome, and in 1983 terrorists destroyed the American embassy in Beirut.

The United States, as a major target of left-wing discontent, has been disproportionately victimized over the years, even aside from Teheran. Between 1971 and 1989, the State Department listed more than 1,000 significant terrorist actions against American diplomatic installations or individuals. Five top officials were killed, including the ambassadors to Afghanistan and Pakistan as well as the president of the American University in Beirut. In December 1988, a high United Nations official was killed in the terrorist bombing of a Pan American flight, claiming 270 casualties. The terror on embassy row everywhere took its toll on the morale of career diplomats. Diplomacy had suddenly become a very dangerous profession.

Perhaps most frightening is the fact that some of the most devastating acts of terrorism in the 1980s were apparently initiated not by crazéd individuals but by coldly calculating leaders of sovereign states. By the mid-1980s, for example, the would-be assassin of Pope John Paul II confessed that he had been on the payroll of the Bulgarian KGB. Since the Bulgarian KGB was clearly a puppet of its Soviet master, strong circumstantial evidence pointed to Yuri Andropov, the deceased Soviet leader and ex-KGB boss, as the prime mover to eliminate the troublesome Polish pope. The destruction of the Korean airliner in 1983 and the murder of 269 innocent people must also be cited as an example of state-initiated terrorism. And the suicide mission that led to the deaths of hundreds of American and French soldiers in Beirut was apparently of Iranian origin. A case could in fact be made that a car bomb triggered the American withdrawal from Lebanon.

Perhaps the most painful dilemma of modern diplomacy is whether one should negotiate with terrorists. There are no clear or simple answers. Virtually every Western country, including the United States, has declared that it will not negotiate and then, contrary to its public pronouncements, has in fact negotiated. If one says no, one may be right to stand on principle and to adhere to the ideals of moral courage. If one says yes, one may be right by being compassionate and placing precious human lives above abstract principles. It is easy to stand on principle, of course, if one's loved ones are not at risk. But if a person's spouse, child, or parent is held captive in a dungeon in Beirut, such a principled stand becomes a lot more difficult. President Reagan became impaled on the horns of this dilemma in the mid-1980s when he agreed to sell arms to the Iranians in order to obtain the release of hostages in Lebanon. When the arms negotiations began in

1985, seven American hostages were incarcerated in Lebanon. During the subsequent two-year negotiations, two were killed, two were freed, and four more were kidnapped. Thus, in the end, the Iranians wound up with the American arms and with more hostages than before. The president had lost on both counts, and the United States had been played for a sucker.

The Western democracies, by placing a high value on each individual human life, are particularly vulnerable to the modern terrorist who has contempt for life. Perhaps the most appropriate policy for the United States may be a public declaration that any of its private citizens who insist on living in countries such as Libya, Iran, or Lebanon do so at their own risk. And even then there would have to be exceptions for embassy personnel or passengers of hijacked airliners. Civilized countries will have to continue to wrestle with this terrible dilemma of courage versus compassion.

It is clear from the preceding examples that, apart from state-initiated terrorism, most of this kind of violence has emanated from post-colonial Third World countries. Not only have most terrorists perceived themselves as freedom fighters, but the new nations of the Third World have been less inclined than Western states to abide by the old rules of discourse among nations. Modern diplomacy was, after all, a Western invention developed by European diplomats. The "inviolability" of embassy grounds and diplomats was a Western concept. In the aftermath of the Hungarian revolution in 1956, for example, Cardinal Jozsef Mindszenty sought asylum in the American embassy in Budapest. In London, on the other hand, the Libyan embassy became a source of terrorism when gunmen sprayed the streets below with machine-gun fire, killing a policewoman. The British had to let the killers go because the Libyans threatened to take reprisals against the British embassy in Tripoli. It appeared that Libyan leader, Muammar el-Qaddafi, was in personal charge of the operation. In 1985 Qaddafi offered to support black American servicemen with weapons if they plotted to overthrow the government of the United States.

Thus, traditional principles of diplomacy were no longer accepted by many of the new nations, such as Khomeini's Iran and Qaddafi's Libya. In short, the West wanted to export its diplomatic way of life, and this simply did not work. A custom that had evolved over five hundred years of time had virtually broken down in a single decade. And, as a consequence, as we move toward the year 2000, diplomacy itself is now on trial.

Conclusion

The human element is the last though most crucial link in the fateful chain that leads to war. In the Persian Gulf region, most of the "fundamental causes" of war were already present: military arsenals, alliance systems, and competition over territorial and economic resources, as well as power rivalries and terrorism. But these "fundamental causes" do not precipitate a war unless personalities and misperceptions come into play. It took men like Saddam Hussein of Iraq and Khomeini of Iran to ignite the witches' brew in 1980. Each man believed himself to be the defender of the one true faith and his adversary to be Satan. Each believed the enemy's intent to be entirely malevolent, yet his capacity for fighting weak. Little wonder that the war quickly bogged down in a bloody stalemate, a kind of microcosm of 1914. But imagine for a moment what might have happened if Khomeini's delusions about the United States had infected that nation as well? After all, Khomeini had blamed America, "the Great Satan," for the Iraqi invasion of his country. It is not impossible to conceive of an American president, enraged and distracted by Iranian "criminals and kidnappers," driven to push the button. And would the Soviet leaders look on passively if war raged on their borders?

The point here is not the correctness or incorrectness of a particular policy. Rather, it is this: the road to war is paved with numerous "objective causes." But the final step across the threshold is taken by an individual leader, whose character is all-important. If a leader's personality, at the turning point, is flawed by misperceptions about himself and his adversary, war is very likely. That is why people like Khomeini and Saddam Hussein are so dangerous. Like matches thrown into a tinderbox, such fanatics can ignite everything around them. The preservation of the peace thus depends on the personalities of those who are provoked. Can they pursue that hardest of all courses, patience and strength?

The most convincing scenario for World War III is not World

War II, but World War I. When the European nations fell into the abyss in August 1914, no one quite knew how and why the tragedy had occurred. After all, the "objective causes"—the power rivalries and the alliances—had been around for a long time. Why, then, August 1914? Because at that particular time, mediocre men with little courage and no vision were in power. These men did not cause the war; they *precipitated* it.

The "fundamental causes" of war are painfully apparent in the Persian Gulf today. Whether our planet has a future will depend on the personalities of those who have the power to precipitate a world war. Paranoia and self-delusion will surely kill us. Quiet strength based on a healthy sense of self-esteem may see us through the year 2000.

NOTES

1. Mohammad Reza Pahlevi, *Answer to History* (Briarcliff Manor, N.Y.: Stein and Day, 1980), p. 175.
2. *Ibid.,* p. 176.
3. *Ibid.,* p. 158.
4. *Ibid.*
5. *Time,* November 15, 1977.
6. *The New York Times,* January 1, 1978.
7. Pahlevi, *op. cit.,* pp. 145–174.
8. *Time,* May 5, 1980, p. 14.
9. *The New York Times,* December 29, 1980.

SELECTED BIBLIOGRAPHY

BILL, JAMES A. *The Eagle and the Lion: The Tragedy of American-Iranian Relations.* New Haven: Yale University Press, 1988.

COTTAM, RICHARD W. *Iran and the United States: A Cold War Case Study.* Pittsburgh: University of Pittsburgh Press, 1988.

JANSEN, G. H. *Militant Islam.* New York: Harper & Row, 1980.

KHADDURI, MAJID. *The Gulf War: The Origins and Implications of the Iraq-Iran Conflict.* New York: Oxford University Press, 1988.

LEDEEN, MICHAEL, and LEWIS WILLIAM. *Debacle: The American Failure in Iran.* New York: Knopf, 1981

LEWIS, BERNARD. *The Political Language of Islam.* Chicago: University of Chicago Press, 1988.

O'BALLANCE, EDGAR. *The Gulf War.* London: Brassey's, 1988.

PENROSE, EDITH, and E. F. PENROSE. *Iraq: International Relations and National Development.* Boulder, Colo.: Westview Press, 1978.

RAMAZANI, R. K. *The Persian Gulf and the Strait of Hormuz.* Alphen aan der Rinj, Netherlands: Sijthoff, 1979.

RUBIN, BARRY. *Paved With Good Intentions: The American Experience in Iran.* New York: Oxford University Press, 1980.

SEGAL, DAVID. "The Iran-Iraq War: A Military Analysis." *Foreign Affairs,* Summer, 1988.

8

Why Nations Go to War

Even in our sleep
Pain that we cannot forget
Falls drop by drop upon the heart
Until in our own despair
Against our will
Comes wisdom
Through the awful grace of God.   Aeschylus

"If you look too deeply into the abyss," said Nietzsche, "the abyss will look into you." The face of war in our time is so awesome and terrible that the first temptation is to recoil and turn away. Who of us has not despaired and concluded that the entire spectacle of war has been the manifestation of organized insanity? Who of us has not been tempted to dismiss the efforts of those working for peace as futile Sisyphean labor? Medusa-like, the face of war, with its relentless horror, threatens to destroy anyone who looks at it for long.

Yet we must find the courage to confront the abyss. I deeply believe that war is a sickness, though it may be humankind's "sickness unto death." No murderous epidemic has ever been conquered without exposure, pain, and danger, or by ignoring the bacilli. But in the end human reason and courage have always prevailed, and even the plague was overcome. The Black Death that ravaged our planet centuries ago today is but a distant memory.

I know that the analogy between sickness and war is open to criticism. It has been fashionable to assert that war is not an illness, but, like aggression, an ineradicable part of human nature. I challenge this assumption. Whereas aggression may be inherent, war is learned behavior, and as such can be unlearned and ultimately selected out entirely. Humans have dispensed with other habits that previously seemed impossible to shed. For example, during the Ice Age, when people lived in caves, incest was perfectly acceptable, whereas today incest is almost universally taboo. Cannibalism provides an even more dramatic case. Thousands of years ago, human beings ate one another and drank one another's blood. That, too, was part of "human nature." Even a brief century ago, millions of Americans believed that God had ordained white people to be free and black people to be slaves. Why else would He have created them in different colors? Yet slavery, once considered part of "human nature," was abolished because human beings showed a capacity for growth. Growth came slowly, after immense suffering, but it *did* come. "Human nature" had been changed. Like slavery and cannibalism, war too can be eliminated from humankind's arsenal of horrors.

It seems, however, that people abandon their bad habits only when catastrophe is close at hand. The intellect alone is not enough. We must be shaken, almost shattered, before we change. A grave illness must pass its crisis before it is known whether the patient will live or die. Most appropriately, the ancient Chinese had two characters for crisis, one connoting danger and the other opportunity. The danger of extinction is upon us, but so is the opportunity for a better life for all people on this planet.

We must therefore make an effort to look Medusa in the face and to diagnose the sickness. Diagnosis is no cure, of course, but it is the first and the most necessary step. I shall attempt this diagnosis by suggesting certain common themes from the seven case studies.

When I first began work on the cases, I did not know what conclusions I would draw. I was afraid, in fact, that I might reach no general conclusions whatsoever. The landscape of war differed so much from case to case that I despaired of finding a reliable road map. As my work progressed, however, certain common themes emerged. Gradually, they took shape and meaning, and as I reached the end of my journey, they thrust themselves before me with clarity and force. Rather than state these themes as definitive conclusions, I prefer to set them forth in the hope that they might engage the reader in a dialogue. If the reader is challenged and pursues my quest to greater depths, I shall have been served well.

The first general theme that compels attention is that no nation that began a major war in this century emerged a winner. Austria-Hungary and Germany, which precipitated World War I, went down to ignominious defeat; Hitler's Germany was crushed into unconditional surrender; the North Korean attack was thwarted by collective action and ended in a draw; although the Vietnam war ended in a Communist victory, it would be far too simple to blame the Communists exclusively for its beginning; the Arabs who invaded the new Jewish state in 1948 lost territory to the Israelis in four successive wars; Pakistan, which sought to punish India through preemptive war, was dismembered in the process. And Iraq, which invaded Iran in 1980 hoping for a quick victory, had to settle for a costly stalemate eight years and half a million casualties later.

In all cases, those who began a war took a beating. Neither the nature nor the ideology of the government that started a war made any difference. Aggressors were defeated whether they were capitalists or Communists, white or nonwhite, Western or non-Western, rich or poor.

In the nineteenth century, by contrast, most wars were won by the governments that started them. Only those who, like Napoleon, aspired to the big prize suffered ultimate defeat. Then war was still a rational pursuit, fought for limited objectives. Twentieth-century aggressors, on the other hand, have tended to be more demanding and more ruthless: they have fought for total stakes and hence made war a question of survival. Those who were attacked have had to fight for life itself. Courage born of desperation has proved a formidable weapon. In the end, those who began the war have been stemmed, turned back, and in some cases crushed completely. In no case has any nation that began a war in our time achieved its ends.

In the atomic age, war between nuclear powers is suicidal; wars between small countries with big friends are likely to be inconclusive and interminable; hence decisive war in our time has become the privilege of the impotent. It has become almost banal to say that the atomic age has fundamentally altered the nature of war. No nuclear power can tell another: "Do as I say or I shall kill you," but is reduced to saying: "Do as I say or I shall kill us both," which is an entirely different matter. Thus, when everybody is somebody, nobody is anybody. But it is not only nuclear countries that cannot win wars against each other. A small country with a close tie to a big ally also can no longer be defeated. The wars in Korea, Vietnam, and the Middle East all illustrate this point. The North Koreans were unable to defeat South Korea so long as the United States was willing to support the South and neutralize the North's successes. And the South Koreans could not defeat the North so long as China and the Soviet Union were willing to render assistance. Thus the Korean War ended with the frontiers virtually unchanged. The main difference was the large number of dead Koreans on *both* sides. In Vietnam, the Soviet Union and China sent enough supplies to offset the results of American bombings; and the deserts of the Middle East became veritable proving grounds for the testing of new superpower weapons. Thus wars between small nations with big friends will be interminable so long as the ally of the weaker side is willing to continue his support. Neither side can win; only the casualties mount. In our time, decisive victories seem possible only for nations without big friends or for the impotent. Bangladesh was able to break away from Pakistan because none of the great powers considered the issue important enough to restore the status quo by force of arms. Nor did the genocidal violence perpetrated by the Tutsi tribe against the Hutu people in Central Africa stir the great powers into action. Thus the paradox of war in the atomic age may be summarized as follows: the power of big states vis-à-vis each other has been reduced, if not altogether canceled out, while the power of small and friendless states vis-à-vis each other has been proportionately enhanced.

In our time, unless the vanquished is destroyed completely, a victor's peace is seldom lasting. Those peace settlements that are negotiated on a basis of equality are much more permanent and durable. In 1918 Germany was defeated but not crushed. Versailles became the crucible for Hitler's Germany, which was then brought down only through unconditional surrender. The Korean settlement was negotiated between undefeated equals. Both sides were unhappy, but neither side was so unhappy that it wished to overturn the settlement and initiate yet another war. An uneasy armistice or truce was gradually recognized as a possible basis for a peace settlement. The relative insecurity of each side thus became the guarantor of the relative security of both. Israel learned this lesson in October 1973. The victor's peace of 1967 had left the Arabs in a state of such frustration that they were compelled to try their hand at war once more. With their dignity restored in 1973, they found it psychologically possible, a decade and a half later, to confront the Israelis with a new and most effective challenge: the Palestinian uprising.

With regard to the problem of the outbreak of war, the case studies indicate the crucial importance of the personalities of leaders. I am less impressed by the role of abstract forces, such as nationalism, militarism, or alliance systems, which traditionally have been regarded as the causes of war. Nor does a single one of the seven cases indicate that economic factors played a vital part in precipitating war. The personalities of leaders, on the other hand, have often been decisive. The outbreak of World War I illustrates this point quite clearly. Conventional wisdom has blamed the alliance system for the spread of the war. Specifically, the argument runs, Kaiser Wilhelm's alliance with Austria dragged Germany into the war against the Allied Powers. This analysis, however, totally ignores the role of the Kaiser's personality during the gathering crisis. Suppose Wilhelm had had the fortitude to continue his role as mediator and restrain Austria instead of engaging in paranoid delusions and accusing England of conspiring against Germany. The disaster might have been averted; the conventional wisdom would then have praised the alliance system for saving the peace instead of blaming it for causing the war. In truth the emotional balance or lack of balance of the German Kaiser turned out to be absolutely crucial. Similarly, the relentless mediocrity of the leading personalities on all sides no doubt contributed to the disaster. If one looks at the outbreak of World War II, there is no doubt that the victor's peace of Versailles and the galloping inflation of the 1920s brought about the rise of Nazi Germany. But once again, it was the personality of Hitler that was decisive. A more rational leader would have consolidated his gains and certainly would not have attacked the Soviet Union. And if Russia had to be attacked, then a rational man would have made contingency plans to meet the Russian winter instead of counting blindly on an early victory. In the Korean War the hubris of General MacArthur probably prolonged the conflict by two years, and in Vietnam the fragile egos of at least two American presidents who could not face the facts first escalated the war quite disproportionately and then postponed its ending quite unreasonably. In the Middle East the volatile personality of Gamal Abdel Nasser was primarily responsible for the closing of the Gulf of Aqaba, the event which precipitated the Six-Day War of 1967. In 1971 Yahya Khan, the leader of West Pakistan, took his country to war with India because he would not be cowed by a woman. And in the 1980s, Saddam Hussein of Iraq and the Ayatollah Khomeini of Iran—both zealots and fanatics—fought a holy war against each other. In all these cases, a fatal flaw or ego weakness in a leader's personality was of crucial importance. It may, in fact, have spelled the difference between the outbreak of war and the maintenance of peace.

The case material reveals that perhaps the most important single precipitating factor in the outbreak of war is misperception. Such distortion may manifest itself in four different ways: in a leader's image of himself; a leader's view of his adversary's character; a leader's view of his adversary's intentions toward himself; and finally, a leader's view of his adversary's capabilities and power. Each of these is of such importance that it merits separate and careful treatment.

There is a remarkable consistency in the self-images of most national leaders on the brink of war. Each confidently expects victory after a brief and triumphant campaign. Doubt about the outcome is the voice of the enemy and therefore inconceivable. This recurring optimism is not to be dismissed lightly by the historian as an ironic example of human folly. It assumes a powerful emotional momentum of its own and thus itself becomes one of the causes of war. Anything that fuels such optimism about a quick and decisive victory makes war more likely, and anything that dampens it becomes a cause of peace.

This common belief in a short, decisive war is usually the overflow from a reservoir of self-delusions held by the leadership about both itself and the nation. The Kaiser's appearance in shining armor in August 1914 and his promise to the German nation that its sons would be back home "before the leaves had fallen from the trees" was matched by similar expressions of overconfidence and military splendor in Austria, Russia, and the other nations on the brink of war. Hitler's confidence in an early German victory in Russia was so unshakable that no winter uniforms were issued to the soldiers and no preparations whatsoever made for the onset of the Russian winter. In November 1941, when the mud of autumn turned to ice and snow, the cold became the German soldier's bitterest enemy. Tormented by the Arctic temperatures, men died, machines broke down, and the quest for warmth all but eclipsed the quest for victory. Hitler's hopes and delusions about the German "master race" were shattered in the frozen wastes of Russia. The fact that Hitler had fought in World War I and seen that optimism crumble in defeat did not prevent its reappearance. When North Korea invaded South Korea, her leadership expected victory within two months. The Anglo-French campaign at Suez in 1956 was spurred by the hope of a swift victory. In Pakistan Yahya Khan hoped to teach Indira Gandhi a lesson modeled on the Six-Day War in Israel. In Vietnam every American escalation in the air or on the ground was an expression of the hope that a few more bombs, a few more troops, would bring decisive victory. And in the Middle East, Saddam Hussein of Iraq expected a quick victory over Iran. What he got instead was a bloody stalemate.

Thus leaders on all sides typically harbor self-delusions on the eve of war. Only the war itself then provides the stinging ice of reality and ultimately helps to restore a measure of perspective in the leadership. The price for this recapture of reality is high indeed. It is unlikely that there ever was a war that fulfilled the initial hopes and expectations of *both* sides.

Distorted views of the adversary's character also help to precipitate a conflict. As the pressure mounted in July 1914, the German Kaiser explosively admitted that he "hated the Slavs, even though one should not hate anyone." This hatred no doubt influenced his decision to vacate his role as mediator and to prepare for war. Similarly, his naive trust in the honesty of the Austrian leaders prompted him to extend to them the blank-check guarantee that dragged him into war. In reality the Austrians were more deceitful than he thought and the Russians more honest. Worst of all, the British leadership, which worked so desperately to avert a general war, was seen by Wilhelm as the center of a monstrous plot to encircle and destroy the German nation. Hitler too had no conception of what Russia really was like. He knew nothing of the history and depth of the Russian land and believed that it was populated by subhuman barbarians who could be crushed with one decisive stroke and then made to serve as slaves for German supermen. This relentless hatred and contempt for Russia became a crucial factor in Hitler's ill-fated assault of 1941. Perhaps the most important reason for the American military intervention in Vietnam was the misperception of the American leadership about the nature of Communism in Asia. President Lyndon Johnson committed more than half a million combat troops to an Asian land war because he believed that Communism was still a monolithic octopus with North Vietnam its tentacle. He did this more than a decade after the death of Stalin, at a time when Communism had splintered into numerous ideological and political fragments. His total ignorance of Asia in general and of Vietnam in particular made him perceive the Vietnam war in terms of purely Western categories: a colossal shoot-out between the forces of Communism and those of anti-Communism. The fact that Ho Chi Minh saw the Americans as the successors of French imperialism whom he was determined to drive out was completely lost on the president. Virtue, righteousness, and justice were fully on his side, so Johnson thought. America, the child of light, had to defeat the child of darkness in a twentieth-century crusade. Mutual contempt and hatred also hastened the outbreak of the wars between the Arab states and Israel and between India and Pakistan. In the former case, the Arab view of Israel as an alien and hostile presence was a precipitating cause of conflict. In the latter, the two religions of Hinduism and Islam led directly to the creation of two hostile states that clashed in bloody conflict three times in a single generation. And religious conflict between Sunni and Shi'ite Moslems hastened the coming of the war between Iraq and Iran.

When a leader on the brink of war believes that his adversary will attack him, the chances of war are fairly high. When both leaders share this perception about each other's intent, war becomes a virtual certainty. The mechanism of the self-fulfilling prophecy is then set in motion. When leaders attribute evil designs to their adversaries, and they nurture these beliefs for long enough, they will eventually be proved right. The mobilization measures that preceded the outbreak of World War I were essentially defensive measures triggered by the fear of the other side's intent. The Russian czar mobilized because he feared an Austrian attack; the German Kaiser mobilized because he feared the Russian "steamroller." The nightmare of each then became a terrible reality. Stalin was so imprisoned by the Marxist dogma that capitalists would always lie that he disbelieved Churchill's truthful warnings about Hitler's murderous intent to the extent that Russia almost lost the war. Eisenhower and Dulles were so convinced that the Chinese would move against the French in Indochina as they had against MacArthur's UN forces that they committed the first American military advisers to Vietnam. The Chinese never intervened, but the Americans had begun their march along the road to entrapment in the Vietnam quagmire. Arabs and Israelis and Indians and Pakistanis generally expected nothing but the worst from one another, and these expectations often led to war. The conviction held by Syria and Egypt after 1967 that Israel intended to hold onto the occupied territories forever was the immediate precipitating cause of the October War of 1973, in which the Arabs made a desperate attempt to reconquer their lost lands. And Yahya Khan's perception of India's intention to fight on the side of the secessionist movement in Bengal led directly to his abortive and suicidal air attack.

A leader's misperception of his adversary's power is perhaps the quintessential cause of war. It is vital to remember, however, that it is not the actual distribution of power that precipitates a war; it is the way in which a leader thinks that power is distributed. A war will start when nations disagree over their perceived strength. The war itself then becomes a dispute over measurement. Reality is gradually restored as war itself cures war. And the war will end when the fighting nations perceive each other's strength more realistically.

Germany and Austria-Hungary in 1914 had nothing but contempt for Russia's power. This disrespect was to cost them dearly. Hitler repeated this mistake a generation later, and his misperception led straight to his destruction. One of the clearest examples of another misperception of this kind took place in the Korean War. MacArthur, during his advance through North Korea toward the Chinese border, stubbornly believed that the Chinese Communists did not have the capability to intervene. When the Chinese did cross the Yalu River into North Korea, MacArthur clung to the belief that he was facing 40,000 men, while in truth the figure was closer to 200,000. And when the Chinese forces temporarily withdrew to assess their impact on MacArthur's army, the American general assumed that the Chinese were badly in need of rest after their encounter with superior Western military might. And when the Chinese attacked again and drove

MacArthur all the way back to South Korea, the leader of the UN forces perceived this action as a "piece of treachery worse even than Pearl Harbor." The most amazing aspect of this story is that the real facts were quite available to MacArthur from his own intelligence sources, if only the general had cared to look at them. But he knew better and thus prolonged the war by two more years. Only at war's end did the Americans gain respect for China's power and take care not to provoke her again beyond the point of no return. Yet in the Vietnam war, the American leadership committed precisely the same error vis-à-vis North Vietnam. Five successive presidents believed that Ho Chi Minh would collapse if only a little more military pressure were brought to bear on him either from the air or on the ground. The North Vietnamese leader proved them all mistaken, and only when America admitted that North Vietnam could not be beaten did the war come to an end. In both Korea and Vietnam the price of reality came high indeed. As these wars resolved less and less, they tended to cost more and more in blood and treasure. The number of dead on all sides bore mute testimony to the fact that America had to fight two of the most terrible and divisive wars in her entire history before she gained respect for the realities of power on the other side. In 1948 the Arabs believed that an invasion by five Arab armies would quickly put an end to Israel. They were mistaken. But in 1973 Israel, encouraged to the point of hubris after three successful wars, viewed Arab power only with contempt and its own as unassailable. That too was wrong, as Israel had to learn in the bitter war of October 1973. In Pakistan Yahya Khan had to find out to his detriment that a woman for whom he had nothing but disdain was better schooled in the arts of war than he, did not permit her wishes to dominate her thoughts, and finally managed to dismember Pakistan. And in the Persian Gulf, the invading Iraqis were amazed at the "fanatical zeal" of the Iranians, whom they had underestimated.

Thus, on the eve of each war, at least one nation misperceives another's power. In that sense the beginning of each war is a misperception or an accident. The war itself then slowly, and in agony, teaches the lesson of reality. And peace is made when reality has won. The outbreak of war and the coming of peace are separated by a road that leads from misperception to reality. The most tragic aspect of this truth is that war has continued to remain the best teacher of reality and thus has been the most effective cure for war.

As we move toward the close of the twentieth century, we face an awesome paradox: never before in history have we prepared so feverishly for a war that no one wants. No analysis of war in our time would be complete without at least a glance at our simultaneous efforts to build—and then destroy, or at least control—weapons that could incinerate the earth.

The following is an eyewitness description of Hiroshima shortly after the city was destroyed by an atomic bomb in August 1945:

> People are still dying, mysteriously and horribly—people who were uninjured in the cataclysm—from an unknown something which I can only describe as the atomic plague.
>
> Hiroshima does not look like a bombed city. . . . I write these facts as dispassionately as I can, in the hope that they will act as a warning to the world. In this first testing ground of the atomic bomb . . . it gives you an empty feeling in the stomach to see such man-made devastation. . . . I could see about three miles of reddish rubble. That is all the atomic bomb left. . . . The Police Chief of Hiroshima . . . took me to hospitals where the victims of the bombs are still being treated. In these hospitals I found people who, when the bomb fell, suffered absolutely no injuries, but now are dying from the uncanny aftereffects. For no apparent reason their health began to fail. They lost appetite. Their hair fell out. Bluish spots appeared on their bodies. And then bleeding began from the ears, nose and mouth.
>
> At first, the doctors told me, they thought these were the symptoms of general debility. They gave their patients Vitamin A injections. The results were horrible. The flesh started rotting away from the hole caused by the injection of the needle. And in every case the victim died.
>
> A peculiar odour . . . given off by the poisonous gas still issues from the earth soaked with radioactivity; against this the inhabitants all wear gauze masks over their mouths and noses; many thousands of people have simply vanished—the atomic heat was so great that they burned instantly to ashes—except that there were no ashes—they were vaporised.[1]

The bomb mentioned here, it should be noted, is now considered obsolete. Its capacity for destruction has been dwarfed by an even more total weapon—the hydrogen bomb.

Today, there are about 50,000 such nuclear weapons in the world, shared roughly equally between the United States and the Soviet Union. Each of these has over a hundred times the explosive power of the Hiroshima bomb. According to one highly respected scientist, if only one-tenth of these weapons was ever detonated, the world would be in the grip of a "nuclear winter," with the sunlight blocked by radioactive dust, the ecological chain broken, and human life probably doomed to extinction.[2] In 1985 even the Pentagon itself agreed with this grim assessment.

Thus, even without retaliation by the nation attacked, the attacking nation would probably commit suicide. It may be argued that Hiroshima survived, but in 1945 there was an outside world to come to its aid. In the event of a nuclear war today, no part of the world would remain unaffected. The earth itself would then become the bomb and the bomb the earth.

In light of the preceding paragraph, how probable is a nuclear war between the superpowers in our time? Are we likely to see the year 2000? For the first time since the first edition of this book appeared, I have become an optimist.

When Ronald Reagan and Mikhail Gorbachev signed the Intermediate Nuclear Forces (INF) Treaty in Washington in December 1987, they set two historic precedents: never before in the thorny relations between the two superpowers were its leaders able to agree on the actual elimination of nuclear weapons; and never before was such a scrapping of weapons to be monitored by mutual on-site inspections. This dramatic achievement deserves careful analysis.

One thoughtful journalist boiled down the essence of the treaty in a catchy paragraph:

> Once upon a time the man in the White House said to the man in the Kremlin, "Hey, you've got a whole category of weapons we don't like. We've got a whole category of weapons you don't like. Why don't we just wipe clean the slate?" After 72 months of contentious, suspenseful, stop-and-go negotiations, the man in the Kremlin said, "OK, it's a deal."[3]

The process began with Ronald Reagan's proposal, made in November 1981, that came to be known as the "zero option." That year, Leonid Brezhnev had arrayed against Western Europe a new class of nuclear missiles that could be fired over a distance of 3,000 miles. West Germany, Britain, and France could easily be reduced to heaps of rubble. The Pentagon was planning to offset these Soviet SS-20 missiles by deploying its own "Euromissiles"— cruises and Pershings—while making a good-faith effort to negotiate a compromise that might scale back the missiles on both sides.

Secretary of State Alexander Haig suggested a compromise that would reduce missiles in Europe but not eliminate them entirely. President Reagan, however, was interested in a proposal "that could be expressed in a single sentence and that sounded like real disarmament."[4]

Richard Perle, assistant secretary of defense, gave the president what he was looking for: an all-or-nothing package—zero American missiles in Europe in exchange for zero SS-20s. That plan was at the heart of the president's November 1981 speech: "The United States is prepared to cancel its deployment of Pershing 2 and ground-launched cruise missiles if the Soviets will dismantle their SS-20, SS-4, and SS-5 missiles."

During the next four years, this "zero option" proposal lingered like an orphan looking for adoptive parents. Leonid Brezhnev, Yuri Andropov, and Konstantin Chernenko all angrily denounced the zero option as patently one-sided. The United States, the Soviet leaders asserted, was asking the Soviets to give up real weapons, already deployed at great expense, in return for the United States tearing up a piece of paper. The Americans, losing patience, began to deploy their Euromissiles on schedule in 1983. The Soviets, as a result, walked out of the arms control talks in Geneva and did not return for one-and-a-half years. The subsequent downing of a Korean airliner by Soviet rockets took the Soviet-American relationship to a new nadir. Ronald Reagan now referred to the Soviet Union as an "evil empire" and passionately advocated his "Strategic Defense Initiative," to be deployed in space as a protective shield against Soviet attack. The Soviet press returned the compliment by comparing the American president to Adolf Hitler. Even a productive "walk in the woods in 1982" by two negotiators—Yuli Kvitinsky, a bright Soviet diplomat, and Paul Nitze, an expert in American nuclear strategy—although leading to a tentative arms reduction deal, was repudiated by both men's home offices. Amidst all this hostility the zero option temporarily lapsed into a coma. But then, in 1985, everything changed.

The new Soviet general secretary, Mikhail Gorbachev, began to assert himself, subtly at first, and then spectacularly. Slowly, and then with amazing speed, the glacial ice of Soviet policy toward the zero option began to melt. The Soviet leader developed a new order of priorities. First and foremost, he was intent on modernizing the Russian economy. If toward that end, some missiles would have to be sacrificed, so be it. Second, he saw some intrinsic merit in the zero option: it would leave the United States without any ground-based missiles in Europe capable of hitting Soviet territory. Accordingly, Soviet policy under Gorbachev now became a great deal more flexible. A game of defensive chess suddenly changed to an offensive game with a dash of daring poker.

In May 1985, Gorbachev asserted that the Soviet Union would be willing to freeze its SS-20 forces east of the Ural Mountains. In October, he made a more far-reaching concession by allowing that an INF agreement might be possible "outside of direct connection with the problem of space and strategic arms." In plain English, the Soviet leader decided not to make an INF treaty contingent upon an American decision to abandon "Star Wars."

Slowly but steadily, the initiative on arms negotiations now shifted to the Soviet side. More and more the United States found itself on the defensive, being bombarded with ever bolder and more comprehensive Gorbachev proposals. In 1986, for example, the Soviet leader proposed a three-stage, fifteen-year plan for total nuclear disarmament. The first stage called for cancellation of "Star Wars," a 50 percent reduction in strategic weaponry, and "complete liquidation" of Soviet and American INF missiles "in the European zone." By now, the superpowers had traded places. The Soviet Union was making disarmament proposals, and the United States was rejecting them.

The Soviet proposal produced an outbreak of guerrilla warfare within the Reagan administration. Various interim and compromise proposals were drafted by the Pentagon, the State Department, and the Arms Control and Disarmament Agency. The Europeans, at first rather friendly to the zero option, had become increasingly ambivalent since the removal of American missiles would expose their countries to a vastly superior Soviet conventional force. Yet the Reagan administration was reluctant to back away from the zero option altogether. After all, it had been the president's own proposal to begin with.

Finally, early in 1987, Gorbachev made a final concession that tilted the negotiations toward acceptance of the zero option. He decoupled once and for all the INF treaty from the issue of "Star Wars." He was willing, in short, to accept a separate agreement along the lines of President Reagan's original zero option proposal made six years earlier.

And thus, in December 1987, the two leaders met in Washington and signed the first real disarmament accord in the postwar world. Just before the ceremony, the president led Mikhail Gorbachev to a little study next to the Oval Office and produced a baseball that Joe Dimaggio had hoped to have autographed by the Soviet leader. Reagan was not just fulfilling the old Yankee slugger's request. He had a metaphor in mind. Are we, he asked, going to play ball? Yes, Gorbachev firmly agreed. Then the two men signed the documents, exchanged pens, smiled warmly, and shook hands, obviously moved by the occasion. When it was all over, Gorbachev called the three-day Washington summit a "major event in world politics," and Reagan declared that the meeting had "lit the sky with hope for all people of goodwill."

In the cooler light of political analysis, what did the INF treaty in fact achieve? On the credit side of the ledger, it eliminated an entire class of nuclear weapons, the Euro-missiles. The Soviets agreed to scuttle about 1,500 warheads on its medium-range SS-20 and SS-4 missiles, while the United States agreed to give up about 350 warheads on its Pershing 2 and ground-launched cruise missiles. An elaborate monitoring system was decided upon under which American and Soviet inspectors were stationed outside missile factories in each country to make sure no banned missiles were illegally produced. Inspectors were also permitted to visit missile bases and installations. After the missiles had been removed from bases by each side, special close-out inspections were arranged to make sure that the missiles were really gone. And finally, the actual physical destruction of the missiles was subject to rigorous supervision and inspection as well.

On the debit side, it might be said that the total number of missiles destined for the scrap heap amounted to a mere 4 percent of the entire superpower arsenals. Moreover, "Star Wars" remained untouched by the treaty, as did the strategic weapons that could incinerate each superpower from across the Atlantic, although both countries continued negotiations in order to attain deep cuts in these weapons. And, of course, the huge conventional arsenals of both superpowers remained untouched as well. Having said all this, however, the net result was still historic. Each side got something that it wanted badly. The United States removed a major threat to its European NATO allies, and the Soviet Union removed a major threat to its own territory. The political circumstances and the timing were excellent as well. Mikhail Gorbachev's first priority was the Soviet economy, not superfluous "overkill" missiles. Rubles could now be spent on making the Soviet Union an economic superpower as well. Ronald Reagan assured himself the legacy of being the first American president to sign a genuine disarmament treaty with the Soviets and to have it ratified by the Senate. Nor did he have to abandon his fondest dream of "Star Wars."

In larger historical perspective, the final truth perhaps is this: the problem of disarmament is not disarmament at all. Disarmament is the by-product of decisions by national leaders to reduce political tensions between their countries. Once this is done, disarmament becomes a possibility, and ultimately a reality. No amount of technical formulas can substitute for such leadership and courage. Gorbachev and Reagan found that kind of courage. For forty years, the doomsday clock had ticked away relentlessly toward Armageddon. On Christmas Day of 1987, at long last, humanity was granted a reprieve.

Mikhail Gorbachev's farewell visit to Ronald Reagan in New York in December 1988 was no doubt his most dramatic. In an eloquent and audacious speech before the United Nations, the Soviet leader offered a sweeping vision of a "new world order" for the twenty-first century, including specific initiatives on a variety of Western concerns, such as Afghanistan, emigration, and human rights. Most compelling was a unilateral decision to reduce, within two years, the total Soviet armed forces by 10 percent, withdraw 50,000 troops from Eastern Europe, and cut in half the number of Soviet tanks in East Germany, Hungary, and Czechoslovakia. What was memorable about Gorbachev's address was not only the package of specific proposals but also his departure from the shopworn slogans and ideological dogmas that had driven Soviet foreign policy for more than half a century. "Today the preservation of any kind of closed society is hardly possible," he declared.

This statement was put to the test the very day after Gorbachev uttered it, when a powerful earthquake hit Soviet Armenia, destroying several cities and killing more than 50,000 people. The Soviet leader immediately returned to his homeland to lead the rescue effort. Significantly, however, with *glasnost* well entrenched, the magnitude of the disaster and its consequences were relayed promptly to the West and Moscow accepted help from abroad—even from the United States, which it had not done since the days of World War II. This reaction stood in sharp contrast to Moscow's response to the Chernobyl nuclear disaster of March 1986 during which the Soviet Union had shrouded itself into its traditional secrecy. Not surprisingly, the American response to the catastrophe in Soviet Armenia was openhearted and generous. In 1986, the world was suspicious and angry; in 1988, it shared in the grief and helped as best it could.

As American leaders were quick to point out after they studied Gorbachev's speech, the troop and tank reduction proposals still left the Soviet Union with a sizable margin of superiority in conventional military strength over the NATO countries. But what was perhaps more important than these numbers was the growing conviction in the United States that Gorbachev was not just seeking a breathing space, but a fundamental change in the Soviet system. The big question in the West about the Soviet leader was no longer "Is he sincere?" but "Can he last?"

And indeed, the philosophical base of Mikhail Gorbachev's speech made one wonder whether a Soviet leader could in fact have spoken those words. The following statements from his United Nations address could easily have been made by an American president. Here are some that are worth quoting:

> The use of threat of force no longer can or must be an instrument of foreign policy. . . . All of us, and primarily the stronger of us, must exercise self-restraint and totally rule out any outward-oriented use of force. . . . It is now quite clear that building up military power makes no country omnipotent. What is more, one-sided reliance on military power ultimately weakens other components of national security.
>
> It is also quite clear to us that the principle of freedom of choice is mandatory. Its nonrecognition is fraught with extremely grave consequences for world peace. Denying that right to the peoples under whatever pretext or rhetorical guise means jeopardizing even the

fragile balance that has been attained. Freedom of choice is a universal principle that should allow for no exceptions. . . . As the world asserts its diversity, attempts to look down on others and to teach them one's own brand of democracy become totally improper, to say nothing of the fact that democratic values intended for export often very quickly lose their worth.

What we are talking about, therefore, is unity in diversity. . . . We are not abandoning our convictions, our philosophy or traditions, nor do we urge anyone to abandon theirs. But neither do we have any intention to be hemmed in by our values. That would result in intellectual impoverishment, for it would mean rejecting a powerful source of development—the exchange of everything original that each nation has independently created.

We are, of course, far from claiming to be in possession of the ultimate truth.[5]

Not only did Presidents Reagan and Bush warm up to Gorbachev, but so did the American people. According to a Gallup poll 65 percent of the respondents believed that the Soviet Union was undergoing major rather than cosmetic changes, and 76 percent believed that Moscow was now more likely to live in peace with its neighbors.[6] Perhaps most important, Americans began to perceive the Soviet leader as a real human being, not a cardboard figure waving feebly from the Kremlin Wall. As a New Yorker put it, "To me, he is more like a human being than the other people who have held power there. He showed more of a human side when he went home where he belonged to deal with the Armenian earthquake. He didn't go with politics."[7]

Roy Medvedev, the dissident Soviet historian, observed that Gorbachev's speech was the best of any world leader since John F. Kennedy. And indeed, there were parallels: the wit, the crowd appeal, and a latent dread that this man was risking too much and might be pushing his luck.

For forty years, the United States had proposed initiatives, and successive Soviet leaders had scowled and said *nyet.* Now Mikhail Gorbachev was proposing sweeping initiatives, and the United States, delighted but taken aback, was saying "maybe." By the time Ronald Reagan left office and the new president was sworn in, the entire choreography had changed. The year 1988 had clearly become a watershed year from the Cold War to something better and more humane.

Yet despite all the progress made, war is still a very real danger. In the past the anarchic nature of the nation-state system was chiefly responsible for wars. Now the future may bring new challenges to our survival that emanate from nonstate entities. Self-styled patriots, liberation groups, criminal elements, and even individual terrorists may soon have access to nuclear technology and subject national leaders to atomic blackmail. When one considers the fact that in 1976 an undergraduate physics student at Princeton University was able to write, with the use of publicly available materials, a paper describing how to build an atom bomb, that possibility does not seem at all farfetched. If the world's poor and hungry remain unable to persuade the world's rich to share their wealth more equitably, then violence becomes an increasingly probable scenario. Hence, as the twentieth century draws to a close, wars may erupt in the cracks of the state system as easily as among sovereign states themselves.

Perhaps the most likely scenario for disaster is a "nuclear Sarajevo." Equipped with a nuclear device, fanatics like Qaddafi or Khomeini would be more dangerous than either superpower. Men with so much Hitler-like hatred might not hesitate to destroy themselves if those they hate are destroyed as well. The "kamikaze" attacks on the American marines in Beirut by Moslem terrorists in 1983 may be forerunners of such nightmare scenarios.

Despite the persistence of so much human tragedy and folly, it is nevertheless possible to conclude this study on a note of hope. Neither the American people nor the Russian people want a nuclear war. In both nations the level of consciousness against war has been raised. In the United States, if the nation's leaders get too close to the brink, the people tend to act as a corrective. In the Soviet Union, the memory of war and devastation acts as a similar corrective. This popular sentiment against nuclear death finally led to some meaningful disarmament. And there is hope now for more. Certainly all men and women of goodwill must continue to work in that direction. *There has been a slow dawning of compassion and global consciousness over humanity's bleak skies in our generation.* This has manifested itself both in a new awareness of and even resistance to the havoc that war wreaks on the human spirit. Our sense of logic no longer finds it acceptable to consider throwing a human being into a fire an atrocity, while condoning the military operation of throwing fire on many human beings.

We can no longer quite understand how one individual who kills another is punished as a murderer, while another who murders thousands anonymously from the sky can be acclaimed as a patriot or hero. This new dawn has risen out of dreadful suffering, but it *has* arisen.

The most fundamental challenge of this generation is to prevent another world war. At the very moment when we have the power to destroy the earth, we must begin to perceive the planet as a whole.

It is this new, slow dawning of compassion and of global consciousness that is our greatest hope. From this new spirit stirring deep within us we shall forge the weapons against war. For we have built *both* cathedrals and concentration camps. Though we have descended to unprecedented depths in the modern age, we have also soared to greater heights than ever before. We are not burdened with original sin alone; we also have the gift of original innocence.

NOTES

1. Peter Burchett, the London *Daily Express,* September 5, 1945.
2. Carl Sagan, "Nuclear Weapons and Climatic Catastrophe," *Foreign Affairs,* Winter 1983–84.
3. Strobe Talbot, "The Road To Zero," *Time,* December 14, 1987.
4. *Ibid.*
5. *Time,* December 19, 1988.
6. *The New York Times,* December 12, 1988.
7. *Ibid.*

SELECTED BIBLIOGRAPHY

BIALER, SEWERYN, and MICHAEL MANDELBAUM. *The Global Rivals.* New York: Knopf, 1988.
BLAINEY, GEOFFREY. *The Causes of War.* New York: Free Press, 1973.
CLAUSEWITZ, KARL VON. *On War.* New York: Modern Library, 1943.
DYSON, FREEMAN. *Weapons and Hope.* New York: Harper & Row, 1984.
GORBACHEV, MIKHAIL. *Perestroika: New Thinking for Our Country and the World.* New York: Harper & Row, 1987.

HOUGH, JERRY. *Russia and the West.* New York: Simon & Schuster, 1988.

KAHN, HERMAN. *On Thermonuclear War.* Princeton: Princeton University Press, 1960.

KENNEDY, PAUL. *The Rise and Fall of the Great Powers.* New York: Random House, 1987.

KISSINGER, HENRY. *White House Years.* Boston: Little, Brown & Company, 1979.

SCHELL, JONATHAN. *The Fate of the Earth.* New York: Knopf, 1982.

SCHELLING, THOMAS C. *Arms and Influence.* New Haven: Yale University Press, 1966.

WALZER, MICHAEL. *Just and Unjust Wars.* New York: Basic Books, 1977.

WRIGHT, QUINCEY. *A Study of War.* Chicago: University of Chicago Press, 1942.

About the Author

On the eve of World War II, John G. Stoessinger fled Nazi-occupied Austria to Czechoslovakia. Three years later he fled again, traveling via Siberia to China, where he lived for seven years. In Shanghai he served with the International Refugee Organization.

John Stoessinger came to the United States in 1947, received his B.A. degree from Grinnell College in 1950, and then earned a Ph.D. from Harvard in 1954. He entered academic life immediately and has taught at Harvard, M.I.T., Columbia, Princeton, and the City University of New York. In 1969 he led the International Seminar on International Relations at Harvard University, and in 1970 received an Honorary Degree of Doctor of Laws from Grinnell College, Iowa, and from the American College of Switzerland. He is now Distinguished Professor of International Affairs at Trinity University in San Antonio, Texas.

Dr. Stoessinger is the author of ten leading books in international relations, including *The Might of Nations: World Politics in Our Time,* which was awarded the Bancroft Prize by Columbia University in 1963 as the best book in international relations published in 1962. The book has gone through nine editions. He is also the author of *The Refugee and the World Community; Financing the United Nations System; Power and Order; The United Nations and the Superpowers; Nations in Darkness: China, Russia, America; and Henry Kissinger: The Anguish of Power.* Dr. Stoessinger also served as Chief Book Review Editor of *Foreign Affairs* for five years and is a member of the Council on Foreign Relations.

From 1967 to 1974 Dr. Stoessinger served as Acting Director of the Political Affairs Division at the United Nations. During the academic year 1978–1979, he served as Presidential Professor at the Colorado School of Mines.

Dr. Stoessinger's autobiography, *Night Journey,* was published in 1978. His latest book, *Crusaders and Pragmatists: Movers of Modern American Foreign Policy,* was published by W. W. Norton in 1979 and again in 1985.